AIPPI FORUM SERIES

Strategic Issues of Industrial Property Management in a Globalizing Economy

AIPPI FORUM SERIES

Strategic Issues of Industrial Property Management in a Globalizing Economy

Abstracts & Selected Papers

THOMAS COTTIER and PETER WIDMER (editors)
KATHARINA SCHINDLER (assistant editor)

1st AIPPI Forum/Interlaken-Switzerland

HART PUBLISHING
OXFORD – PORTLAND, OREGON – 1999

Hart Publishing
Oxford and Portland, Oregon

Published in North America (US and Canada) by
Hart Publishing c/o
International Specialized Book Services
5804 NE Hassalo Street
Portland, Oregon
97213-3644
USA

Distributed in Netherlands, Belgium and Luxembourg by
Intersentia, Churchillaan 108
B2900 Schoten
Antwepen
Belgium

Distributed in Australia and New Zealand by
Federation Press
John St
Leichhardt
NSW 2000

Hart Publishing is a specialist legal publisher based in Oxford, England.
To order further copies of this book or to request a list of other publications please write to:

Hart Publishing, 19 Whitehouse Road, Oxford, OX1 4PA
Telephone: +44 (0) 1865 434459 Fax: +44 (0) 1865 794882
email: hartpub@janep.demon.co.uk

British Library Cataloguing in Publication Data
Data Available

ISBN 1 84113-066-4 (cloth)

Typeset by John Saunders Design & Production, Reading

Foreword and Acknowledgements:

THE 1ST AIPPI-FORUM 1996

In the course of the 35th AIPPI Bureau Meeting held in 1993, the idea was born to organize a new type of event within the AIPPI activities: to set up a forum not only for AIPPI members but also for non-members in order to

- promote industrial property as an element of business-strategy,
- foster the general understanding for intellectual and industrial property matters among private industry and governments and to
- create a platform to meet during the intervals between congresses.

If successful, the AIPPI Forum should be organized regularly.

Martin J. Lutz (Switzerland), the past Secretary General of AIPPI appointed Vincenzo M. Pedrazzini (Switzerland) to call a committee which should develop a concept for the realization of this idea. Thus, our committee was formed and listed as Q 125 of the AIPPI organization.

The concept for the first AIPPI Forum was then presented at the AIPPI EXCO meeting 1994 in Copenhagen and approved. At the same time the AIPPI Foundation was founded in order to take responsibility for the organization of the AIPPI Forum. In the course of the preparation of this first AIPPI Forum the close co-operation with LES International turned out to be very fruitful.

Finally, the first AIPPI Forum took place from 10 September through 14 September 1996 in Interlaken, Switzerland. The success of this first Forum and – above all - the interest expressed by the participants encouraged the AIPPI Foundation to organize other such events, the next to take place in early March 1999 in Lyon (France). It was also decided to publish all abstracts and a selection of the final papers submitted by the speakers of the 1st AIPPI Forum.

The authors of all contributions deserve our wholehearted thanks and highest recognition for their commitment and for the quality of their work. The selection of the final papers included within this book had to inevitably be arbitrary and we present our apologies to all speakers of the 1st AIPPI Forum whose contributions could not be published.

Finally, we want to cordially express our thanks to the 'editing team' which made this publication possible: First of all to Thomas Cottier, Professor of European and International Economic Law at the University of Berne, who arranged for the support of his assistant, Barbara Rutz. Our special thanks go to Dr. Katharina Schindler of Fuhrer Marbach & Partners, Berne, who took responsibility for the final editing.

The Organizing Committee of the AIPPI Forum (Q 125)

Berne/Zurich, 30 November 1998

Vincenzo M. Pedrazzini, Peter A. Pestalozzi, Peter Widmer

Introduction

"Strategic Issues of Industrial Property Management in a Globalizing Economy". The topic of the first AIPPI Forum, the presentations and papers which resulted from the conference, all share a common goal: to discuss and advance insights into strategic issues of intellectual property protection and management. While intellectual property issues are frequently dealt with from a technical or legal point of view, it was felt necessary to broaden the context and look further ahead in this important field: to engage into an inquiry with regard to strategy. This term, of course, was originally coined in rather military context. The science of planning and co-ordinating all operations of war in order to render them compatible with political objects and decisions. Fortunately, we need not refer to this definition to be found in Clausewitz's standard treatise on war. We refer to the term in a peaceful, albeit strongly competitive environment of business operations and transactions in a globalizing economy. Strategy, today, is commonly used to depict planning and decisions relating to the defining of the structure and organization of companies, to allocation of human and capital resources, to motivation of personnel, and to the determination of competitive markets. All of this is essentially linked to creative development of products, goods and services. This is exactly the point where strategies relating to intellectual property development and management enters the scene. Innovation and tools to protect competitive advantages created by such innovation, are an essential part of strategic thinking in companies. True, a willingness and ability of a company to innovate and compete is an essential starting point. Yet, a willingness and ability to properly utilize and implement the fruits of such labours eventually is of equal importance. These qualities entail in particular the providing of means to communicate innovative achievements to markets, the capacity to translate innovative ideas into products and practice, and to safeguard these achievements and benefits by legal and managerial tools. In each of these areas of innovation management, there are interfaces with traditional industrial property protection. Yet, it is no longer a matter of merely looking into specific aspects of intellectual property protection, but to focus on these interfaces, and bring intellectual property protection into play and interaction with a much broader scenery. This is a call for interdisciplinary thinking and approaches. It requires an exchange of ideas and views between high-level decision makers, specialists in communication, corporate finance, banking and law in the broadest sense.

Some of these interdisciplinary aspects were addressed and covered in the 1st AIPPI Forum held in September 1996 in Interlaken, Switzerland.

Panel I on *Strategies of Industrial Property Protection in the U.S.A., Japan, Europe and Developing Countries* addressed the concept and use of industrial property rights in a strategic context. What is the role assigned to these rights within companies in order to protect the competitive edge and to secure innovative assets? What is their role to encourage and stimulate research and to advance the reputation of a company? The panel sought to achieve a comparison of different corporate strategies with respect to Industrial Property rights around the globe and among countries with different cultural backgrounds.

Panel II on *Selected Financial Aspects of Industrial Property* addressed financial aspects of industrial property rights related both to creation and use of such rights. The role of industrial property rights to secure loans, particularly in European countries, is still in its beginnings. The exchange of views and experiences made in this field will help to advance the issue. Moreover, there are close relations of Industrial Property rights and taxation, particularly in the context of licensing.

Panel III on *Industrial Property Rights in the Context of Antitrust Legislation* addressed the relationship of industrial property rights and antitrust legislation and practise in mayor countries, including the European Union. Whereas industrial property rights are a necessary condition for competition, they may at the same time also impede free markets. Particularly, where industrial property rights are systematically and strategically used to displace and remove competitors, tension arises with national and international antitrust rules.

In the globalizing market, intellectual property rights have to be adequately protected and enforced. Panel IV on *Strategies of Dispute Settlement in Industrial Property* explored aspects relating to dispute settlement in this field. It discussed the pros and cons of different methods of dispute settlement (litigation, arbitration, mediation, negotiation). Rather than highlighting legal and procedural issues, the panel examined how different methods help to ensure strategic advantages and at what financial and transactional costs this can be achieved.

With the advent of genetic engineering and biotechnology, new issues relating to the protection of industrial property rights have emerged. Perhaps for the first time, the industrial property right community is confronted with ethical and ecological challenges. Panel V on *Ethical and Ecological Aspects of Industrial Property Rights* addressed these challenges in relation to patenting of life forms. It also dealt with implications for developing countries. How can co-operation and technology transfer best be achieved? Further, the discussion focused on how these questions should be strategically approached and dealt with in public relations of corporations.

The topics addressed in the five panels are of basic importance in the context of long-term strategy. Abstracts and papers address valuable experience, or issues which have remained unresolved ever since, and the various contributions have not lost any of their timeliness. We hope that they will assist in further developing strategies not only in board rooms of companies, but also in governments and international organizations with a view to promote and secure appropriate tools fit for a globalizing economy.

Peter Widmer
Thomas Cottier

Contents

PART ONE
Selected Papers

Panel I
Strategies of Industrial Property Protection in the USA, Japan, Europe and Developing Countries

1

GLOBAL APPROACH TO BUILDING STRONG TRADE MARKS

*W. Dexter Brooks**

I am very privileged to participate in your programme today and tell you about the Coca-Cola Company and our famous trade marks.

I plan to provide you with an overview of (1) our company's scope of operations, (2) our portfolio of trade mark rights, and, finally, (3) our company's licensing and policing activities, including (4) global trends/decisions in the trade mark area.

I What is the Scope of Operations of the Coca-Cola Company?

In simple terms, our core business consists of *selling* soft drink syrups and concentrates and, *licensing* our trade marks to our bottling partners and fountain customers around the world. The company thrives, however, by expanding and reinforcing the *image* of the Coca-Cola *trade mark*; by offering top-quality products and service to our customers; and, ultimately, by providing consumers worldwide with a consistent, inexpensive source of top-quality refreshment.

Coca-Cola is the world's best-known trade mark. The company is the world's leading marketer of soft drink syrups and concentrates, with 1995 retail sales of *$18 billion* and a total sales volume *double* that of our nearest competitor.

Syrup and concentrate sales, however, only hint at the scope of the company's business. The company is also the hub of the largest production and distribution system in the world. Through a global network of over *1,000* independently owned bottlers, Coca-Cola is available in more than *195* countries; and company brands account for more than *45* per cent of all

* Senior Staff Counsel, Legal Division, The Coca-Cola Company, Atlanta, USA.

soft drinks sold worldwide. Each day, consumers enjoy more than 724 million servings of Coca-Cola.

While the company itself employs approximately *30,000* people worldwide, the global Coca-Cola system provides more than *1 million jobs* around the world. In 1995, our *Coca-Cola system* generated approximately *$90 billion* in retail sales. For more than a century, we have been developing business relationships, and investing in a global Coca-Cola system, that is conservatively estimated to be more than *$100 billion* in replacement value.

The international headquarters of the company are located in Atlanta, Georgia.

And the company employs *110* in-house counsel, worldwide, who in turn legally manage over *200* outside counsel around the world and we, as lawyers, do what you would expect:

- Protect the assets;
- Resolve disputes;
- Enhance the value of the business and the trade mark; and
- Ensure regulatory compliance and corporate maintenance.

II What is the Portfolio of Trade Mark Rights of the Company?

As many know, Coca-Cola was originated and introduced in Atlanta, Georgia, in *1886*, by Dr John Pemberton, a local pharmacist, who concocted the secret soft drink formula in this brass kettle. This formula still remains today as one of the most *reverend* "trade secrets" in the world.

The trade mark "Coca-Cola" was first used in the market-place at Jacobs' pharmacy in Atlanta and Coca-Cola was dispensed from a unique dispenser.

"Coca-Cola" and "Coke" were registered as trade marks in *1893* and *1945*, respectively and registration has been renewed periodically since then. In fact, we celebrated our 100th anniversary of the trade mark "Coca-Cola" in 1993.

The never-ending battle against *substitution* was the major factor in the evolution of the distinctive *"contour bottle"* that was developed in *1915*. The now familiar *"contour bottle"* shape was granted registration as a US *patent* in *1915* and as a *trade mark* in *1977*, an honour accorded to only a handful of other packages.

The Chicago world's fair of 1933 marked the introduction of the first automatic fountain dispenser, and in 1938, the first coin-operated vendor was introduced into the market-place.

Together, all products bearing the Coca-Cola trade mark and which are based upon proprietary formulations make up the Coca-Cola *megabrand*, the most powerful force in the history of the soft drink industry. For example, a recent independent *"brand power"* survey by *Landor and Associates* found

Coca-Cola to be not only the *best* known *brand name* in the world, but the most *admired* and *most esteemed* as well. Also, *Financial World* recently reported that as at 1995, the Coca-Cola megabrand was estimated to be an asset worth over *$42.8 billion.*

Thus, in protecting our most valuable asset, our *trade mark* group takes a number of steps to make certain that the company's trade marks are properly *registered* and *maintained* through renewals, and that our licenses are properly recorded where required by governmental authority, and that our trade marks are properly used, *whenever* and *wherever* they are used.

The magnitude of the trade mark operations is illustrated by the fact that we have in force at present over 13,000 registrations throughout the world, with 1,800 registrations pending. In recent years, we have renewed our trade mark registrations in China, Vietnam, Budapest, Prague and other Eastern European markets that have opened up with the fall of the Berlin Wall.

III What are the Licensing and Policing Activities of the Company?

The majority of our company's *licensing* activities typically involve agreements with:

- Our bottlers, wholesalers and advertising agencies concerning the manufacture, sale and distribution of our beverage products;
- Our suppliers concerning the manufacture, sale and distribution of merchandise for non-beverage use, and
- Our suppliers concerning the development of improved technology for use throughout the Coca-Cola system.

These bottler agreements are highly confidential and time does not permit me to share all of the details of these agreements with you today. However, suffice it to say, a typical bottler agreement will generally authorise the bottler for a perpetual or specified term to bottle and sell our soft drinks in designated packages within certain *territorial* boundaries, and contain other condition that ensure the highest standards of *quality* and *uniformity*. You should particularly note that generally we only license our bottlers the right to *use* our trade marks and not our trade names. We also include *"confidentiality"*, *"termination upon default"* and *"no contest clauses"* that survive the termination of the agreement. Also, we always retain all *enforcement* rights concerning our valuable trade marks.

Another important licensing activity involves our Olympics and World Cup contracts, global advertising and other marketing-related activities. These licensing activities require expertise, not only in trade mark and copyright laws, but also advertising and entertainment law.

Another important function of the trade mark group is to file various types of trade mark litigation designed to protect the company's trade marks and trade dress. First are the infringement and *counterfeiting* actions, such as have occurred recently in:

- USA—Stew's Cola
- US Export to Asia—Coli Cola
- USA—contour bottle
- Eastern Europe—contour bottle
- Sofia (Bulgaria)—different pricing:
  - real coke
  - fake coke
- Far East—contour bottle
- UK—Sainsbury Cola (trade dress)
- Korea—Fanta orange product
- Korea—Sprite product
- Eastern Europe—Joy and Joke Cola were introduced. I can assure you that this was no *"joke"* to "coke"!

Incidentally, we have adopted certain international *trade dress criteria* for protection of our products, including, inter alia, (1) colour, (2) verticality as primary package description, (3) script-spencerian, (4) device—dynamic ribbon or original circles, and (5) trade mark—primary or secondary—cola (etc.). Big or little—our primary objective is to eliminate any product or source of confusion in the market place.

Next are the syrup piracy or *substitution* or *passing off* actions involving substitution of *bogus* syrup in our bag-in-box and stainless steel figal containers. For example, we have recently obtained *injunctive* relief and *seizure* orders against syrup pirates in four sets of cases filed in *New York, Puerto Rico*, the *United Kingdom* and *Australia.* The law prohibits these types of piracy activities and provides that when a consumer orders a product by a brand name, the consumer must be served that product or be advised that it is unavailable.

Note: in the UK, we were told that it would be difficult to obtain *Anton Piller* orders—ex parte seizures. However, persistence paid off and we were successful in establishing a new trade mark/counterfeiting precedent in the UK!

Another type of trade mark litigation that we frequently encounter concerns *trade disparagement* cases. This involves the improper use of our trade marks, trade dress, or simulations thereof, on various items. For example, we have *enjoined* the use of:

- "Enjoy cocaine" advertising
  - Posters/T-shirts
- Minute mud advertising and
- Coca-Cola stash cans for hiding drugs.

Another type of licensing activity involves our merchandise licensing programme. For example, in order to prevent the registration and use of our trade marks in *non-soft* drink categories, the company initiated in *1982*, a MLD programme of registring its marks in a variety of classes. In order to ensure that these registrations can be maintained, the company has licensed over 100 manufacturers in *27* countries to produce non-beverage articles displaying "Coke" and "Coca-Cola" such as:

- Clothing
- Trays and clocks and
- Bottle radios.

The company charges a royalty for the use of its trade marks on these articles and received over *$10 million* in 1994.

Incidentally I should also mention that our trade mark group also includes investigators or super spies, as they are called, who are very active in gathering intelligence and evidence for use in these trade mark actions. They were extremely effective during recent world cup games in the USA, relative to halting "ambush marketing" activities by our competitors.

During 1995, we brought over 600 cases against trade mark infringers, and defended over 200 cases alleging infringement by our company.

The third type of licensing activity is handled by our *patent* group. The patent group is responsible for all worldwide patent filings, all secret ingredient procurement, all development, licensing, engineering design, computer, patent and trade secret litigation. The technical contract area generated over 3,500 technical agreements and $25 million dollars in royalty income during 1995.

Everyone knows that international business transactions, and the associated acquisition and licensing of intellectual property are often considered the *glamorous* side of our law practice. However, be that as it may, special problems and legal pitfalls exist which are unique to these endeavours.

Thus, as international licensing practitioners, we are required to work closely with our counterparts around the world to ensure that we stay abreast of the relevant tax and cartel laws, particularly those that affect, "exclusivity", cross-licensing, and "field of use" licensing. Also, we must remain prudent in *"selection and clearance of a mark"*, using three key criteria: (1) *market appeal of the mark*, (2) the mark's *distinctiveness*, and (3) the mark's *availability*. Careful attention should be afforded to *"establishing rights to mark"* a critical factor being "proper use of the mark". US law was changed several years ago to allow applications based upon a *''good-faith intent''* to use the marks. Although registrations do not issue until actual use has begun by this method, an intent-to-use application can obtain a "notice of allowance" indicating probable registration after clearing the examination by PTO and the public opposition period. This gives applicants greater comfort in proceeding with new marks.

Advertising of the mark or slogan can be burdensome, particularly in those countries involving language issues. For example, "can't beat the feeling" in Japanese translates to "I feel coke". Comparative advertising is acceptable in the USA but not in many foreign countries. The ideal situation is to perfect "one mark throughout the world", and standardise your advertising and licensing agreements so that at least the essential trade mark provisions and control factors are reduced to writing and that procedures are in place for periodic supervision of the manner of use of trade marks.

For example, to protect the validity of a licensed trade mark in most countries, a trade-mark owner should require a *written agreement* in which:

- Every licensed use is identified;
- The owner has the contractual right to control the character or quality of the licensee's wares or services;
- Exclude unsafe or dangerous products;
- A mechanism is provided for the owner to exercise control—for example, a right of inspection and testing coupled with a right to terminate for non-compliance with the owner's quality standards; and
- The licensee is required prominently to identify the trade mark owner and the existence of the licence on packaging and on advertising or promotional materials used in connection with the licensee's wares or services; and
- Insurance—loss payable to licensor;
- Disclaimer—limitation of liability.

IV What are the Global Trends that Affect Trade Mark Owners?

Communication media: first, one of the most recognised trends going into the 1990s is that communication media will continue to *change* technologically and the audience will continue to be *fragmented.* That trend is substantiated by the following:

- There are fewer newspapers;
- Network TV have a shrinking share of viewers;
- Cable viewers and VCR usage continue to increase;
- Phone, cellular phones, fax machines, video text, computers—may all merge into a single medium; and
- The number of available media alternatives continue to grow and become globalised.

Secondly, *decline of mass market*: another trend that impacts on trade marks is that consumers are harder to reach. They are more isolated, more regionalized, more fragmented, more individualistic, more demanding, more informed, more stressed, more discriminating. We are seeing shorter market life for products. More *"niche"* products.

Our slogan—place our products within arm's reach of desire becomes more difficult to realise!

Thirdly, *global market*: the *cliché* of the 1990s is that we are in a global economy. One of the manifestations of the global economy in the consumer retail area is that we are seeing the creation of large multinational retail enterprises, including grocery stores, retailers like *Wal-mart* going international. Couple that to the decline of centralised economies and we see fertile ground for the practitioners of trade mark law.

Finally, *trading blocks*: another trend that is accelerating is the creation of multinational trading blocks. The European Union, NAFTA and other groups of countries are implementing their own trading blocks and, no doubt, will be adding new members. Naturally, the objective of these trading blocks is to lower trade barriers among the participating states.

V US Trade Marks Recent Decisions

Communication media: there is a recent case that underscores the changes in what we consider communication media. *Playboy Enterprises, Inc.* v. *Frena*, 839 F. Supp 1552 (MD Fla 1993). In the playboy case, the defendant George Frena operated a subscription bulletin-board service that allowed subscribers to download files containing unauthorised copies of photographs in digitised form to their home computers. The defendant used the trade marks "playboy" and "playmate" to identify many of the files. The court had no problem in finding *trade mark infringement*. Even though a different medium was used, the services they provided were "virtually identical". The court also found that it did not matter whether a subscriber was the person who used the trade mark "playboy" to describe the file.

Decline of mass markets: with the segmentation of consumers and the development of niche markets, *product differentiation* is critical, and consequently *trade dress* becomes significantly more important.

The Supreme Court recently decided a trade dress case, *Two Pesos. Inc.* v. *Taco Cabana, Inc.*, 112 S Ct. 2753 (1992). The case involved an assertion of *trade dress infringement* against Two Pesos. The court held that trade dress "may include the shape and general appearance of the exterior of the restaurant, the identifying sign, the interior kitchen floor plan, the decor, the menu, the equipment to serve food, server's uniforms and other features reflecting the total image of the restaurant". The court held that inherently distinctive trade dress is protectable without a *showing of secondary meaning*. However, it should be pointed out that there was evidence that the defendant had intentionally copied the features asserted as trade dress.

Another recent case dealt with the issue of whether colour can be protected as a trade mark: *Qualitex Co.* v. *Jacobson Products Co.*, 13 F 3d 1297 (9th Cir. 1993). Qualitex sold pads for dry-cleaning presses in a green gold colour under the "sun glow" mark. The green-gold colour was federally registered as a trade mark. Jacobson began making a pressing pad with the same colour. The court held that registration of a colour as a trade mark was appropriate only in unusual circumstances such as were present in the Owens-Corning fibreglass case (vast sums of money spent in advertising and no competitive need for the colour pink). However, despite traditional "colour confusion" and "colour depletion" arguments against such trade mark protection, the court found that the sale of the defendant's product constituted unfair competition under the Lanham Act, section 43(a). The court found that the trade dress was *non-functional*, had acquired *secondary meaning* and there was a *likelihood of confusion*. This case has recently been upheld by the US Supreme Court who found that "color can be registered as a trade mark".

Reaching the consumer with creative advertising is one way to overcome the fragmentation of markets; however that has its risks. An interesting recent case involved a "Vanna White" look-alike robot: *White* v. *Samsung Electronics America, Inc.*, 989 F 2d 1512 (9th Cir 1993). The case involved the use of a television advertisement showing a robot dressed in a wig and gown similar to the hair and dress of Vanna White. The set was similar to the wheel of fortune and the advertisement used a caption "longest running game show. 2012 A.D." The plaintiff brought a case alleging misappropriation of her likeness under California state law and under the Lanham Act. The District Court granted summary judgment for the defendant. The 9th Circuit reversed. In respect of misappropriation of likeness, the appeals court found that the district court had improperly limited the rights to a name or likeness. The important inquiry is whether the identity was appropriated. In respect of the Lanham Act claim, the court found a celebrity's persona is a "mark". The court also reasoned that the reasons or source of a celebrity's fame are "goods" for the purpose of a Lanham Act analysis. The court found that there was a genuine issue of fact and remanded.

Global markets: one of the consequences of the "global markets" is the increasing number of parallel imports that are taking place.

A recent case held that importation of grey goods could constitute unfair competition: *Ferrero USA Inc.* v. *Ozak Trading, Inc.*, 753 F. Supp 1240 (D NJ 1991), aff'd 935 F 2d 1280. Ferrero USA was the exclusive distributor of Tic Tac in the USA. The US version of Tic Tac had only 1.5 calories. Ozak bought the genuine Tic Tac product in the UK and imported it into the USA. The UK product had two calories. Ferrero USA brought suit for unfair competition and false advertising (Lanham Act, section 32(1) and 43(a)). The court found in favour of the plaintiff on the basis that the products were materially different.

I mention these cases because, unfortunately, I doubt whether any of these decisions would have favoured the trade mark owner if they had been litigated outside the USA.

Trading blocks: there have been a number of recent developments in the area of trading blocks.

NAFTA: first, NAFTA defines trade marks as consisting of "any sign, or any combination of signs, capable of distinguishing the goods or services of one person from those of another, including personal names, designs, letters, numerals, colors, figurative elements, or the shape of goods or of their packaging".

NAFTA requires the parties to provide a system for registration which requires examination of applications, notice of any refusal to register, a reasonable opportunity for the applicant to respond to the notice, publication of trade marks either before or promptly after registration, and a reasonable opportunity for interested persons to petition to cancel the registration of a trade mark. Opposition prior to registration is optional.

GATT developments: in December of 1993 the Uruguay Round of GATT negotiations concluded with a number of agreements including an accord on trade-related aspects of intellectual property rights (TRIPS Agreement). Among the relevant trade mark provisions the accord will require participating countries to:

- Register service marks in addition to trade marks;
- Enhance protection for internationally well-known marks;
- Prohibit mandatory linking of trade marks; and
- Prohibit compulsory licensing of trade marks.

EU developments: one of the effects of the European trade mark harmonisation initiative is the new UK trade mark law (the Act of 31 October 1994) that will allow for the registration of *three-dimensional shapes* and provide for easier registration of trade marks. In fact, our famous trade mark bottle was recently registered as the first trade mark under the new UK trade mark law.

VI Future Legal Issues

What issues will we be dealing with in the future? Here is a sample:

Communication media: if a bulletin board operator in *Russia* offers products for sale EXW Russia under a trade mark owned by another in the USA, and ships directly to the customer, is that operator infringing the US trade mark? What will constitute usage in the new media?

Decline of mass market: if products have a shorter market life and consumers are fragmented, how do you show *secondary meaning*? Will *trade dress be given* similar protection everywhere? Even in China? Will large retailers infringe trade dress as a way of growing *private labels*? Will other countries afford the same protection to personality rights?

Please note that the INTA task force is challenging "look-alikes" in the *UK.*

Global markets: how will trading groups address intra-group transshipments?

Trading blocks: how will the trade mark laws change as a result of harmonisation? How will parallel imports be treated in large trading groups? Will all countries require *use* to maintain trade mark rights? Will we have an *international* trade mark register?

Given these issues the trade mark practitioner will not be bored in the 1990s and the trick will be to ensure that the scales holding your *intellectual property* and *contractual* rights are preserved and decidedly weighed in your favour. That will help you "go global with your trade mark practice without going crazy".

2

INDUSTRIAL PROPERTY PROTECTION – LIFELINE FOR THE PHARMACEUTICAL INDUSTRY

*Thomas B. Cueni**

British Biotech plc is a rather unique company in Europe. Having neither sold a product yet, nor made a profit ever, the British start-up company is quoted at more than £1 billion at the London Stock Exchange. British Biotech is unique because in most other European countries, in contrast to the United States, a company could not go public without having a product on the market. It is also unique because its strength derives solely from the stock market's valuation of the patents which the company holds on a series of biotech-derived products.

Patents and the pharmaceutical industry form a symbiosis which is inseparable. Industrial property protection, and, in particular patents, form the lifeline for the research-based pharmaceutical industry. Investment of, at present, more than $500 million for the research and development of one new medicine which reaches the market can only be justified because industrial property protection grants a limited exclusivity for the commercial exploitation of such an invention. At the same time, no other industrial property right gives as much cause for controversy as do pharmaceutical and, more recently, biotechnology patents. The inherent tension between the limited monopoly of the patent which gives the successful innovator a fair chance to recoup its investments and many governments interest in containing health care cost is evident in many patent controversies.

In my introduction, I want to address the industrial property protection (IPP) theme from various angles. I want to go beyond the technical patent issues and focus on some of the more political aspects, such as the current industry problems, communicating its messages in the European and, more particularly, the Swiss biotech debate. My papers includes the following aspects:

- I shall talk about some of the myths which clouded much of the debate during the Uruguay Round;
- I will touch on recent achievements in the efforts to improve intellectual property protection world-wide, such as the minimal standards of

* Secretary General, Interpharma, Basle, Switzerland.

TRIPS, the successful US pressure to gain pipeline protection in key developing countries, the European introduction of a Supplementary Protection Certificate (SPC) for medicinal products and, *per* 1 January 1997, for agrochemical products;
- I will address some of the current IPP issues as seen from the perspective of the European R&D-based pharmaceutical industry; and
- I plan to conclude by highlighting some of the communication problems which have been exemplified in the debate about biotech patents in Europe, and, in particular, in my own country, Switzerland.

I Patents—Myths and Realities

Trade-related aspects of industrial property rights (TRIPS) were for a long time an unloved child of the Uruguay Round. For many diplomats struggling with the intrinsically difficult task of successfully completing the Round, TRIPS were a nuisance rather than an essential part of trade negotiations. The pharmaceutical industry was in the forefront of the fight for the inclusion of minimal standards of IPP as a safeguard against the trade-distorting aspects of the lack of such standards. To put the case for the industry's interest simply, two factors have to be borne in mind: first, it is relatively easy to copy a pharmaceutical product, and, secondly, no other industry spends as much on research on development as the pharmaceutical industry, namely 17 per cent of its sales. In contrast, the computer industry spends just above 8 per cent, the electronics industry less than 6 per cent, and the huge run-up costs to the building of a new aeroplane amounts to less than 4 per cent of sales. On average it takes ten to 12 years from patent filing to market launch of a new medicine, and R&D investments of products reaching the markets today probably exceed $500 million per product.

The patent debate in Argentina may serve as an example of some of the myths which were used to protect the invested interests of a powerful national copier industry which still controls about 60 per cent of the Argentine market with its pirate copies.

A first such myth is that patents create monopolies. In reality, patent protection offers protection only for a limited time. The exclusivity is limited to eight to ten years and, in reality, most new introductions compete with similar products. Competition is fierce in almost all therapeutic areas, and even new chemical entities which introduce a novel therapeutic concept are followed by competitor products within a short time. In fact, over the last two decades the time lag in which a company enjoys real exclusivity has shortened considerably: from several years in the case of the beta-blockers, calcium channel blockers, or H2-antagonists, to just a few weeks when the protease inhibitor used in the fight against AIDS was introduced recently.

A second myth is that patents are a significant factor in escalating health-care costs. This argument ignores the fact that there is a clear and established link between patent protection and the rate of innovation, but no such link between the strength of IPP and price levels. France and the USA are two countries with traditionally strong patent protection, yet the price of medicines in these two countries is quite different. Furthermore, the introduction of patents does have no effect on products already marketed. It is estimated that in Argentina 85 to 90 per cent of pharmaceutical sales cover products whose patent protection has already expired in industrialised countries. Moreover—and I shall return to this—it will take at least ten years before the effect of product patents is really felt in developing countries. It is also a reality that pirate products in countries such as Argentina were occasionally sold at a higher price than the original product. According to a study done by CAEME, the organisation of multinational companies, unit prices of national products in Argentina exceeded those of multinational companies by an average of 14 per cent and 48 per cent in the years between 1982 and 1993. Another myth is the alleged domination of countries by multinational companies, an argument used to hide the real motive, the protection of vested interests of powerful local families which became rich pirating R&D investments of others. First, a major part of the market, the off-patent segment, will continue to be free, and countries such as Germany show the potential for companies focusing on the generic sector. Secondly, the introduction of product patents may lead to new forms of co-operation in the form of licences and co-marketing, as was done in the cases of Italy and Spain.

There are more myths, such as that only international companies are able to engage in research and development of pharmaceuticals. The fact of the matter is that there is no true innovation without proper industrial property protection. Pharmaceutical research in Canada almost came to a standstill following the introduction of the most arbitrary system of compulsory licensing. Many developing countries do have a pool of first class scientists. For years, these scientists had to emigrate if they wanted to see any benefit in their research.

II Achievements

The pharmaceutical industry, working in an environment which is highly regulated, has a strong track record of complaining about adverse effects of government policy. However, it has to be said that the industry has had some notable achievements in its ongoing struggle for improved protection of industrial property.

For all the patent lawyers who for many years had been engaged in a rather frustrating debate about patent harmonisation in the WIPO context, the acceptance of the *TRIPS agreement* with its minimal standards of IPP, is quite remarkable. For the first time, all signatory states of the World Trade Organisation committed themselves to 'patents for both products and process inventions in all fields of technology'. These standards are based on a:

- minimal 20 years term,
- guarantee national treatment,
- offer protection irrespective of whether a product is imported or locally manufactured, and
- contain objective and concise criteria for the issuing of compulsory licences.

Although the TRIPS agreement, from an industry point of view is far from perfect and has many shortcomings, the significance of the World Trade Organisation requiring minimal standards on industrial property protection which are an enforceable part of the multilateral trade system cannot be overestimated.

Many observers and, in particular, many of my former diplomat colleagues view the tough *bilateralism which the United States* applied in the IPP area with a great deal of frustration. They saw the US pressure on many of the newly industrialised countries as anathema to a well-functioning multilateral trade system. Having spent quite a bit of time travelling through the Latin Americas in the early 1990s and spreading the gospel of IPP with conviction but no '301' to follow, I tend to disagree. The breakthroughs which American trade officials reached in Korea and Mexico were an extremely persuasive argument for recalcitrant newly industrialised countries as well as for European governments which were afraid of being left on the sidelines. And even today, it is fair to admit that few people other than my persistently stubborn American colleagues would have bet on the recent remarkable patent victory in Brazil, including a provision for pipeline protection. The importance of US pressure is still the main factor in speeding up the implementation of the TRIPS agreement.

Whereas many of the patent achievements in the US are the result of remarkable co-operation between companies are the very professional lobbying of our American sister association, PhRMA, and USTR, European industry has had its success too. In 1993, following years of lobbying by the research-based pharmaceutical industry, the European Community introduced a *supplementary protection certificate* (SPC) granting a maximum patent protection of 15 years following market introduction. It is fair to acknowledge the reference to the competitiveness of European industry compared to industries in Japan and the US, both which enjoy patent term restoration legislation in their home countries, which played a major part in the SPC's introduction. It is also fair to state that the European industry won this battle without having to offer concession similar to Hatch-Waxman or "Bolar" in the United States.

III Current Issues

Having won the battle for minimum standards for an effective patent protection within the World Trade Organisation gives no reason for industry complacency. In contrast, one might be quite surprised about the multiplicity of issues we are still faced with as just a cursory glance at some of the current IPP issues will demonstrate.

From a global perspective, the *TRIPS agreement*, as already mentioned, needs attention and, hopefully, the review of the TRIPS agreement will allow some improvements. These include the need to shorten the transitional periods. Transition for implementing TRIPS standards should correspond to individual country's level of development, and whereas few people would bother to pressure countries such as Mali, Burundi, or Bhutan, a ten-year transitional option for countries such as India, Argentina or Egypt is unacceptably long. A country such as India which has a well-developed chemical and pharmaceutical industry should not be allowed to exploit the disclosure of inventions in Europe and the USA to produce bulk and processed pharmaceuticals and sell them all over the world where the patent system is defective.

Pipeline protection is another very important issue for the pharmaceutical industry because the lack of administrative protection for products new to the market of the respective country and patent elsewhere unduly delays the benefits of the introduction of product patents.

Other concerns by the industry are the necessary clarification regarding the protection of registration data (ten years from registration), the patentability of plants and animals, and the prohibition of testing for commercial purposes. It should be clarified that the existing exception for "experimental use" only applies to genuine research, at least outside the US. Finally, the review of TRIPS should clarify that exhaustion of rights should be applicable only to national states or regional areas that have achieved full economic integration.

A second area of concern is the discussion about giving *preferential treatment to generics*. The fact that generic companies in the United States can prepare their "abridged new drug application dossiers" (ANDAs) prior to patent expiry is no excuse for accepting a similar infringement of patent rights in Europe. It is quite clear, e.g., that conducting commercial bioequivalence studies with a substance which is still patent-protected violates basis industrial property rights. Fair generic competition following patent expiry is legitimate, speeding up the introduction of generics by undermining patents is not. It must be hoped that the European Commission will adhere to its present position.

Whereas discussion about this so-called "Bolar-type" amendment focuses so far on Europe, the issue of generics and respect for proper patent terms must be seen in a global context. It would be much easier to argue the patent case in Europe if Bolar did not exist in the USA. Furthermore, the renewed Canadian discussions about facilitating generic market entry by abolishing the existing "linkage" regulation is another area of great concern.

The third area of concern is the erosion of patent rights within the European Community through *parallel trade*. Based on the notion that the patent holder's rights are exhausted, once a company introduces voluntarily a product in any given market of the European Community, the European Court of Justice has in the past consistently put free trade rules above the protection of industrial property. It would go beyond a brief introduction to address the issue of parallel trade in pharmaceuticals in its full complexity. However, two problems must be addressed:

A The case of Spain

Spain introduced patent protection for pharmaceuticals only in late 1992. Because it takes about ten to 12 years from patent filing to pharmaceutical product launch, the first patented medicines will not reach the Spanish market before 2002. Thus, in the case of Spain, low-price products marketed in Spain which never enjoyed patent protection in Spain may be exported and undermine the intellectual property protection of medicines which are still patented in other countries.

The Spanish case is primarily a case of intellectual property protection. However, the lack of adequate patent protection in Spain is aggravated by the very low prices in Spain which are the result of:

- government price controls at the time of introduction,
- competition by Spanish copy products exploiting the lack of patent protection (e.g. for a company's major product, two copies received marketing approval in Spain six months ahead of the originator),
- adverse effects of the devaluation of the Spanish Peseta,
- an inability of pharmaceutical companies to adjust their prices to inflation or currency fluctuation,
- an inability of companies to withdraw their products from the Spanish market.

Whereas it is true that the European Court of Justice has ruled in favour of the free flow of goods when a similar case (*Merck/Stephar*, 1981) was raised in Italy, the situation—as the Commission has acknowledged—has changed since then. Over the last few years the Commission has consistently upheld the importance of strong protection of intellectual property worldwide and demonstrate this through:

- the introduction of the Supplementary Protection Certificate (SPC) for medicines on 2 January 1993,

- its support for minimal IPP standards in the GATT TRIPS agreement,
- its support for efforts to speed up the implementation of these standards in newly industrialised countries such as Argentina, Brazil, and Turkey,
- Commissioner Monti's recent affirmation, although qualified, of the Commission intention not to introduce a Bolar amendment in the EU.

However, the European Court of Justice did not follow the recommendation of the Advocate General and confirmed the Merck/Stephar decision in its *Merck/Primecrown Ltd.* decision (1996).

B The Trade-distorting Impact of Administered Prices and Currency Fluctuation

Parallel trade is a symptom rather than a cause of the industry's problem. It is symptomatic for the industry's inability to react to price discrepancies which are primarily the result of government price controls and currency fluctuations. Pharmaceuticals are a special case for a number of reasons:

- First, the price differences that make parallel trade worthwhile arise not from the decision of manufacturers but from those of governments. Therefore, parallel trade is not a result of market arbitrage but a trade distortion resulting from government price controls.
- Secondly, parallel trade in pharmaceuticals can lead to confusion for the patient because of differences in labelling and patient information. Furthermore, they would hinder recall procedures or even make them impossible because a manufacturer does not know where a wholesaler sells his product.
- Thirdly, the benefactor of parallel trade is, in general, neither the social security system nor the patient, but the parallel trader.
- Fourthly, because of the special nature of pharmaceutical products, the manufacturer, by law or since he has an ethical obligation to market, may not be at liberty to withdraw a product from a market where his price has been eroded through a combination of price controls, inflation and currency devaluation.
- Fifthly, parallel trade undermines patent protection because it exposes patented products to arbitrary price controls of other countries through the back door. It also amplifies the effect of currency erosion without allowing the manufacturer to adjust prices in line with competitive market forces.

So far, in the inherent tension between the Community's objectives regarding health (sustainable growth rates of health budgets), trade (free trade) and industrial policy (foster innovation), the latter has always had to give in.

Finally and maybe the most complex issue the industry has been faced with was the debate about the so-called *"Biotech Directive"* 98/44/EC, eventually adopted in July 1998. It would be oversimplifying to say that the lack of a strong biotech sector in Europe is due to the uncertainty created by the controversies surrounding patentability of biotechnology derived products. Other aspects such as the missing venture-capital markets, obstacles to IPOs (initial public offering), different attitudes to technology transfer among European universities and a lack of entrepreneurs among many continental academics may be as important or even more important. It is also true that many of the traditional European pharmaceutical companies such as the Swiss, the British, and Novo-Nordisk are on a level par with or even more advanced than their American competitors. But it is a fact that effective patent protection is even more of a lifeline to a start-up company than for the traditional pharmaceutical industry. To use an example from Switzerland, transgenic animal models are used as a matter of routine in many research products of Novartis and Roche. So far, none of these animal models is patented, the reason being that they are part of early phases of pre-clinical trials, the companies are not in the business of selling transgenic mice and these mice are used as instruments but are of no commercial interest *per se*. For an academic, however, who invented an animal model for an important disease, effective protection of his invention may be an essential prerequisite for establishing a start-up company.

IV The Communication Challenge

Personally, I have no doubt that Europe needs the "Biotech Directive", 98/44/EC, adopted in 1998, clarifying that inventions derived from biotechnology are patentable as are any other inventions.

Very much involved in the debate on the biotech referendum in Switzerland, which the Swiss People voted on in summer 1998, I am, however, also very much aware of the communication challenge which industry experts have so far struggled with. The rather radical Swiss biotech referendum had called for a total ban:

- on the production, sale, and use of transgenic animals,
- on deliberate release of genetically modified organisms, and
- on patenting of plants and animals.

This referendum was a matter which questioned the future of modern biomedical research in Switzerland, not only in the laboratories of the big Basle companies but, even more so, because they do not have the alternative of moving, the research laboratories at Swiss universities. A study by the Zurich Polytechnic which we had commissioned estimated the potential job losses if this referendum had passed at more than 40,000 for the year 2005. And yet, if it had been just on the patent issue, the fight against this referendum would have been a very tough one. Switzerland may be an extreme case, but a lack of understanding for the IPP biotech case is widespread. The problem is real when it is known that many Swiss university professors questioned about the importance of intellectual property protection state that patents are of little concern to them. The message from a Swiss Nobel laureate who states that living organisms should not be patentable because they will never be of exactly the same structure creates a tough communication challenge. And it is not confined to Switzerland, as can be seen from a quotation of the Chairman of the German Doctors Federation that he regarded the notion of human gene patenting as absurd.

The Swiss People finally voted approximately 2:1 against the biotech referendum.

However, the debate about the biotech referendum in Switzerland had shown that, so far, the industry has been relatively inept in responding to this communication challenge. We have failed to admit that the discussion on biotech patents goes beyond the traditional arguments. Yes, it is true that huge investments in research and development will only be made if the resulting inventions bring not only hope and benefit to patients suffering from as yet uncurable diseases but also to the successful innovator. However, perhaps some over-zealousness in claiming intellectual property rights may have done more harm than we would wish for. And it is true that a mere technocratic response to the biotech patent discussion may be inadequate to respond to some real concerns which are expressed in this context.

Although I am not a patent expert myself, as someone who is frequently engaged in discussions on political issues, I would like briefly to address some of the key issues.

First, patentability of human genes: the human body or parts thereof *per se* are not patentable. However, DNA molecules which do occur in nature can be patented after they have been isolated and can be reproduced subject to their novelty, their inventiveness (non-obviousness), and their industrial applicability (utility). These patent criteria are strict and, in my view, should clearly limit excessive claims on genes based on computerised mapping of genes or gene sequences. In my view, the frequent criticism that discoveries rather than inventions are submitted in patent filings cannot always be dismissed out of hand. But I am confident that all major patent offices in the world, including the US patent office, will apply these criteria in their original and strict sense and not grant patents for mere discoveries.

Secondly, patenting of animals and plants: here, we do suffer from a peculiar European problem. The exclusion of plant and animal varieties from patentability which is part of the European Patent Convention creates difficult problems of terminology. Why, for instance, should the Harvard Mouse be considered a new animal rather than a different breed of mouse? And how can a new plant be distinguished from a new plant variety if, as shown in the PGS case, not even the European Patent Office Appeal Board can agree on the definition of plant *v.* variety?

Thirdly, we may also have to go beyond existing concepts. Our Swiss debate showed that the classic value system is being increasingly challenged and that many people make little distinction between men and animals. Thus, the patent notion that you cannot patent "men" but that you can patent animals as a whole is called into question. Is it not conceivable to admit that the invention is not the animal as such, be it the "oncomouse" or the Immutran "pig", but rather what does not occur in nature, namely the genes artificially introduced into these transgenic animals, the "oncogene" or the "DAF" gene?

Fourthly, industry may have and may still show too little respect for concerns by traditionally friendly constituents such as European farmers. A few years ago, the industry's reluctance to accept the political necessity of plant breeder's rights and farmer privileges were the main sticking points in blocking a desired revision of the Swiss patent law. The main concessions were now made in the European Union without much fuss as part of the new Biotech Directive. Furthermore, company policies which make genetically modified plants resistant to agrochemicals of the same company, thus creating new dependencies, are again seen as problematic examples of restrictive business practices. Having said this, past experience shows that such new crops will have to face competition soon.

Fifthly, the debate about the practical application of the Biodiversity Convention will not be easy. Whereas it is generally agreed that exploration and exploitation of genetic resources must take place based on prior informed consent and mutually agreed terms, the exact nature and scope of such contracts are still subject to debate.

In the course of the very heated debate about biotech patentability some of the basic truths tend to be forgotten, first that patents encourage disclosure of information as against secrecy, secondly that patents encourage investment in research and development for the benefit of mankind, and thirdly that they give no right to use inventions where other regulations such as, e.g., animal protection laws, are involved. Maybe, we must repackage these home truths and communicate them to a public which is still apprehensive about the potential risks as well as benefits of new technologies. But perhaps, we must go beyond repackaging and accept some limitations which may still be regarded as heresy by purist patent experts.

Panel II
Selected Financial Aspects of Industrial Property

3
INDUSTRIAL PROPERTY RIGHTS AND PRIVATE SECTOR DEVELOPMENT: LESSONS FOR DEVELOPING COUNTRIES

*Carlos A. Primo Braga**

I Introduction

Industrial property rights (patents, utility models, industrial designs and trade marks) are at the core of the intellectual property systems of developing and industrialized nations. The value ascribed to intellectual property rights (IPRs) by private agents, the quality of substantive laws and enforcement vary significantly across countries, however. In the case of developing countries, for example, the level of resources committed to the protection of these rights is often inadequate and the demand for protection by local entrepreneurs is limited.

The globalisation of economic activities and the expansion of international transactions involving knowledge-intensive products have generated many frictions in this area, reflecting differences in national approaches toward IPRs protection. This has fostered a movement for international convergence toward higher standards of protection at world-wide level. Over the last few years, many developing countries began to reform their IPRs regimes, in response to new international commitments (e.g., the "Agreement on Trade Related Intellectual Property Rights, including Trade in Counterfeit Goods" (TRIPS) negotiated in the Uruguay Round of multilateral trade negotiations), domestic economic reforms and external pressures.

This paper reviews what are the potential implications of stronger IPRs

* Manager of the Information for Development Programme and of the TechNet (Technology Network) initiative at the World Bank. The assistance of C. Fink is gratefully acknowledged. The views expressed here are the author's own and they should not be attributed to the World Bank, its Executive Board of Directors, or any of its member countries.

(particularly, industrial property rights) for economic development.[1] It begins by analysing some aspects of the contemporary debate on the economics of intellectual property rights. It goes on to discuss the above-mentioned patterns of convergence. The paper ends with a discussion of what is needed to transform this process of convergence into effective levers of innovation in the developing world. Its main message is that changes in substantive laws are just the first step in the process of transforming IPRS systems in the developing world. Unless adequate resources are committed to the administration and enforcement of these rights and local entrepreneurs become convinced of the benefits of these new regimes, these reforms will fall short of their potential.

II The Economics of IPRs

The conventional economic rationale for the protection of IPRs is often framed in terms of Arrow's (1962) seminal work concerning the incomplete appropriability of knowledge. IPRs can be understood as second-best solutions to the problems created by the "public good" nature of knowledge. To the extent that they enhance "appropriability", IPRs are expected to foster investment in research and development (R&D) and knowledge creation. They create, however, a static distortion as they constrain the current consumption of knowledge, by enhancing the market power of title-holders. In short, IPRs involve a "bargain" between the producers of knowledge and society, which is mediated by the government.[2]

The above rationale is typically used to explain the economics of patent and copyright laws. With respect to trade marks and industrial designs, the basis for protection is more often framed in terms of incentives for investments in reputation (quality/distinctive features) rather than innovation *per se*. Trade secrets, in turn, are rationalised as a necessary supplement to the patent system. Their main positive role is to foster innovations that do not comply with the strict requirements for patentability of products and processes. In this paper, we focus our analysis on industrial property rights as instruments to promote innovation.

The long-term trend with respect to IPRs protection in developed economies has been clearly in the direction of the strengthening of these rights. As pointed out by Winter (1989), however, there is no clear theoretical presumption that a movement towards stronger standards of protection will always be welfare-enhancing. Patent races may lead to over-investment in R&D. Private returns may exceed social returns as protection increases and inventors can appropriate additional gains in assets that are complementary to

[1] This paper relies extensively on Primo Braga (1996) and Primo Braga and Fink (1996).

[2] For an early discussion of the terms of this bargain, see the "monopoly profit incentive" and the "exchange for secrets" theses as presented in Machlup (1958).

the innovation. And the increase in static distortions in the consumption of knowledge (because of monopolistic practices) may overcome the dynamic benefits of additional R&D.

In spite of these considerations, there is broad recognition that IPRs systems play an important role in the promotion of technological progress. It is true that other institutional arrangements can be used to foster the generation of knowledge without necessarily relying on property rights. The direct production of knowledge by the government and the reliance on subsidies and/or government procurement to foster R&D activities by the private sector illustrate some of the available alternatives.[3] But historical hindsight suggests that market-driven incentives (as exemplified by the *proprietary* approach) provide the most effective way to organize economic activities, including the creation of knowledge through R&D.

IPRs are territorial in nature. Nations must reach accommodation as their residents seek protection for their works abroad. The caveats that apply to the desirability of ever stronger protection for IPRs at the national level gain an additional dimension when the analysis moves to the international level. If the existing (or potential) title-holders are predominantly foreigners, the strengthening of protection raises the possibility of an international rent transfer.[4] The net welfare impact of the reform for a developing country will depend on how local consumers and producers are affected, not to mention the implications of the reform for world levels (and composition) of R&D. Generalisations can only be made if strong assumptions are adopted. For example, if one assumes that the supply of innovations in the South (i.e. in the developing world) is rather inelastic and that IPRs regimes are of limited relevance in influencing trade, foreign direct investment and technology transfer, then it follows that reforms geared to strengthen IPRs are in essence exercises in rent transfer. A much more optimistic view of the welfare implications for developing countries of such reforms emerges, if one assumes that trade, investment and technology flows, as well as R&D expenditures, will be positively affected by the strengthening of protection (Sherwood 1993).

There are some aspects of the economics of IPRs that are less controversial, however. First, the economic interests affected by the availability and quality of protection are significant. After all, "at some level nearly all legitimately traded goods and services operate under patent, copyright, or trade mark protection" (Maskus 1994, 13). Moreover, trade in knowledge-intensive goods and services has been among the most dynamic components of international trade over the last few decades. Figure 1 illustrates this in the

[3] For a discussion of these issues see Dasgupta and Stoneman (1987).

[4] Available statistics suggest that this is a valid description of the situation of developing countries. By 1982, of the 200,000 patents awarded by developing countries, for example, 175,000 (87.5 per cent) were awarded to foreign patentees. For the major developing countries, the share was around 79 per cent. See WIPO (1983) and Subramanian (1994).

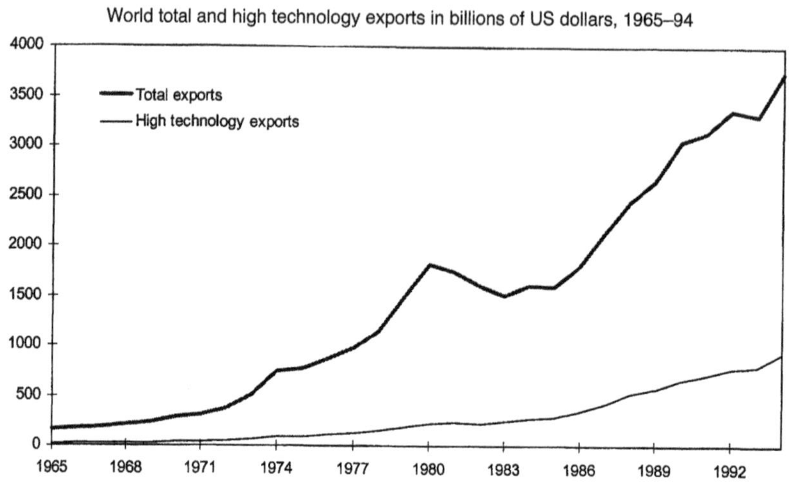

Figure 1: *The growing importance of knowledge-intensive activities in international goods trade*

Note: The definition of high technology exports relies on the approach described in Primo Braga and Yeats (1992).

Source: Comtrade Database (United Nations).

context of the growing share of high-tech trade (products that are R&D-intensive) in global merchandise trade.

Secondly, as economies become more integrated, the potential for international conflicts over IPRs tends to increase. A look at the number of Special 301 cases initiated by the United States in the 1990s highlights this trend.

Thirdly, as markets expand and competition in the R&D sector increases, the amount of R&D per patented innovation tends to increase (Kortun 1993) while the capacity of IPRs holders to deter the introduction of competitive products and processes tends to shrink. The experience of the pharmaceutical industry exemplifies this trend. In the 1960s, a patented drug was often able to enjoy as much as ten years of market exclusivity. Currently, a competitive drug—covered by other patents—often comes to the market in less than four years after the introduction of the original drug (Mossinghoff 1996).

All of these considerations suggest that the pressure for international convergence toward minimum standards of protection on a global basis are here to stay. Moreover, the efficiency with which any given national system of protection will promote innovation will be increasingly affected by the timeliness of the associated administrative and enforcement procedures.

II International Convergence

Since the early 1990s, many developing countries have reformed their IPRs regimes, strengthening the rights of innovators and creators. A detailed analysis of these events is beyond the scope of this work. International trade agreements (e.g. NAFTA and association agreements with the European Union) and bilateral negotiations have been instrumental in this process. The outcome of the TRIPS negotiations will further promote this trend. TRIPS implies the acceptance of minimum standards of protection (not only in terms of coverage of subject matter and scope of protection, but also with respect to administration and enforcement) and the "universal" coverage of the agreement (special and differential treatment for developing countries is limited to the concession of generous transition periods). It will promote a much greater level of "harmonisation" of IPRs protection than was believed feasible a few years ago.

If one focuses, for example, on patents and trade marks, many countries will be required to adapt their legislations, administrative and enforcement practices to comply with the new standards: Among the most relevant changes one can mention[5]:

- a number of developing countries will have to extend patent protection to pharmaceutical and chemical products (among the 98 developing countries that signed the Marrakesh Agreement in April 1994, 25 did not provide patents for pharmaceutical products and 13 did not allow patents for chemical products).
- many developing countries will have to alter the term of protection of their patents that often are smaller than the 20-year term from filing mandated by the Agreement.
- absence of local production can nolonger be invoked as an acceptable cause for the grant of compulsory licences in the case of patents; accordingly, many developing countries will have to revise their compulsory licences regulations.
- clarification of the requirement of protection of well-known trade marks against registration/use by others (Article 16.3) will require additional enforcement efforts countries were speculative registration is common.
- many countries will have to extend protection to new types of marks, encompassing graphical designs and logos.
- the requirement of prompt publication of trade marks after registration will require changes in practices in the registries of many developing countries.

[5] For details see Primo Braga (1996).

IV Costs and Benefits

There are costs and benefits for developing countries reforming their IPRs regimes. Among the main costs one should take into account the additional administrative and enforcement costs, increase in payments for foreigners' proprietary knowledge, price increases associated with greater market power for knowledge producers, the costs of displacement of "pirate" activities, and the opportunity cost of additional R&D. Potential benefits include new inventions fostered by higher levels of R&D at domestic and international level, and greater technology and foreign direct investment (FDI) flows.[6] Moreover, convergence is expected to affect trade flows in products that rely on IPRs protection.

In what follows, the discussion focuses on the main potential implications of the TRIPS agreement. First, the potential impact of strengthening IPRs on trade, FDI and the transfer of technology is discussed. The basic premise is that these effects may generate allocative and dynamic benefits for the countries in question. After that, attention is given to the rent transfer aspects of the Agreement, its impact on local producers and on R&D investments in the North and in the South.

A IPRs and Trade Flows

IPRs regimes may influence trade flows. Stern (1987), for example, points out that discrepancies among national IPRs regimes generate effects analogous to non-tariff barriers. Exporters in the North have additional costs when exporting to the South (as compared to North–North trade) as they have to engage in activities designed to inhibit local imitation. It can also be argued that the international harmonisation of IPRs regimes diminishes the transaction costs of operating in different regulatory environments.

The net impact on trade flows of strengthening protection of IPRs in the South is, however, ambiguous. As pointed out by Maskus and Penubarti (1994), the higher level of protection fosters two conflicting effects. First, it will enhance the market-power of the title holder, reducing the elasticity of demand for his/her products. Secondly, it will expand the net demand for the protected products as imitators are displaced. The net trade impact will depend on which effect dominates. If the market-power effect is bigger than the market-expansion effect then trade flows may decrease in the aftermath of the reform. If the opposite holds, then strengthening IPRs protection will lead to trade expansion. In other words, the net trade effect of the TRIPS Agreement is in essence an empirical question.

[6] For a detailed discussion of each one of these potential costs and benefits see Primo Braga (1990).

Using bilateral data for the USA from 1989 covering 35 partner countries, Primo Braga and Fink (1996) estimated a gravity model for the same dependent variables analysed in Ferrantino (1993): arm's length trade, intra-firm trade, and "establishment trade" for US companies. The explanatory variables used were GDP, population, geographical distance from the USA, an estimate of trade barriers, dummies for Europe and landlocked countries, and the Rapp and Rozek index for strength of patent protection.[7] Positive coeffcients for the IPRs index are found in all equations, but the coefficient is statistically significant only with respect to arm's length trade. Taking this result at its face value, it seems that market expansion dominates market-power effects—that is, stronger IPRs protection promotes more trade.

This result is confirmed by Maskus and Penubarti (1994), who use an augmented version of the Helpman–Krugman model of monopolistic competition in examining bilateral trade flows. The results obtained suggest that firms are influenced by the strength of importing countries' patent regimes when engaging in export activities. Countries with stronger patent regimes import more than what is predicted by the Helpman–Krugman model. Moreover, the impact of patent protection on trade flows is found to be bigger in the larger developing countries.

Following Maskus and Penubarti's (1994) methodology, Primo Braga and Fink (1996) estimated a similar model with bilateral trade flows as a share of aggregate expenditure as dependent variable.[8] Explanatory variables were exporter output, importer *per capita* income, an estimate for trade barriers and the Rapp and Rozek index of the importing country interacted with dummy variables dividing the importing countries into high income, large developing, and small developing countries. In accordance with Maskus and Penubarti (1994), they show a positive impact of patent protection on trade flows within the Helpman–Krugman model.

In sum, there is mounting evidence "that IPRs are indeed "trade-related" (Maskus and Penubarti 1994, 22). These results are, of course, model specific and should be interpreted with care.[9] They suggest, however, that the implementation of TRIPS will have a net trade creating impact. Although no precise welfare predictions can be derived from them, they suggest that TRIPS may have a positive allocative impact at global level and

[7] Rapp and Rozek (1990) rated the patent laws of 157 countries on a scale from zero (for countries with no protection) to five (for countries with patent laws which fully conform to the minimum standards in U.S. Chamber of Commerce (1987).

[8] However, their country set and data source were much different from Maskus and Penubarti (1994). 1988 total manufacturing trade flows from 91 reporter (exporter) countries to 65 (importer) countries as reported to the UNSO Comtrade Database were used by Primo Braga and Fink (1996). Maskus and Penubarti (1994) relied on 1984 exports of 22 OECD members to 77 partner countries as reported to the OECD Comtap Database.

[9] The results may be misleading as the strength of an IPRs regime is correlated with the level of economic development and thus the estimated coefficients may pick up other development-related effects in the dependent variables.

that market expansion will dominate the market-power effect in developing countries.

B IPRs and FDI

It is often argued that foreign firms avoid investing in countries with weak IPRs regimes (OECD 1989). The magnitude of the impact of weak protection on FDI decisions is an empirical issue. Evidence based on surveys of foreign investors that identify IPRs as a relevant variable for FDI decisions tends also to point out that other considerations—in essence the overall investment climate of the country—are more important (Frischtak 1989). Moreover, FDI may replace trade flows as firms try to maintain control of proprietary information in countries with weak IPRs protection.

Mansfield (1994, 1995) provides some new insights on the IPRs–FDI link. His analysis, based on survey data collected from patent attorneys and executives of major US, Japanese and German manufacturing firms, makes clear that IPRs regimes are relevant for some, but not all, types of FDI decisions. Not surprisingly, IPRs protection was found to be much more relevant for decisions on investment in R&D facilities than for FDI in sales and distribution outlets. Sharp differences were also found concerning the perceptions of different industries on the importance of IPRs regimes in influencing their decisions on FDI. While the chemical (and pharmaceutical) industry reported that IPRs played a major role in their decisions with respect to investment in joint ventures abroad, the metals and food industries considered IPRs protection to have marginal significance.

Mansfield (1994) also reports econometric work that tries to explain US foreign direct investment flows to the 16 countries encompassed by his survey, using the host-country GDP and his own index of protection as independent variables (a dummy for Mexico is also included in the model). The overall results are not particularly robust, but when Japan and Spain are excluded from the sample, he does find that both aggregate manufacturing FDI flows as well as FDI flows to certain industries (particularly machinery and food) are sensitive to weaknesses in IPRs regimes—that is, US FDI flows increase with the perceived strength of the IPRs regime.

A similar exercise was implemented by Primo Braga and Fink (1996), relying on a larger set of countries and the Rapp and Rozek index. Total assets of US firms in 1992 for total manufacturing and certain manufacturing industries were used as dependent variable. As explanatory variables GDP, a dummy for Canada and Mexico, and the Rapp and Rozek index were used.[10] The results are most powerful with respect to manufacturing as a

[10] Trade barriers and growth rates were also tested as explanatory variables, but they did not contribute to the overall explanatory power of the model—mostly the coefficients were statistically insignificant—and nor did they change the result with respect to the other explanatory variables.

whole. All coefficients are statistically significant and the R-square lies in the 80th percentile. The coefficient on the Rapp and Rozek index shows IPRs to have a positive impact on the level of US investment abroad. The sectoral results are less robust, although the coefficient on the Rapp and Rozek index always shows a positive sign and is statistically significant for "primary and fabricated metals" and "electric and electronic equipment".

These results are tentative and additional work needs to be done in this area. In particular, a formal model of equilibrium of the international distribution of FDI is needed for one to derive more precise inferences about the IPRs–FDI link. It can be argued, however, that in a world characterised by growing competition for FDI flows, future compliance with the minimum standards of the TRIPS Agreement will be perceived as a threshold indicator. It will influence perceptions of foreign investors about the relative attractiveness of competing investment locations, even though its direct impact on FDI flows at country level remains an open question.

C IPRs and Transfer of Technology

Probably the most traditional argument for intellectual property rights protection in developing countries is that technology owners are less willing to transfer proprietary knowledge to countries with weak protection because of the risk of "piracy". Support for this proposition typically comes from surveys of firms in industrialised countries. Mansfield (1994, 11), for example, finds that US firms "tend to regard intellectual property protection as being more important in decisions regarding the transfer of advanced technology than in investment decisions".

Some analysts, however, remain sceptical about the relevance of this effect. Subramanian (1990) points out that conflict occurs mainly in those fields (e.g. pharmaceutical and chemical products, software) where imitation is possible independently of technology transfer. Accordingly, the potential benefits of higher IPRs protection are disputed to the extent that imitation is argued to be a sound alternative for formal transfer of technology. It must be noted, however, that lack of protection in sectors that are imitation-prone influences the overall perception of the IPRs regime in the developing country. If the country is perceived not to be playing by the "rules of the game", it will find it increasingly difficult to obtain the transfer of technology in fields in which the co-operation of the inventor is fundamental. Moreover, imitation as a "mode" of technology transfer will be of limited efficacy to the extent that knowledge about a particular technology is "tacit" and "circumstantial".[11] On balance, one should expect more North–South transference of technology in response to the ongoing reforms in developing countries.

[11] See, for example, Evenson and Westphal (1994) and United Nations (1993).

D IPRs and Investments in R&D

Evidence of the response of investments in R&D in developing countries to changes in IPRs protection remains scarce.[12] Still, there is growing appreciation of the role played by innovation in economic development. Gould and Gruben (1994), for example, have found evidence that IPRs protection has a marginally significant positive effect on economic growth. They attribute this to the role of IPRs in fostering R&D investments. They also find that the contribution of IPRs to economic growth increases with the openness of the economy. Based on these results, an argument can be made that the trade liberalisation fostered by the Uruguay Round will enhance the potential dynamic benefits of the TRIPS Agreement. More research, however, is needed to confirm this proposition.

Another aspect is the potential impact of higher protection of IPRs in developing countries on R&D investments in the North (industrialised countries). The small-country assumption may not be appropriate on aggregate terms or with respect to products of special relevance to developing countries (e.g., drugs to fight tropical diseases). The relevance of such a proposition remains an empirical question, but in theory it opens the door for "Pareto-efficient" bargains between developed and developing countries (Subramanian 1994).

E IPRs and Rent Transfer

One of the main concerns of developing countries with respect to the TRIPS Agreement is related to the potential impact of higher standards of protection on domestic prices and with respect to rent transfer abroad.[13] The potential for rent transfer is significant to the extent that, as already noted, non-residents account for most of the patents granted in developing countries.

The introduction of patents for pharmaceutical inventions, for example, has attracted considerable attention.[14] This is an area in which many developing countries did not offer IPRs protection and where price levels are closely monitored in the context of health policies and other social objectives. Estimates of price increases, domestic welfare losses (encompassing consumer surplus and domestic producer surplus losses) and potential rent transfers (as measured by the rise in foreign profits) are available in the literature. As expected, the static effects of the introduction of patent for pharmaceutical inventions in developing countries imply domestic welfare losses for the South which are larger than the benefits accrued to innovators

[12] It is worth noting, however that there are examples of countries that have significantly increased the R&D-intensity of their economies, before reforming their IPRs regimes under external pressure (e.g., South Korea and Taiwan, China).

[13] See, for example, Rodrik (1994).

[14] See, for example, Nogues (1993), Subramanian (1994) and Maskus and Konan (1994).

in the North. The estimates, however, are quite sensitive to assumptions concerning market structure and firm behaviour.

A worst case scenario in terms of welfare losses and rent transfer can be developed if one assumes that a domestic competitive industry becomes a foreign-owned monopoly as a consequence of the introduction of patents (Nogues 1993). The domestic welfare loss is determined by the significant price increase that occurs in such a scenario. If the original market structure is characterised by a duopoly with a domestic and a foreign firm that evolves into a foreign controlled monopoly as a result of the strengthening in protection, the scope for a price increase is limited, but a significant welfare loss may still ensue, mainly as a consequence of the loss in domestic producer surplus.

As Maskus and Konan (1934) point out, however, these scenarios do not capture in a realistic fashion the market for pharmaceutical products in most developing countries. Once one assumes that in the pre-reform situation the dominant foreign firm faces a competitive fringe of imitators and, eventually, of producers of generic drugs that are close substitutes for the patented drugs, the results change. First, the price impact and consumer surplus losses are significantly reduced. They will be larger in countries in which the competitive fringe of imitators is relatively bigger (e.g., India, Argentina) than in others where imitators have a more limited market share to start with (e.g., Brazil).[15] Secondly, the potential for rent transfers also decreases dramatically.

F IPRs and the Displacement of "Pirates"

Estimates of revenues foregone by innovators in industrialised countries due to weak IPRs protection in the South vary widely, but there is no doubt that the values involved are significant.[16] In the same vein, the economic interests of "pirates" (that is those free riding on intellectual property of others, independently of the legality of their actions) in developing countries are substantial, particularly in those industries in which imitation is relatively easy (e.g. trade-marked goods, software).

The displacement of "pirates" *per se* does not necessarily entail a social welfare loss, as these producers may be replaced by others operating under licences from foreign title-holders. For trade-marked goods there is some evidence, from countries that have reformed their IPRs regimes (e.g. Singapore), that "pirates" often are well positioned to switch to legitimate activities once the legal environment changes, particularly in industries characterised by low barriers to entry.[17]

[15] In all these exercises, information on market size and relative importance of patented, copied and non-patented drugs relies on Gadbaw and Richards (1988).

[16] See, for example, US International Trade Commission (1988) and IIPA (1994).

[17] Note that the net welfare impact of combating counterfeiting can be negative under certain assumptions. See, for example, Grossman and Shapiro (1988a; 1988b).

G Administrative and Enforcement Costs

The ongoing process of reforms to strengthen IPRs in developing countries will only deliver the benefits identified above if in addition to the reforms in substantive law, governments commit the necessary resources to administer and enforce the new IPRs regimes. This is particularly true in the area of industrial property rights. Most developing countries are ill equipped to respond to the new administrative responsibilities that their patent and trade marks offices will have to deal with. The increase in the scope of patentability, for example, will add a significant number of new applications (increases of the order of 35 per cent in the number of new applications are expected in countries like Brazil). In many countries this will tend to add to existing backlogs, increasing the stress of the system.

Similar concerns arise with respect to the capacity of over-stretched judicial systems properly to enforce these rights. The lack of familiarity and training of judicial authorities with IPRs issues is more the rule rather than the exception. Moreover, court systems in developing countries are often unable to process their case loads in a timely fashion.

These considerations suggest that the strengthening of patent and trade mark offices and of judicial courts should receive special attention by governments engaged in the process of reform. One should try to explore economies of scale and scope available through international treaties such as the Patent Cooperation Treaty and the Trade mark Law Treaty. At the same time, governments should foster the administrative and financial independence of their patent and trade mark offices. Technical assistance by WIPO and multilateral financial institutions may play an important role in this process. In essence, however, these reforms require a high level of commitment by the governments involved.

V. Concluding Remarks

The trend toward strengthening IPRs in developing countries identified in this paper is here to stay. Moreover, the TRIPS Agreement will further promote international convergence between developed and developing countries with respect to their IPRs regimes. Actually, international convergence in terms of substantive law is happening at a much faster pace than most analysts thought possible ten years ago.

From a static perspective, these reforms have the danger of becoming exercises in rent transfer from the South to the North. There are, however, positive-sum games that can be explored by developing and developed countries in the areas of trade, foreign direct investment, and transfer of technology as protection of IPRs is strengthened. Dynamic benefits will tend to dominate short-term costs, as long as these reforms become effective levers for innovation.

The main challenges at this stage are: (a) how to foster proper administration and enforcement of the new IPRs regimes—particularly with respect to industrial property rights; and (b) how to raise awareness among private entrepreneurs of developing countries concerning the proper use of IPRs protection.

References

Arrow, Kenneth, 1962, "Economic Welfare and the Allocation of Resources for Inventions", in R.R. Nelson, ed., *The Rate and Direction of Inventive Activity* (Princeton, NJ, Princeton University Press).

Dasgupta, P., and Stoneman, P., 1987, "Introduction" in P. Dasgupta and P. Stoneman, eds., *"Economic Policy and Technological Performance"*, (Cambridge: University of Cambridge).

Evenson, R. E., and Westphal, L. E., 1994, "Technological Change and Technology Strategy", Forthcoming chapter in T.N. Srinivasan & Jere Behrman, eds.,*Handbook of Development Economics*, Vol. 3 (Deventes North-Holland Publishing Company).

Ferrantino, M.J., 1993, "The Effect of Intellectual Property Rights on International Trade and Investment", 129 *Weltwirtschaftliches Archiv*, 300–31.

Frischtak, C.R., 1989, "The Protection of Intellectual Property Rights and Industrial Technological Development in Brazil", World Bank Industry Series Paper No. 13, (World Bank, Washington, DC).

Gadbaw, R.M., and , Richards, T., 1988, *Intellectual Property Rights: Global Consensus, Global Conflict?* (Boulder, Co: Westview Press).

Goldstein, P., 1994, *Copyright 's Highway* (New York, Hill and Wang).

Gould, D., and Gruben, W., "The Role of Intellectual Property Rights in Economic Growth", Research Department Working Paper No. 94–09 (Dallas, Tx: Federal Reserve Bank of Dallas).

Grossman, G.M., and Shapiro, C., 1988a, "Counterfeit-Product Trade", 78 *American Economic Review* 59–75.

—— ——, 1988b, "Foreign Counterfeiting of Status Goods", 103 *Quarterly Journal of Economics* 79–100.

IIPA, 1994, 1994 *Special 310 Recommendations and Estimated Trade Losses* (Washington, DC: International Intellectual Property Alliance).

Machlup, F., 1958, "An Economic Review of the Patent System", *Subcommittee on Patents, Trade marks and Copyrights, Committee on the Judiciary*, US Senate Study No. 15, (Washington, DC: US Government Printing Office).

Maskus, K.E., and Eby Konan, D., 1994, "Trade-Related Intellectual Property Rights: Issues and Exploratory Results," in Deardorff and Stern, eds., *Analytical and Negotiating Issues in the Global Trading System* (Ann Arbor, Mich.: University of Michigan).

——, and Penubarti, M., 1995, "How Trade-Related Are Intellectual Property Rights?" 39 *Journal of International Economics* 227–48.

Nogues, J.J., 1993, "Social Costs and Benefits of Introducing Patent Protection for

Pharmaceutical Drugs in Developing Countries", 31 *The Developing Economies*, 24–53.
OECD, 1989, "Economic Arguments for Protecting Intellectual Property Rights Effectively", TC/WP(88) 70, (Paris: OECD).
Primo Braga, C.A., 1990, "The Developing Country Case for and against Intellectual Property Protection", in Siebeck, ed., *Strengthening Protection of Intellectual Property in Developing Countries: A Survey of the Literature*, World Bank Discussion Paper No. 112 (Washington, DC: The World Bank).
— —, and Yeats, A., 1992, "How Minilateral Trading Arrangements May Affect the Post-Uruguay Round World", *Policy Research Working Paper*, WPS 974, (Washington, DC: International Economics Department, The World Bank).
— — — —, 1996, "Trade-Related Intellectual Property Issues: The Uruguay Round Agreement and its Economic Implications", in W. Martin and L.A. Winters, eds, *The Uruguay Round and the Developing Economies* (Cambridge: Cambridge, University Press).
— —, and Fink, C., 1996, "The Economic Justification for the Grant of Intellectual Property Rights: Patterns of Convergence and Conflict" 72 *Chicago-Kent Law Journal* 439–61.
Rapp, R., and Rozek, R., 1990, "Benefits and Costs of Intellectual Property Protection in Developing Countries", Working Paper No. 3 (Washington, DC: National Economic Research Associates, Inc.).
Rodrik, D., 1994, "Comments", in Deardorff and Stern (eds.), *Analytical and Negotiating Issues in the Uruguay Round* (Ann Arbor, Mich.: University of Michigan).
Sherwood, R.M., 1993, "Why a Uniform Intellectual Property System Makes Sense for the World", in Wallerstein, Mogee and Schoen, eds., *Global Dimensions of Intellectual Property Rights in Science and Technology* (Washington, DC: National Academy Press).
Stern, R., 1987, "Intellectual Property", in Finger and Olechowski, eds., *The Uruguay Round: A Handbook on the Multilateral Trade Negotiations* (Washington, DC: The World Bank).
Subramanian, A., 1990, "TRIPS and the Paradigm of the GATT: A Tropical, Temperate View", 13 *The World Economy* 509–21.
— —, 1994, "Putting Some Numbers on the TRIPS Pharmaceutical Debate", 10 *International Journal of Technology Management* 1–17.
United Nations, TCMD, 1993, *Intellectual Property Rights and Foreign Direct Investment* (New York: United Nations).
United States International Trade Commission, 1988, *Foreign Protection of Intellectual Property Rights and the Effect on US Industry and Trade*, (Washington, DC: US International Trade Commission).
WIPO, 1983, *100 Years of Industrial Property Statistics* (Geneva: WIPO).
Winter, S., 1989, "Patents in Complex Contexts: Incentives and Effectiveness", in Weil and Snapper (eds.), *Owning Scientific and Technical Information* (New Brunswick, NJ: Rutgers University Press).

4

INTELLECTUAL PROPERTY RIGHTS IN THE BALANCE SHEET AND SPECIFIC TAX PROBLEMS IN CROSS-BORDER LICENSING

*Dirk Krüger**

I. Introduction

In the German language intellectual property rights are referred to as "immaterielle Wirtschaftsgüter"—which could lead to the mistaken translation "immaterial assets". As we all well know, intellectual property rights are anything but immaterial in the sense of insignificant and worthless. In fact intellectual property rights can represent the major assets of a business, whether included in the balance sheet or not. These assets are *intangible* but by no means *immaterial.* The word "intangible" stems from the Latin verb *tangere*—to touch. Intangible assets are not capable of being touched, but none the less play a real part in the business world and have real values. The increased application of information technology in all walks of life, product innovation in the services sector and indeed the growing tendency of acquiring competitors in order to take over their trade marks have brought intangible assets to the forefront. Intellectual property rights often represent a considerable proportion of corporate value, so that questions of the accounting and tax treatment of these rights have gained in significance. Today it is my task to relate some of the accounting and tax issues to you, based mainly on developments in the German law in this area. As my fellow speaker Mr. Thierry Sueur will be speaking to you in detail on the valuation of intellectual property rights, I shall not deal with this aspect. I shall be using the term "intellectual property rights" loosely to include assets such as patents, trade marks and copyrights—in fact those intangible assets capable of being licensed for use by third parties.

In addition to the balance sheet treatment of intellectual property rights, inherently connected with the rights themselves are the licences concluded between the owners of the rights and the users. The second part of my lecture today will deal with the tax issues arising in particular in the case of cross-border licences and the application and use of tax treaties to such transactions.

* Professor, Arthur Andersen Wirtschaftsprüfungsgesellschaft Steuerberatungsgesellschaft mbH, Frankfurt am Main, Germany.

II Intellectual Property Rights in the Balance Sheet

The question whether intangible assets may be, must be or may not be capitalised in the balance sheet is closely associated with two accounting principles: one being the protection of the creditors of a business, and the other being the necessity of the balance sheet reflecting the true value of a business. The different jurisdictions are witnessing a "tug-of-war" situation between the inclusion of intangible assets which are of considerable value and importance to a business and the fact that in the case of the collapse of a business, i.e. through bankruptcy, intangible assets vanish into thin air. In addition to this "push-me pull-you" effect comes the added problem of the value of the intangible assets in question shown in the balance sheet and the retention of this value.

Fundamentally, intangible assets are capable of being classed as either fixed assets or current assets in the balance sheet.

In order to assess which class is appropriate some jurisdictions, such as Germany and the UK, look to the intended use/function of the asset for the business, whereas the USA looks to the time lapse between acquisition and sale—applying the 12-month operating cycle in deciding whether an asset is a fixed or a current asset.

A Fixed Assets

Many commercial and tax jurisdictions differentiate between the balance sheet treatment of so-called self-generated or self-created intellectual property rights and purchased intellectual property rights. In particular, the commercial and tax laws of many jurisdictions restrict the capitalisation of self-generated intellectual property rights in the balance sheet and often, therefore, exclude a significant business asset from inclusion in the balance sheet. For instance, one of the oldest German accounting principles is the prohibition on the capitalisation of self-generated intellectual property rights. This principle has its roots in the concept of prudence in connection with the overriding intention to protect creditors. Capitalisation is permitted/required only when the intangible property has been acquired for consideration. The requirement to capitalise purchased intangibles is based on the theory that an asset in the equivalent value has been acquired in connection with the expense incurred. An acquisition for consideration generally requires the acquisition of the intangible asset from a third party on the basis of a contract on the payment of consideration to that third party. The consideration received will generally be the value of the capitalised right in the balance sheet. The further rationale behind the prohibition against capitalising intangible assets not acquired for consideration lies in the assumption that an intangible fixed asset which has never been the subject of a transaction and for which a consideration has ever been paid cannot be valued.

It is not necessary that the intangible asset acquired for consideration was previously a capitalised asset of the vendor, but rather it is sufficient that the asset actually emerges as a result of the acquisition transaction.

Example

Parent company A in the USA sells the exclusive right to use its self-generated know-how in connection with the production of certain products to its subsidiary B in Germany. The know-how is not shown as an asset in A's balance sheet, but must be capitalised in B's balance sheet on acquisition.

Often, in practice, the exact differentiation between acquisition for consideration and self-generation is not an easy task, in particular as acquisition and own-production may flow together. Theoretically, the differentiation is simpler, as an acquisition requires the transfer of a right in an asset, whereas in the case of self-generation a process under which the intangible asset is created requires work and other efforts which are invested in the development of the intangible asset.

Example of Self-generation

Rather than paying a third party for the acquisition of a patent, expenditure on labour and other costs (e.g. overhead costs) has been incurred for an invention made by the business itself.

Some apparent exceptions to the requirement of "acquisition for consideration" apply in the case of German tax law, these exceptions also being typical to other jurisdictions. First, the capitalisation prohibition does not apply if the intellectual property right was purchased for consideration by the predecessor and transferred by way of universal succession without consideration.

Example

A German limited liability company is merged into its 100 per cent German parent company. Intangible assets previously purchased for consideration by the GmbH are also capable of being capitalised by the parent company, which is now the owner of the property by way of universal succession.

Further, for German tax law purposes the hidden contribution of intellectual property rights to the assets of a business does not exclude the capitalisation of the self-generated intellectual property right in the balance sheet of the recipient business. A self-generated intellectual property right contributed to a business by the owner is capable of being capitalised in the balance sheet (at market value on the date of contribution).

The capitalisation of *self-generated* intellectual property rights generally comes into play in all cases in which hidden reserves are realised.

Example

A German limited liability company (GmbH) is transformed into a partnership under the realisation of its hidden reserves. Previously uncapitalised self-generated intangible assets of the former GmbH are now capable of being capitalised in the balance sheet of the partnership. The counterpart to the prohibition against capitalising self-generated intangible assets is the compulsory capitalisation of intangible assets acquired for consideration, which is a requirement of German commercial and tax law, whereby the acquisition costs are generally the capitalised value. Thus in deciding whether an intellectual property right *must be* or *may not be* capitalised the German legal jurisdiction asks the critical question "was the right purchased for consideration?" Some other jurisdictions (e.g. USA) have an option whether to capitalise certain self-generated intangible assets. In the USA this option is available to, *inter alia*, software, patents, copyrights and licences on condition that the self-generated intangible assets can be individually defined, have a certain useful life and were not merely created through current business.

Intrinsically connected with the capitalisation of intellectual property rights as a fixed asset, is the question whether such assets, which do not wear out in a physical sense, are capable of being depreciated, and, if so, over what period of time. Further, what happens in the case of those intangible rights which may not be capitalised in the balance sheet? To answer the latter question first, in this case expenses and costs incurred in connection with those intellectual property rights which may not be capitalised are generally immediately deductible business expenses. The question of depreciability cannot be answered so simply.

Some jurisdictions permit the depreciation of intellectual property rights. For German tax law purposes capitalised intellectual property rights may be amortised under application of the general rules of tax amortisation. This requires that the use of the asset be fundamentally limited in time and the depreciation rate be based on this anticipated useful life of the asset. This may be derived from the underlying contract relating to the asset, if any. Presuming that the duration of the useful life cannot be derived from an underlying contract, intangible assets are generally depreciable over varying periods. Standard software may be depreciated over three years. In some instances the depreciability of intellectual property rights will be denied. In such a case only an extraordinary write-down to going concern value will be available if the asset has significantly lost its value. An amendment to US law in 1993 based on the landmark Newark Morning Ledger Company decision of the US Supreme Court permits the depreciation of many intangible assets over a period of 15 years including information basis and know-how. In the case of non-standard computer software, copyrights and patents, and other intellectual property rights the depreciation is only permitted if these intangibles are acquired in connection with the acquisition of a business. Computer software that is readily available for purchase by the general public is not depreciable. Self-created intangibles are generally excluded from the list of depreciable assets.

Summarising this point on intellectual property rights intended for long-term use in a business these intangible assets must generally be capitalised as fixed assets to the extent that they were acquired for consideration. The depreciability of these assets and the period, over which they may be depreciated vary from jurisdiction to jurisdiction. As regards expenses incurred in connection with the creation, maintenance, or enhancement of intangible assets, these may generally be deducted as ordinary business expenses in the year in which the costs were incurred.

B Current Assets

An intellectual property right will generally be classed as a current asset if the asset is not intended continuously to serve the purposes of the business. This generally covers assets which are used or sold in one act. The prohibition on capitalising self-generated intangible assets as stated for fixed assets does not apply to current assets. An example of intellectual property rights which will typically be classed as current assets are computer programs intended for sale. Such assets will be capitalised as current assets, and will generally not be depreciable, except in the case of an extraordinary depreciation due to a reduced market value.

III Cross-border Licensing

This section of my lecture deals with the often complex tax issues arising when the use of an intellectual property right is transferred to a third party, by way of a licence agreement between the owner of the right and the user.

When this transaction takes place within one country, i.e. both owner and user are taxed as such in the same jurisdiction, the tax issues arising are comparatively straightforward. More sophisticated tax aspects come into play when owner and user are in different jurisdictions, thereby giving rise to a cross-border licence.

Two major tax issues arise in connection with cross-border licensing. I shall focus on these two issues in this second half of my lecture. First, and I believe one of the most significant tax issues giving rise to the greatest headaches for international groups, and an issue with theoretical answers which are at times hardly capable of being applied in practice, is the question of transfer pricing. Obviously, transfer pricing is a topic which is so extensive that it is a never-ending theme for the publications of the OECD and a subject which alone could be the theme of this five-day forum, and in no way will I today attempt to give you a comprehensive picture of current transfer pricing. However, as it plays a significant role in licensing agreements concluded within international groups I will attempt to give you a short analysis of the specific transfer-pricing issues arising in connection with inter-group licensing.

The second major tax issue arising in connection with cross-border licensing is the question of treaty protection for the royalties received by the licensor, regardless of whether the parties to the licence are related or unrelated. In connection with the issue of treaty protection I shall also deal with the closely related question of the existence and application of anti-treaty shopping provisions and the effect of controlled foreign companies legislation within the national jurisdictions which may present an impediment to treaty protection.

A Transfer Pricing

Article 9 of the OECD Model Convention deals with the adjustment of income of affiliated companies if transactions between the companies are not based on arm's length principles. The arm's length principle requires that in contractual and business relations affiliated enterprises observe those standards that would be applied by unrelated third parties, in particular with regard to the level of remuneration charged for a supply or service.

Most tax treaties contain this article or an article based on Article 9 of the OECD Model Convention which allows the tax authorities of contracting states to adjust the profits of related companies which in contractual relations have not observed the arm's length principle. The actual legal basis for the profit adjustment is then derived from the laws of the countries concerned. In Germany this is section 1 of the International Transactions Tax Act and as a supplement to this, the Administration Principles on Income Allocation. In the USA the domestic profit adjustment provision are in section 482 of the Internal Revenue Code and the administrative regulations issued in connection with this provision.

With regard to licences concluded by affiliated parties relating to intellectual property rights, transfer pricing is a significant issue in that the royalty must be based on arm's length principles, which means that the royalty charged must be of an amount that a third party would have paid for the licence under the same circumstances.

The requirement of an arm's length royalty can give rise to significant problems in practice. The German Administration Principles accept that turnover/sales as a basis for the royalty calculation can lead to "arm's length" remuneration and also accept that a lump-sum payment for the use of intangible property may be appropriate. The Administration Principles cite the comparable uncontrolled price method, the resale price method and the cost plus method as possible methods of calculating arm's length remuneration, whereby the facts of each individual case may influence the appropriateness of the method applied.

The practice has shown, at least in Germany, that the tax authorities will challenge what they consider to be excessive royalty payments made by German companies to foreign related companies and will require a detailed explanation and justification of how and on what basis the royalty was calculated, in order to assess whether the royalty is at "arm's length".

In my experience the royalties charged between related companies are based more on a "hit and miss" principle due to the fact that the solutions offered by the treaties and domestic legislation take no account of the practical difficulties faced by international groups in calculating an "arm's length" royalty.

B Treaty Protection

Remuneration paid in connection with the use of intellectual property rights is generally classed as a royalty and not as business income of the recipient according to Article 12 of the OECD Model Convention. Thus Article 12 takes precedence over Article 7 of the Model Convention which deals with the taxation of business profits.

The main features of the OECD Model Convention are that:

- the right to tax royalties is generally attributed exclusively/primarily to the country of residence of the recipient licensor;
- the possibility of tax being imposed by the country of source (the licensee's state of residence) is excluded. This country is therefore obliged to refund any withholding tax undertaken by it on the royalty income. (Some exceptions apply to this whereby a limited withholding tax by the source country is permitted);
- An exception applies if the royalties are paid in respect of an underlying right (e.g. intellectual property right) which form part of the fixed assets of a permanent establishment of the licensor. In this case the country in which the permanent establishment is located is allocated the right of taxation.

The "golden rule" that the country of residence of the licensor has the primary right to tax the royalty income opens wide scope for tax planning, which I would like to demonstrate on the basis of the following example:

Example

Company X is a resident of Country A, which has a corporate income tax rate of 50 per cent. Company X is the owner of certain intellectual property rights which it uses in its business activities. Company X sells these rights to its newly established subsidiary (Company Y) in Country B, a tax haven. Company X and Company Y conclude a licence under which Company X pays a royalty to Company Y for the use of the rights. The royalty paid by Company X is a deductible business expense in Country A, and subject to low or no taxation at the level of Company Y in Country B.

Obviously this example is very simplified and does not deal with the issue of a potential taxable capital gain at the level of Company X on sale of the intellectual property right to Company Y; however, it does demonstrate the fundamental possibility of implementing tax planning in the area of licensing.

However, the tax authorities of many jurisdictions have not remained oblivious to the use of tax treaties in the implementation of advantageous tax structures as just described. Two areas of legislation are increasingly being introduced into national tax legislation in order to curb the use of such structures. These two areas of legislation are anti-treaty shopping provisions and controlled foreign companies provisions. Using Germany as an example I would like to describe the function and results of such provisions.

1 Anti-treaty-shopping Provisions

Anti-treaty-shopping legislation has been developed on the basis that tax treaties are intended to promote international trade and commerce by eliminating double taxation, but should not promote tax evasion and tax avoidance. As at 1 January 1994 Germany has introduced its own anti-treaty shopping provision within national tax law. This provision states (*inter alia*) that a foreign company is not entitled to tax relief in Germany pursuant to a double tax treaty if the company is held by persons who would not be eligible for such tax relief if they had generated the income directly and if there is no economic or other justification for use of the foreign company and if the company does not carry on its own economic activities.

In relation to licences, this anti-treaty-shopping provision would lead to the withholding of taxation of the royalties in Germany at 25 per cent under the following scenario:

Company X is resident in Country A, which has not concluded a tax treaty with Germany. Company X establishes a subsidiary, Company Y, in The Netherlands. Company Y concludes a licence agreement with Company Z, a resident of Germany. The royalty payments made to Company Y are exempt from withholding taxation in Germany on the basis of the German/Netherlands tax treaty. Presuming that Company Y does not carry on its own economic activities and no commercial or other justification for the implementation of Company Y exists, the exemption from German withholding tax will not be granted.

2 Controlled Foreign Companies Provisions

An increasing number of countries have introduced controlled foreign companies provisions into their tax legislation. The purpose of such legislation in Germany is to tax passive income in Germany which has been earned by German-controlled foreign companies in low tax regimes. In the German controlled foreign companies provisions "low taxation" is deemed if the foreign company is subject to less than 30 per cent income tax on its income in its country of residence.

In Germany this legislation is highly complex and to a certain extent controversial, in that recent amendments to widen the scope of income/activities caught by its provisions are directly aimed at subsidiaries of German groups which have been established in the Irish International Financial Services Centre in Dublin.

In relation to royalty income, the German controlled foreign companies provisions are highly relevant in that royalty income in connection with licences for the use of intellectual property which is not self-created by the foreign company is classed as passive income and therefore potentially subject to German taxation at the level of the German shareholder.

Example

Company X resident in Ireland is the 100 per cent subsidiary of Company Y resident in Germany. Company X is the owner of purchased intellectual property rights which it licenses to group companies throughout Europe. The royalties received are taxed at 10 per cent at the level of Company X in Ireland.

Although the German controlled foreign companies legislation potentially covers this situation, the royalty income is not subject to taxation in Germany as it is treaty protected under the tax treaty concluded between Germany and Ireland. Treaty protection is available as the treaty itself does not have an activity clause requiring that the Irish company derives income for non-passive activities. The treaty-overriding provision in the German controlled foreign corporation legislation applies only to passive income with a capital investment character, such as interest and dividend income. Royalty income does not fall within this definition.

IV Closing Comments

Ladies and gentlemen, as I come to the close of my lecture on the selected financial aspects of industrial property, I would like to emphasise the word "selected". I have merely touched the tip of the iceberg of the many, many accounting and tax issues arising in connection with intellectual property rights. In particular, the tax issues arising in connection with cross-border licences can be complex, and costly if the correct tax planning is not undertaken beforehand. I hope that I have increased your awareness for the difficulties in calculating arm's length royalties and the possible impact of treaty overriding national legislation. The prohibition against capitalising self-created intangibles remains a controversial issue likely to become an even greater issue in view of the ever growing significance of industrial property rights in the business world.

5

SECURITY INTERESTS IN INTELLECTUAL PROPERTY

*Harry C. Sigman**

I Introduction

The world's wealth is increasingly becoming embodied in intangible assets, particularly in intellectual property ("IP"). At the same time, owners increasingly seek to maximise the leverage available from their assets. Therefore, the ability to grant effective security interests in IP becomes increasingly important. Legal systems that recognise or provide meaningful enforcement only to security interests in immovable property or to only tangible movable property, needlessly limit the amount of secured credit available. By effective security interests I mean a legal system that allows the secured party's rights to be created easily, quickly and inexpensively, that provides clear rights *inter partes* and predictable and certain priorities *vis-à-vis* third parties, and that provides efficient and reliable enforcement mechanisms. This entails, ideally, a sophisticated financial market-place and a well-designed legal regime. Even, and perhaps especially, developing countries, however, will find it advantageous to create the legal environment necessary to facilitate such transactions. The ultimate goal is a modern, efficient and harmonised world-wide system for effectuating (creating, publicising and enforcing) security interests in IP.

This paper assumes that the reader is familiar with the substantive concepts of IP law—there will be no discussion of the substantive law or procedural rules applicable to patents, copyrights, trade-marks, trade secrets and other forms of IP recognised in various countries. Rather, its scope will be limited to a description of personal property (i.e. movables) security law in the United States—first generally and then focussing on security interests in IP under that law. Given the time constraints, it will of course not be possible to discuss the applicable law in detail; my goal will be to introduce this subject and to stimulate and provoke.

I should state at the outset that I do not discuss US personal property security law for chauvinist reasons. Rather, it is described in order to present a picture of a legal regime that has successfully facilitated the development of an innovative and extremely efficient secured credit market-place in the

* Attorney-at-Law, Los Angeles, USA.

context of a highly sophisticated, and highly leveraged, economy. The message is that it works. Theoretical discussions about the "best" legal concepts are not likely to be useful in developing a legal structure whose purpose is to facilitate beneficial economic results in the real world. Countries that wish to modernise their personal property security legal structures can benefit from this model, while at the same time avoiding, particularly with respect to security interests in IP, the defects in the US system that are largely the result of historical accident, the fact that the US is a federal country and the fact that the filing systems were created decades ago, before the advent of the modern technology that is presently available.

With respect to US substantive IP law, I will simply observe that because the USA is a federal nation, rather than a unitary one, it is always necessary to take into account the respective roles of federal and state law. Generally speaking, most of the substantive patent and copyright law is federal, trademark law is far more of a mix and trade secret law is mostly state law. Personal property security law, on the other hand, is primarily state law. Fortunately, it is far less variegated than other state law subjects in America, because it is largely embodied in Article 9 of the Uniform Commercial Code ("UCC"), drafted in the early 1950s, which has been adopted, in substantially identical text, in all 50 states. Nevertheless, there may well be an overlay of federal involvement with respect to security interests in IP collateral, particularly with respect to the publicising of security interests. Generally speaking, state, not federal, law governs substantive issues relating to security interests in IP. For example, over forty years ago, in *Republic Pictures Corp.* v. *Security-Pacific Nat 'l Bank*, 197 F.2d 767 (9th Cir. 1952), a federal appellate court ruled that state law governs the enforcement of a security interest in a copyright. None of the federal IP statutes provides a comprehensive body of security law such as to totally displace the UCC.

II UCC Article 9

I will now discuss the key principles and features of UCC Article 9.

In 55 Code sections, Article 9 sets forth a single coherent comprehensive legal framework for security interests in personal property, both tangible and intangible. Subject to a very limited number of exclusions, Article 9 governs all such security interests, no matter the nature of the debtor, no matter the nature of the secured party, no matter the nature of the collateral, including property not yet owned by the debtor and even not yet existing, and no matter the nature of the obligation secured, which need not be quantifiable or even in existence at the time the security interest is created. It covers both possessory and non-possessory security interests, with respect to the latter usually providing for public notice by means of filing. This comprehensiveness and flexibility has facilitated the development of creative and sophisticated financing techniques that maximise the leverage that may be obtained from personal property.

Article 9 governs consensual security interests in personal property regardless of the form of the transaction and regardless of the language used by the parties—that is, the economic substance and reality, rather than the apparent legal structure or the terminology of the documents, determines the nature of the transaction as a secured transaction. Thus, a vendor who retains title to goods (*Eigentumsvorbehalt, réserve de propriété*) in order to secure payment of the purchase price is treated as a secured party, having no greater rights than a third party lender who finances the acquisition of goods by a user, and Article 9 will govern these transactions. The location of title will make no difference in this context (although it may for tax or other purposes). Likewise, a purported lessor whose status as such is, similarly, for the purpose of securing payment of the price (though denominated as rent), under circumstances where the lessor has no expectation of a residual value at the end of the lease term, is treated as having a security interest, and such transactions are governed by Article 9. The notion of a unitary security interest, where all transactions serving the purpose of providing security are treated alike, is a functional one. US personal property security law is not burdened with the rigidity of a *numerus clausus* concept or with distinctions that are based on form or that have a historical or conceptual basis.

In the creation of security interests, Article 9 provides for a minimum of formality and allows *inter partes* rather broad party autonomy, with very few mandatory provisions. A single sentence, e.g., "I grant to X a security interest in all my present and future equipment, wherever located, to secure any obligation of any nature that I now or hereafter may owe to X", is, when signed by the debtor, sufficient to create a valid security interest. This exemplar illustrates, besides the absence of formality other than signature, an essentially revolutionary feature of Article 9—the "floating lien". This concept allows the efficient present creation (by a simple agreement that uses general descriptions of the collateral and of the secured obligation) of a security interest covering both present and future property and securing both present and future obligations. There is no requirement of notarisation, collateral need not be described specifically, and no maximum value of secured debt need be specified.

Article 9 provides a detailed regime of priorities, spelling out who prevails in contests between a secured party, on the one hand, and various competing interests, ranging from another secured party to a lien creditor (a creditor who has obtained a lien on a particular asset by means of a judicial levy), a buyer of the collateral, a donee of the collateral, etc. The level of refinement leaves little to the courts and thus provides maximum predictability. A lender or seller who knows that his position is vulnerable to no or only a few specified competitors can measure his risk on an informed basis and extend a greater amount of credit at a lower price, i.e. the value of the asset as collateral is maximised.

Generally speaking, Article 9 uses the term "perfection" as a touchstone in spelling out certain priority rules. Typically, perfection is based on publicity; in most cases it is achieved by filing a public notice, although it may in some cases be achieved by the secured party's taking of possession, and in other cases it occurs automatically without either filing or possession. Perfection, however, is not synonymous with invulnerability. A perfected security interest is subordinate to certain competitors (for example, a buyer of inventory in the ordinary course from a dealer in such goods takes free of a perfected security interest in those goods), and an unperfected security interest prevails against many other competitors (for example, a non-ordinary course transferee will prevail over an unperfected security interest only to the extent that the transferee gives value (and, in the case of tangibles, receives delivery) without knowledge of the security interest). Perfection is irrelevant between debtor and secured party. On the other hand, an unperfected interest is vulnerable to the nemesis—the bankruptcy trustee. This is true both under Article 9 and, independently, under federal bankruptcy law, which gives the trustee powers to avoid certain transactions.

Article 9 also deals with rights and obligations after default, i.e. enforcement remedies. I will say very little about this, observing simply that in addition to the familiar judicial remedies (such as seizure and sale by a judicial officer), Article 9 provides a seemingly revolutionary enforcement mechanism. This is the power of the secured party to realise on the collateral, commonly after a peaceful taking of possession by the secured party without judicial assistance, foreclosing the debtor's interest in it, by means of a non-judicial disposition, subject only to two overarching principles—good faith and commercial reasonableness. This flexible realisation process reflects Article 9's policy determination that both debtors and secured parties are better off with an efficient market-oriented realisation process (which may entail a public auction or a private disposition), rather than a mandatory expensive and usually inefficient (in terms of likelihood of achieving the best possible price) judicial sale.

As stated above, the priorities regime, generally speaking, depends on notoriety, typically provided by the filing of a financing statement in a statewide public office. Article 9 provides basic filing rules, but does not provide a detailed system implementation design. Article 9 was written around 1950, well before the computer age. Each state designed its own filing system. There is a great variation in the financial resources of the different states, and the states moved into the computer age in different ways and at different speeds. Thus, today, in the United States there exist a variety of systems ranging from a rather primitive uncomputerised paper system to, at the other extreme, several states that already accept paperless electronic filings. Indeed, there now exists a national standard format for electronic filing (ANSI X12 154); this agreed protocol offers the potential to facilitate not just nationwide, but worldwide, efficient filing and searching, using shared databases. Electronic filing is not a dream of the future—it is technologically feasible, inexpensive to implement (in the United States, most filing offices today produce excess revenues, even at very low filing fee rates) and makes the filing office extremely efficient (minimising need for personal contact, eliminating delay in getting the data into the searchable index and reducing costs and risk of error for both filer and filing office). Most of the Canadian provinces have adopted Personal Property Security Acts modeled on Article 9, primarily during the last 15 years. In Canada, electronic filing is the norm rather than the exception; indeed, in New Brunswick, the province that most recently adopted a PPSA, the registry accepts only electronic filings.

The paper financing statement under Article 9 is a simple one-page form calling for minimal information—essentially, the name and address of the debtor, the name and address of the secured party, and a general description of the collateral. As with the security agreement, there is no requirement of notarisation, collateral need not be described specifically, and no maximum value of secured debt need be specified. Under the present version of Article 9, the financing statement must be signed by the debtor. Revisions currently contemplated will eliminate this requirement.

Unlike registries familiar to most legal regimes, the Article 9 filing system is not a repository of the underlying security agreements. The financing statement does not create real rights (as that term is understood in civil law regimes) in the collateral; it simply serves a notice function. Attached is a form of financing statement currently accepted in virtually all of the statewide UCC filing offices. It is easy to prepare and publicises very little information. These features underscore its purpose. It is not intended to provide strangers with details of the financial arrangement. Indeed, it is often not possible to disclose many details—Article 9's sophisticated flexibility contemplates that the precise pool of collateral and the exact amount of the secured debt may vary from time to time, even daily. All prospective creditors need to learn from the public record is that there may be someone who might, by virtue of the prior filing, have now or at some time in the future a security interest in assets of the debtor that would have priority over that of the later filing creditor. The searcher learns this from the financing statement; he may then act on this information in whatever way is appropriate to the nature and amount of credit he expects to extend. The prospective secured party may get more information from the debtor, may confirm it with the prior filer, may even make priority arrangements directly with the prior filer. This is an extremely inexpensive system. For a $5–20 filing fee and the minutes that it takes to complete this form, a secured party can obtain the priority position accorded to a filed security interest that may cover millions of dollars of credit secured by millions of dollars' worth of collateral over a long period of time (typically, the filing must be continued every five years by the presentation of an even simpler form). The State of Texas handles over 250,000 filings annually with a small staff and is a net revenue generator. In the ideal world, all filing will be done electronically, instantaneously, from anywhere, with no bureaucratic intervention to cause delay or error or impose additional requirements.

IP falls within the UCC category of "general intangibles". Filing is required to perfect a security interest in that category of collateral. The proper place to file against general intangibles is the debtor's "location". Although intangibles have no *situs*, a debtor is located in only one place (at any given point in time) and that place is usually easy to determine. Article 9 provides that a debtor is located for this purpose "at his place of business if he has one, at his chief executive office if he has more than one place of business, otherwise at his residence". (The current draft of proposed revised Article 9 would change this location concept to designate the place of legal organisation as the location of a debtor that is an entity of the type, such as a corporation, that comes into being by virtue of the public filing of constitutive documents.) There is a four-month grace period in which to re-file in the new location if the debtor's location changes.

III Intellectual Property as Collateral under US Law

What has been said up to this point about Article 9 is valid with respect to ordinary collateral, such as inventory, equipment, accounts, etc. This description articulates the modern effective regime that prevails in the United States with respect to most collateral. Unfortunately, the picture with respect to IP collateral is less clear. This is due to historical accident and also to the general unfamiliarity of personal property security law experts with IP substantive law and vice versa. Although lawyers and scholars are beginning to focus on the need for a comprehensive effort, primarily at the legislative level but also looking to the modification and improvement of the recording systems operated by the Copyright Office and the Patent and Trade Mark Office, the various statutes relevant to IP have not yet been revised to integrate them with the UCC and to eliminate the existing doubts and anomalies that render IP less certain as collateral in the United States than they would be were they governed exclusively by Article 9. A more detailed description of the issues and a proposed possible solution can be found in the 1993 Report of the American Bar Association Task Force on Security Interests in Intellectual Property.

The Patent Act long antedates the UCC. The federal trade mark laws, revised extensively in 1946 by the Lanham Act, also antedate Article 9. The Copyright Act was enacted in 1975, after Article 9 was already in effect in 49 states, and it does use the term "security interest". However, the Act's substantive provisions, particularly those relating to transfers, and the structure of the Copyright Office index (organised not by debtor, as are the UCC filing system indices, but rather by copyrighted item and number), make clear that, even in the case of copyrights, Congress did not focus on the issue of financing and did not create a satisfactory federal regime suitable for modern secured credit on the strength of copyrights.

I will very briefly describe here some of the issues as they relate to the key types of IP collateral.

No federal statute governs trade secrets, and they are clearly creatures of state law. Without doubt, all security interest issues pertaining to this type of IP, including perfection and priority, are governed by Article 9.

Although there are federal trade mark laws, the rights themselves are common law (state created) rights. Indeed, trade marks rights do not exist independently of, and cannot be transferred separately from, the trade or business in connection with which they are employed. See *Visa, U.S.A., Inc.* v. *Birmingham Trust Nat'l Bank*, 696 F.2d 1371 (Fed. Cir. 1982). Thus, the creation of a security interest in a trade mark necessarily must be accompanied by the creation of a security interest in the related goodwill. This will, of course, require perfection by filing under state law, i.e. Article 9, in such goodwill collateral (indeed, such a transfer may well require the related collateral to include not only intangibles, such as secret formulas for producing the trade-marked product but possibly also tangible assets, such as unique tools and dies, which would also be perfected under Article 9, not federal law). Thus, a requirement of a federal filing with respect to the trade mark would inevitably mean a second filing, as there will always be a filing under Article 9 with respect to the related assets. Moreover, the recording requirements of the Lanham Act apply only to federally registered trade marks, not to common law or state-registered marks, and only to assignments of such marks—so it is difficult to characterise these recordation provisions as comprehensive and preemptive. The court in *Roman Cleanser Co.* v. *National Acceptance Co. (In re Roman Cleanser Co.)*, 43 BR 940, 944 (Bankr., ED Mich 1984), aff'd, 802 F.2d 207 (6th Cir. 1986), stated: "since a security interest in a trade mark is not equivalent to an assignment, the filing of a security interest is not covered by the Lanham Act. Accordingly, the manner of perfecting a security interest in trade marks is governed by Article 9 and not by the Lanham Act". See also, all holding that perfection of security interests in trade marks is governed by state law, *Creditors Committee of TR-3 Industries* v. *Capital Bank*, 41 BR 128 (Bankr., CD Cal. 1984); *In re Chattanooga Choo-Choo Co.*, 98 BR 792 (Bankr., ED Tenn. 1989); and *Joseph* v. *1200 Valencia, Inc. (In re 199Z, Inc.)*, 137 BR 778 (Bankr., CD Cal. 1992).

With respect to patents, the issue is more complex. Patents are creatures of federal law. Unfortunately, the language of the Patent Act is archaic. Its recording provision does not use the broad term 'transfer' or refer expressly to security interests, which may not be encompassed within "assignment, grant or conveyance", and its priority rule is stated not in terms of perfection but in terms of specified categories of competing interests. If the recording in the PTO of a security interest is required, a security interest not timely recorded there would not be effective against a subsequent purchaser or mortgagees for valuable consideration who took title from the debtor without notice of the security interest. Several cases have held that a trustee in bankruptcy does not fall within this protected class and that a security interest in a patent was properly perfected *vis-à-vis* a trustee in bankruptcy when the financing statement was filed in the appropriate UCC filing office but not in the PTO. *In re Transportation Design & Technology Inc.*, 48 BR 635 (Bankr., SD Cal. 1985); *City Bank & Trust Co.* v. *Otto Fabric, Inc.*, 83 BR 780 (D Kan. 1988); see also *Chesapeake Fiber Packaging Corp.* v. *Sebro Packaging Corp.*, 143 BR 360 (D Md. 1992), aff'd, 8 F.3d 817 (4th Cir. 1993). Moreover, both the Patent Act and the Lanham Act provide three-month grace (relation back) periods for recording, and the Copyright Act provides a slightly shorter period—such provisions are hardly conductive to efficient financing.

From the standpoint of determining the extent of federal displacement of Article 9, the most difficult issues are presented by copyright collateral. Copyrights are creatures of federal law, although, unlike patents, they come into being upon being fixed in a tangible medium, not upon an action being taken by or at the Copyright Office. Moreover, registration of a copyright is not required, although registration is a prerequisite to filing an action for infringement and being awarded statutory damages.

Furthermore, copyrights are the subject of a relatively recent statute which often uses very sweeping language. The problems of interpretation are exacerbated by a recent (and in my view misguided) opinion in *National Peregrine, Ltd.* v. *Capitol Fed. Sav. & Loan Ass'n (In re Peregrine Entertainment, Ltd)*, 116 BR 194 (CD Cal. 1990); see also, following *Peregrine, Official Unsecured Creditors' Comm.* v. *Zenith Prods., Ltd. (In re AEG Acquisition Corp.)*, 127 BR 34 (Bankr., CD Cal. 1991), aff'd, 161 BR 50 (BAP 9th Cir. 1993). If these cases are correct, the recording provisions of the Copyright Act broadly pre-empt state law with regard to perfection of security interests not only in registered copyrights but also in unregistered copyrights and in royalty income generated by copyrights.

Thus, the state of the law in the United States with respect to the extent of federal pre-emption of Article 9 as it pertains to security interests in IP is at this moment unclear. In terms of practical advice today, a prudent creditor would search and file/record under both regimes and in all possible places, i.e. the appropriate federal IP office in Washington, DC and the UCC filing office in the state in which the debtor is located. There are currently underway efforts to improve the state and the federal filing offices and to clarify the law governing with respect to the "where to file" question.

IV Some Lessons from the US Experience

Some of the US issues described above should not present a problem elsewhere, as most nations are unitary, not federal. Thus, federalism problems and interstate movement of debtors and multistate filing issues present in the U S are all easily avoided elsewhere.

Should there be special filing locations with respect to IP collateral, separate from the office for filing with respect to non-IP collateral? My answer is an emphatic no! The value of IP collateral is enhanced as efficiency and certainty with respect to the perfection of security interests in such collateral are improved. In countries that presently have or hereafter create a registry for security interests in general, i.e. non-IP, collateral, it would be highly inefficient to place IP security interest filings in the specific offices that otherwise govern the issue or ownership of the various forms of IP. Typical financing is not limited to a single patent or a single copyright; rather, all the debtor's IP, together with all its non-IP assets, is likely to be pledged to a lender providing blanket financing. It would be inefficient, costly and likely to lead to errors if perfection of such a collateral package were to require filings in a patent office, a copyright office, a trade mark office and an office for non-IP collateral filings. Also, one or more particular copyrights, trade marks and trade names are likely to be associated with inventory that is being financed. Again, the benefit of requiring only a single filing in a single office is readily apparent. Also, patents usually have their genesis in ideas that are first trade secrets for an extended period before the issue of the patent, and, during this period, the appropriate filing would clearly be done in the general, i.e. non-IP, filing office. Requiring a filing in the patent office when a patent is issued would present problems of potential loss of perfection and priority by the lender who had relied on the predecessor trade secret, and an attempt to ameliorate this problem by establishing a grace period would require subsequent searchers to contend with a secret lien. Furthermore, a lender is likely to want to receive a security interest in future IP obtained by the debtor, not just presently existing IP. A filing/searching system built on a debtor-based index, such as the UCC system, rather than an asset-based system such as is common in copyright and patent registries, is far better suited to facilitate sophisticated financing of multiple types of collateral of a changing composition and including future assets. Thus, it is, generally speaking, more efficient to put all security interest filings in a single office without regard to the nature of specific items of collateral.

Finally, the filing system for publicity with respect to security interests should adopt (1) a "notice filing" approach—a simple, unsigned, non-notarised submission of data that requires only basic information sufficient to alert prospective financiers to the possibility of a potential competing security interest; (2) electronic filing technology that facilitates simple, rapid and inexpensive world-wide filing and remote access searching; and (3) a non-bureaucratic approach that minimises the role of the administrators of the system, holding to an absolute minimum the imposition of arbitrary requirements, exercise of discretion and creation of grounds for rejection or delay.

V The Challenge—and Current International Activities

The challenge is to design, legislate and implement in each country a modern legal regime that facilitates effective security interests in IP (ideally, along with all other forms of personal property), along with an efficiently operated electronic worldwide database. Given the essentially borderless nature of IP (think of the Internet), uniformity of this domestic law is particularly crucial, to provide the greatest possible certainty and to minimise issues of conflict of laws. Such a regime will maximise the value of IP as collateral, making it attractive to lenders wherever located and giving borrowers and lenders everywhere the benefits of a global capital market. The World Bank and other agencies are providing assistance to countries seeking to modernise their domestic personal property security law. Also, there is already activity at the multinational level in the modernisation and harmonisation of personal property security law. Unidroit is working on a convention relating to international security interests in mobile equipment, and Uncitral is working on a convention or model law for international receivables financing.

THIS SPACE FOR USE OF FILING OFFICER

FINANCING STATEMENT — FOLLOW INSTRUCTIONS CAREFULLY

This Financing Statement is presented for filing pursuant to the Uniform Commercial Code and will remain effective, with certain exceptions, for 5 years from date of filing.

A. NAME & TEL. # OF CONTACT AT FILER (optional)

B. FILING OFFICE ACCT. # (optional)

C. RETURN COPY TO: (Name and Mailing Address)

D. OPTIONAL DESIGNATION (if applicable): ☐ LESSOR/LESSEE ☐ CONSIGNOR/CONSIGNEE ☐ NON-UCC FILING

1. DEBTOR'S EXACT FULL LEGAL NAME - insert only one debtor name (1a or 1b)

1a. ENTITY'S NAME

OR

1b. INDIVIDUAL'S LAST NAME	FIRST NAME	MIDDLE NAME			SUFFIX
1c. MAILING ADDRESS	CITY	STATE	COUNTRY	POSTAL CODE	
1d. S.S. OR TAX I.D.# / OPTIONAL ADD'NL INFO RE ENTITY DEBTOR / 1e. TYPE OF ENTITY	1f. ENTITY'S STATE OR COUNTRY OF ORGANIZATION	1g. ENTITY'S ORGANIZATIONAL I.D.#, if any ☐ NONE			

2. ADDITIONAL DEBTOR'S EXACT FULL LEGAL NAME - insert only one debtor name (2a or 2b)

2a. ENTITY'S NAME

OR

2b. INDIVIDUAL'S LAST NAME	FIRST NAME	MIDDLE NAME			SUFFIX
2c. MAILING ADDRESS	CITY	STATE	COUNTRY	POSTAL CODE	
2d. S.S. OR TAX I.D.# / OPTIONAL ADD'NL INFO RE ENTITY DEBTOR / 2e. TYPE OF ENTITY	2f. ENTITY'S STATE OR COUNTRY OF ORGANIZATION	2g. ENTITY'S ORGANIZATIONAL I.D.#, if any ☐ NONE			

3. SECURED PARTY'S (ORIGINAL S/P or ITS TOTAL ASSIGNEE) EXACT FULL LEGAL NAME - insert only one secured party name (3a or 3b)

3a. ENTITY'S NAME

OR

3b. INDIVIDUAL'S LAST NAME	FIRST NAME	MIDDLE NAME			SUFFIX
3c. MAILING ADDRESS	CITY	STATE	COUNTRY	POSTAL CODE	

4. This FINANCING STATEMENT covers the following types or items of property:

5. CHECK BOX (if applicable) ☐ This FINANCING STATEMENT is signed by the Secured Party instead of the Debtor to perfect a security interest (a) in collateral already subject to a security interest in another jurisdiction when it was brought into this state, or when the debtor's location was changed to this state, or (b) in accordance with other statutory provisions [additional data may be required]

7. If filed in Florida (check one) ☐ Documentary stamp tax paid ☐ Documentary stamp tax not applicable

6. REQUIRED SIGNATURE(S)

8. ☐ This FINANCING STATEMENT is to be filed [for record] (or recorded) in the REAL ESTATE RECORDS Attach Addendum [if applicable]

9. Check to REQUEST SEARCH CERTIFICATE(S) on Debtor(s) [ADDITIONAL FEE] (optional) ☐ All Debtors ☐ Debtor 1 ☐ Debtor 2

(1) FILING OFFICER COPY — NATIONAL FINANCING STATEMENT (FORM UCC1) (TRANS) (REV. 12/18/95)

General Instructions for National Financing Statement (Form UCC1) (Trans)

Please type or laser-print this form. Be sure it is completely legible. Read all Instructions.

Fill in form very carefully; mistakes may have important legal consequences. Follow Instructions completely. If you have questions, consult your attorney. Filing officer cannot give legal advice.

Do not insert anything in the open space in the upper portion of this form; it is reserved for filing officer use.

When properly completed, send Filing Officer Copy, with required fee, to filing officer. If you want an acknowledgment, also send Acknowledgment Copy, otherwise detach. If you want to make a search request, complete item 9 and send Search Request Copy, otherwise detach. Always detach Debtor and Secured Party Copies.

If you need to use attachments, use 8-1/2 X 11 inch sheets and put at the top of each additional sheet the name of the first Debtor, formatted exactly as it appears in item 1 of this form; you are encouraged to use Addendum (Form UCC1Ad).

Item Instructions

1. **Debtor name:** Enter only one Debtor name in item 1, an entity's name (1a) or an individual's name (1b). Enter Debtor's exact full legal name. Don't abbreviate.

1a. Entity Debtor. "Entity" means an organization having a legal identity separate from its owner. A partnership is an entity; a sole proprietorship is not an entity, even if it does business under a trade name. If Debtor is a partnership, enter exact full legal name of partnership; you need not enter names of partners as additional Debtors. If Debtor is a registered entity (e.g., corporation, limited partnership, limited liability company), it is advisable to examine Debtor's current filed charter documents to determine correct name, entity type, and state of organization.

1b. Individual Debtor. "Individual" means a natural person and a sole proprietorship, whether or not operating under a trade name. Don't use prefixes (Mr., Mrs., Ms.). Use suffix box only for titles of lineage (Jr., Sr., III) and not for other suffixes or titles (e.g., M.D.). Use married woman's personal name (Mary Smith, not Mrs. John Smith). Enter individual Debtor's family name (surname) in Last Name box, first given name in First Name box, and all additional given names in Middle Name box.
For both entity and individual Debtors: Don't use Debtor's trade name, D/B/A, A/K/A, F/K/A, etc. in place of Debtor's legal name; you may add such other names as additional Debtors if you wish.

1c. An address is always required for the Debtor named in 1a or 1b.

1d. Debtor's social security or tax identification number is required in some states. Enter social security number of a sole proprietor, not tax identification number of the sole proprietorship.

1e,f,g. "Additional information re entity Debtor" is optional. It helps searchers to distinguish this Debtor from others with the same or a similar name. Type of entity and state of organization can be determined from Debtor's current filed charter documents. Organizational I.D. number, if any, is assigned by the agency where the charter document was filed; this is different from taxpayer I.D. number; this should be entered preceded by the 2-character U.S. Postal identification of state of organization (e.g., CA12345, for a California corporation whose organizational I.D. number is 12345).

Note: If Debtor is a transmitting utility as defined in applicable Commercial Code, attach Addendum (Form UCC1Ad) and check box Ad8.

2. If an additional Debtor is included, complete item 2, determined and formatted per Instruction 1. To include further additional Debtors, or one or more additional Secured Parties, attach either Addendum (Form UCC1Ad) or other additional page(s), using correct name format. Follow Instruction 1 for determining and formatting additional names.

3. Enter information, determined and formatted per Instruction 1. If there is more than one Secured Party, see Instruction 2. If there has been a total assignment of the Secured Party's interest prior to filing this form, you may provide either assignor Secured Party's or assignee's name and address in item 3.

4. Use item 4 to indicate the types or describe the items of collateral. If space in item 4 is insufficient, put the entire collateral description or continuation of the collateral description on either Addendum (Form UCC1Ad) or other attached additional page(s).

5, 6. All Debtors must sign. Under certain circumstances, Secured Party may sign instead of Debtor; if applicable, check box in item 5 and provide Secured Party's signature in item 6, and under certain circumstances, in some states, you must also provide additional data; use Addendum (Form UCC1Ad) or attachment to provide such additional data.

7. If filing in the state of Florida you must check one of the two boxes in item 7 to comply with documentary stamp tax requirements.

8. If the collateral consists of or includes fixtures, timber, minerals, and/or mineral-related accounts, check the box in item 8 and complete the required information on Addendum (Form UCC1Ad). If the collateral consists of or includes crops, consult applicable law of state where this Financing Statement is to be filed and complete Ad3b, and Ad4 if required, on Addendum (Form UCC1Ad) and, if required, check box in item 8.

9. Check box 9 to request Search Certificate(s) on all or some of the Debtors named in this Financing Statement. The Certificate will list all Financing Statements on file against the designated Debtor currently effective on the date of the Certificate, including this Financing Statement. There is an additional fee for each Certificate. This item is optional. If you have checked box 9, file copy 3 (Search Request Copy) of this form together with copies 1 and 2. Not all states will honor a search request made via this form; some states require a separate request form.

Instructions re Optional Items A-D

A. To assist filing officers who might wish to communicate with filer, filer may provide information in item A. This item is optional.

B. If filer has an account with filing officer or is authorized to pay fees by means of a card (credit or debit) and wishes to use such means of payment, check the appropriate box and enter filer's account number in item B, or, in the alternative, filer may present this information by a cover letter.

C. Complete item C if you want acknowledgment copy returned and you have presented simultaneously a carbon or other copy of this form for use as an acknowledgment copy.

D. If filer desires to use titles of lessee and lessor, or consignee and consignor, instead of Debtor and Secured Party, check the appropriate box in item D. This item is optional. If this is not a UCC security interest filing (e.g., a tax lien, judgment lien, etc.), check the appropriate box in item D, complete items 1-9 as applicable and attach any other items required under other law.

Panel III
Industrial Property Rights in the Context of Antitrust Legislation

6
TECHNOLOGICAL INFORMATION AND THE ESSENTIAL FACILITIES DOCTRINE OF US ANTITRUST LAW

*David J. Gerber**

I Introduction

This presentation focuses on the potential impact of US antitrust laws on the capacity of dominant firms to protect their technological information. Specifically, our concern here is with the essential facilities doctrine of US antitrust law and its potential impact on the capacity of firms to protect such information. When might the application of this legal doctrine or associated ideas require a dominant firm subject to US laws to provide access to proprietary information?

This issue is obviously critical for many international firms. Protecting technological information is an increasingly important component of international business strategies in many industries, and thus legal principles that might call for duties to provide access to such information could seriously impact on these strategies.

The doctrine has become a major topic of discussion in international intellectual property circles recently for several reasons. Some are related to changing business conditions. For example, the increasing technological and economic inter-relatedness of firms tends to increase the importance of intellectual property rights, which are often instrumental in structuring the frequently complex relationships among related firms. Moreover, the growing importance of technological leadership in business strategies underscores the role of intellectual property rights in maintaining competitive advantages.

Accompanying these changes is concern in some quarters that the

* Professor of Law, Chicago-Kent College of Law, Illinois Institute of Technology, Chicago, USA.

increased importance of intellectual property rights should lead to greater controls on the use of these rights. As such rights become more important—and more valuable, policy concerns about their use inevitably increase. In this context increased concern over "access" to "necessary" technology may well be inevitable. This is particularly likely in industries in which there has been extensive state ownership that has created monopoly positions and, often, technological leadership.

Events in the legal world have also focused attention on the issue of access to essential facilities. On a general level, the expansion of international intellectual property protection through the TRIPS agreement and WTO arrangements raises the issue of whether this significant expansion of potential bases of legal and economic power should be accompanied by additional normative constraints designed to protect against abuse of this increased potential power.[1] More specifically, the *Magill* decision of the European Court of Justicc has highlighted the possibility that the essential facilities doctrine may be applied to intellectual property rights in ways that would significantly influence the scope of those rights.[2]

But why at this international conference pay particular attention to the essential facilities doctrine *under US law?* After all, the *Magill* decision had nothing to do, at least directly, with US law. There are two basic reasons. One involves direct application of US law. The size and technological sophistication of the US market means that most international firms must compete, directly or indirectly, in that market and thus need to know what norms are being applied there and what impact they may have on business operations.

The second reason is the potential influence of US essential facilities ideas on developments in the rest of the world. The doctrine itself—at least in its modern form—can be said to have originated in United States antitrust law, and it is here that experience with it has been most extensive. It is thus to US experience with this doctrine that scholars and officials in other parts of the world are turning in making decisions about the use of the doctrine elsewhere. One need only review recent articles on the issue in European legal and economic journals to realise that US experience is a primary reference point for thinking and decision-making about the concept.[3]

My objective here then is to examine briefly the essential facilities doctrine in US antitrust law in the light of these two kinds of concerns. What kinds of impacts should it have on firms operating in or in relation to the US market, and to what extent and for what purposes is US experience with the

[1] For a recent symposium discussing these issues, see Frederick M. Abbott and David J. Gerber, *Public Policy and Global Technological Integration* (1996),

[2] *Radio Telefis Eireann and Others* v. *Comm'n of the European Communities* (Magill TV Guide Ltd. intervening) [1989] ECR 1141, [1989] 4 CMLR 749.

[3] See, e.g., Mark Furse, "The 'Essential Facilities' Doctrine in Community Law" (1995) 8 *Eur. LR* 469.

essential facilities doctrine likely to influence those outside the US making decisions about the use of such ideas? As directed by the organisers of the conference, I will not be concerned with refinements of legal argument, because I know that many of you are not lawyers, but with the kinds of information that should be most relevant to non-US businesspeople and their advisers. I emphasise that for our purposes here the issue is not "what are the rules" but what are the factors driving decisions that may affect international business.

I will first set the stage by discussing some of the characteristics of the US antitrust law system that are relevant to assessing information about the essential facilities doctrine. I will then look at the basic outlines of experience with these ideas in US law. And, finally, I will examine the actual and potential application of these ideas and doctrines to the specific area of protecting technological information.

My basic message is that most firms under most circumstances are not likely to be affected by the essential facilities doctrine, but that firms with both a high level of dominance in a particular market and control of information that may be necessary for competition on the market may under limited circumstances need to pay attention to the potential applications of the doctrine.

II Relevant Characteristics of United States Antitrust Laws

Before discussing the substantive law relating to the essential facilities doctrine, it is important to describe briefly some of the features of the US antitrust system in which these substantive rules are imbedded. For our purposes here, it will be far more useful to talk about substantive law ideas against the practical background in which they operate. I should mention here that we will be concerned only with the antitrust laws on the federal level. State antitrust enforcement in this area is unlikely to be of relevance for our purposes.

A Enforcement

Of particular importance for foreign observers is the system of enforcement of US antitrust laws. Whereas in most competition law systems in the world bureaucrats are the primary or exclusive agents in enforcing competition laws, this is not the case in the US. The enforcement picture is more complicated. While bureaucratic enforcement is not unimportant in the US, the role of private litigation in enforcing the antitrust laws is far more extensive than in other competition law systems, and it is thus a defining feature of the US antitrust system.

The antitrust laws are enforced by two separate government offices. The federal justice department has been in recent years the centre of attention regarding the application of these laws. This office is authorised to bring civil as well as *criminal* actions in the ordinary courts for violation of the antitrust laws. It will normally bring criminal actions only in cases of wilful violation of the laws, and thus it is unlikely in the area of our concern that criminal sanctions will be sought.

The justice department enforces "the law", but it must also be understood as an often highly political office. It is subject to political control by the government that is in power at any given time, and its policies can vary significantly depending on the political "colour" of that government. It is thus often very important in assessing the likely action of the justice department to keep in mind the political and economic pressures affecting decision-making there. The justice department brings suit not only to enforce "the law", but to change "the law" and to pursue policy objectives.

The same may be said of the Federal Trade Commission, which also enforces elements of the antitrust laws relevant to our concerns. Due to a variety of factors, the FTC has been generally a more peripheral and restrained part of the antitrust picture in recent years, but under its new chairman, Robert Pitofsky, this is changing.

Perhaps the most significant difference between the US antitrust system and other competition law systems is the degree to which enforcement of the antitrust laws takes place through private suits brought in the ordinary courts. For the situations here relevant, enterprises injured by anti-competitive conduct generally may bring suit to recover the losses resulting from such injury, and in order to encourage such suits, the law provides that they can be awarded compensation in an amount three times the amount of the injury sustained. There is thus significant encouragement to bring such suits. This so-called "treble damage" provision is one of the factors that can make US private antitrust litigation so expensive, but there are others, and these are generally related to the peculiarities of the US procedural system.

Most important here are the pre-trial discovery procedures, which are quite unlike anything else in the world in terms of their scope and significance. Basically, once a plaintiff has commenced litigation by filing a complaint (and assuming the defendant intends to defend the suit), the law provides attorneys for both parties with extensive rights to require their opponents and third parties to produce information that might be related to the issues involved in the case. This "discovery" process can become extremely expensive. Moreover, and this is particularly likely in cases involving valuable technology, it can be used to seek to acquire information from one's opponent.

One additional aspect of the US antitrust system that deserves emphasis in an international context is the degree of uncertainty that it can represent. Whereas most competition-law systems in the world are primarily enforced by an administrative office that is likely to be relatively predictable in its enforcement efforts, at least in the short run, the private enforcement of the US laws introduces an additional degree of uncertainty into the system. Competition law cases can often be highly complex, and they may be heard by judges who have little experience with such cases. Moreover, decisions about facts in such litigation may be made by a jury of laymen! These factors tend to reduce the capacity to predict what is likely to happen in a particular case. Finally, the fact that the case law decision-making is based on extremely vague statutory principles and interpretations of existing decisions often means that stating general principles of law is sometimes very difficult.

B Consequences

This combination of factors means that, in general, businesses concerned with the impact of US antitrust laws need to be concerned with a variety of issues other than the substantive content of the norms themselves. For example, what kinds of policy messages are the public enforcement officials sending? Is there enough uncertainty regarding a particular kind of potential violation that a private firm may be tempted to bring suit on the theory that it just might be able to win? To what extent might a firm be likely to sue in order to gain information about a competitor's technology or to impose costs on the competitor that might lead him to take actions that he otherwise might not take? These are some of the factors that make up the background against which the impact of US antitrust law needs to be assessed.

III The Substantive Law Framework of the Essential Facilities Doctrine

Our concern here is with interpretation of the basic statute of US antitrust law, the so-called Sherman Act, which is now more than a century old. Its provisions tend to be very general compared to the competition legislation in many other countries, and thus the law in the area is derived from cases that have applied that statute. For ease of reference, I will identify the two main provisions in the statute. Section one relates basically to agreements to restrict competition, while section two refers basically to single-firm conduct, and here a violation occurs where a firm "monopolises" a market or "attempts to monopolise" a market. There are, of course, merely code words for complex legal issues.

The classic case relating to essential facilities, the one that US lawyers are likely to think of when the term is mentioned, is actually a §1 case, i.e. a case involving an agreement to restrain competition. This was the famous *Terminal Railroad Assn. case*, in which a group of private railroads essentially agreed among themselves to prevent private competing railroads from having access to a major railroad hub in St Louis, a major transportation hub in the center of the country. The Supreme Court held that this was a violation of section 1 because it prevented access to an "essential facility".[4] The essential facilities doctrine evolved from this basic idea.

Our concern here is not, however, with collusive behaviour, but with the conduct of a single firm, and this falls within section 2 of the Sherman Act. The essential facilities concept has also been used in this context, and this will be the focus of the rest of our discussion.[5]

The starting point is that, in general, United States antitrust law does not impose a duty on business firms to transact business. Normally, a firm may unilaterally refuse to sell or deliver services to any other firm if it so wishes. Under some limited circumstances, however, section 2 of the Sherman Act may impose such obligations, and this is our concern.

Two basic principles can lead to such an obligation. The first relates to the intent of the enterprise in engaging in a particular practice. If the firm has a significant degree of market power and engages in conduct with the intent of excluding rivals from the market, it may be violating §2, because it may be said to be "monopolising" or "attempting to monopolise" the market. We need not explore these rather fuzzy issues in detail, but the basic idea is that a firm with significant market power may not engage in conduct which "excludes" its rivals—i.e. which hinders their ability to compete. The definition is negative: "exclusion" is conduct other than competitive conduct.

The essential facilities concept is a related notion, but it fits somewhat awkwardly. Here the idea is that a monopolist's control of an essential facility imposes on it an obligation to permit potential competitors to compete. It is, in effect, a corollary of the idea that a monopolist may not exclude competitors from the market. It says that if a monopolist controls such a facility, it must provide access to it. Both concepts rest on the same basic enmity toward monopoly and the policy decision not to permit monopolists to stifle competition.

The cases under the essential facility doctrine do not present a clear picture of the reach of the doctrine, but in the 1983 *MCI* case the seventh circuit court of appeals established a four-part test for violation of the essential facilities doctrine that has been widely followed. According to the court, the elements of a violation include: control of the essential facility by a monopolist; a competitor's inability practically or reasonably to duplicate the essential facility; denial of the use of the facility to a competitor, and the feasibility of providing the facility to the competitor.[6]

4 *United States* v. *Terminal RR Ass'n*, 224 US 383 (1912).

5 See generally Kenneth L. Glazer and Abbott B. Lipsky, Jr., "Unilateral Refusals to Deal Under Section 2 of the Sherman Act", 63 *Antitrust LJ* 749 (1995); Lawrence A. Sullivan, "Section 2 of the Sherman Act and Vertical Strategies by Dominant Firms", 21 *Sw. UL Rev.* 1227 (1992); Phillip Areeda, "Essential Facilities: An Epithet in Need of a Limiting Principal", 58 *Antitrust LJ* 841 (1989).

6 *MCI Communications Corp.* v. *American Tel. and Tel. Co.*, 708 F.2d 1081 (7th Cir.1983), cert. denied 464 US 891 (1983).

There is no need here to review the case law dealing with the essential facilities doctrine, but it is important for our purposes to note that the doctrine has been applied successfully only in cases involving some kind of "facility", which has thus far been considered to mean something "physical". For example, it has been used to require a monopolist of electrical transmission lines to make access available to competitors,[7] and it has been used to require an owner of a basketball stadium to provide access to a team competing with a team in which it also had an interest.[8]

IV Application to Intellectual Property Rights

How then does this apply to the protection of proprietary information? A preliminary answer is that the essential facilities doctrine does not apply to intellectual property rights. It has not been used to justify a requirement that a firm holding intellectual property rights provide to a competitor access to those rights. In other words, the law today seems to be that control of an intellectual property right does not represent control of a "facility" for purposes of the essential facilities doctrine, and thus there is no general duty to provide information to competitors.

There have been several cases in which plaintiffs have sought to establish claims of monopolisation on this basis, but they have been consistently denied.[9] The basic underlying argument has been that intellectual property rights are the result of competitive effort and investment and their owners should not be required to divulge information or license those rights simply because other competitors have not made similar investments or achieved similar successes. In addition, it has been claimed that the courts could not be expected effectively to draw lines between "essential" rights and others and thus application of the doctrine to the intellectual property rights area would necessarily be confused and likely to discourage technological innovation.

To end our analysis here would, however, be misleading. We need to look at the likelihood that government or private plaintiffs might bring suit on the basis of such claims, and we need to ask whether courts might be inclined to accept such claims.

First, there is occasional language in cases that suggests that the essential facilities doctrine might apply in cases involving intellectual property rights. For example, in a case with some similarities to the *Magill* decision, a publisher of telephone directories sued a local phone company for refusing to provide it with information in its possession that was necessary for the

[7] *Otter Tail Power Co.* v. *United States*, 410 US 366 (1973).

[8] Fishman v. *Estate of Wirtz*, 807 F 2d 520 (7th Cir. 1886).

[9] *SCM Corp.* v. *Xerox Corp.*, 645 F 2d 1195 (2nd Cir. 1981), cert. denied 455 US 1016 (1982).

publisher to publish the phone book. The local phone producer also published a directory, and thus the plaintiff claimed that this violated §2. Although it decided the case on other grounds, the district court found that there was "no reason why it [the essential facilities doctrine] could not apply, as in this case, to information wrongfully withheld".[10] Such language has thus far been in the form of dictum (i.e., not binding on later courts), and it has not been found in the opinions of important courts, but it means that at least some judges have found the idea attractive.

Secondly, there is the issue of whether government enforcement agencies are likely to pursue this type of application of essential facilities doctrine. In many ways, this issue is almost as important for business decision-making as whether courts are likely eventually to accept the arguments being pressed.

There is little doubt that the general issue of the relationship between competition law and intellectual property rights is central at both the Justice Department and the Federal Trade Commission. At the Justice Department there has been renewed enforcement activity in the general area, including, in particular, the Microsoft litigation. The hearings held by the FTC in late 1995 were also focused on these issues.[11]

There is, however, a curious and I think little-noticed, aspect of this discourse. At the level of professed aims and statements of policy, both agencies stress that they support technological progress and wish to avoid uses of the competition laws that might interfere with such progress. They emphasise that earlier thinking that saw competition law and intellectual property rights as antithetical will no longer be followed. This would appear to be good news for intellectual property rights holders.

Yet there may be a more subtle and not necessarily intentional dynamic hidden in this intellectual move—this new discourse of competition law and intellectual property rights. If one seeks a wider perspective on it, one might note that this concern with technological progress focuses on—you may have guessed—preventing impediments to the competition that leads to technological progress. The concept of preventing impediments to competition is, however, the core idea behind the essential facilities doctrine.

The government's recent Microsoft litigation also indicates that the US Department of Justice and at least some members of the Federal Trade Commission have serious concerns about the anti-competitive effects of a monopolist's refusal to allow access to proprietary information.[12] The case

[10] *Bellsouth Advertising & Publishing Corp.* v. *Donnelley Info. Publishing, Inc.*, 719 F Supp. 1551 (SD Fla. 1988), aff'd 933 F 2d 952 (11th Cir. 1991).

[11] For a detailed report on the hearings, see Federal Trade Commission Staff Report, "Anticipating the 21st Century: Competition Policy in the New High-Tech, Global Marketplace", CCH Trade Regulation Reports, 11 June 1996.

[12] See *United States* v. *Microsoft Corp.*, 1995 Lexis 20533, 1995–2 Trade Cas. (CCH) 71, 096 (DDC 1995).

was settled by a consent decree, and thus we do not have a full explanation of the Justice Department's concerns, but the enforcement effort seems designed to require such a monopolist not to hinder competitors from gaining access to the proprietary information and rights without which competition may be impossible.

One somewhat tangential aspect of this case to note is the Justice Department's insistence that Microsoft not be allowed to prevent licensees acquiring information about its products from divulging that information to competitors.[13] A requirement that Microsoft not engage in such practices was included in the consent decree, suggesting that Microsoft's attorneys considered it to have some merit. This further suggests that at the very least a monopolist should refrain from contractually binding others not to reveal information that they have acquired.

Finally, there are some not entirely implausible bases for extending the essential facilities doctrine in the direction of applying it to intellectual property rights. As I have indicated, any such extension would have to overcome the position of a number of courts that the doctrine does not reach that situation, and it would have to overcome the underlying policy arguments mentioned above, but the line between intellectual property rights and "facilities" is not necessarily impenetrable. It rests on the notion that intellectual property rights are "special"—different from "facilities". Under some circumstances, however, an intellectual property right may well create the same anti-competitive concerns created by physical "facilities". It may effectively prevent competition on an entire market. Moreover, if a court were to understand it as analogous to an "essential facility", it is not difficult to identify situations in which the tests for applying the doctrine would be met.

One final point in this regard. The conceptual distance between intellectual property rights and "essential facilities" may be influenced by a current reorientation of the discourse relating to the general relationship between antitrust law and intellectual property rights. Officials of the Justice Department and the FTC are currently emphasising the theme that intellectual property rights should be considered property rights like any other.[14] These discussions seem to be part of a larger effort to undermine the notion of a conflict between intellectual property rights and antitrust law, and I do not mean to suggest that they currently are intended to influence application of the essential facilities doctrine. An unintended consequence of this type of discourse could, however, be to accustom policymakers and judges to the notion that intellectual property rights are not so "special", and this would

[13] See "Proposed Final Judgement and Competitive Impact Statement; *United States of America* v. *Microsoft Corp.*", 59 Fed. Reg. 42845 (19 Aug. 1994).

[14] Anne K. Bingaman, "Antitrust, Innovation and Intellectual Property", Program on Antitrust and Intellectual Property Law, Stanford Law School (7 Oct. 1994) (internet: justice2.usdoj . . . /atr/talks/94-10-07.txt).

tend to undermine the conceptual barrier protecting intellectual property rights from the reach of the essential facilities doctrine.

I emphasise that such arguments have thus far had little success, but in discussing US antitrust law it is important to remember the enforcement context. Major monopolists operating in the US should plan in relation to the operations of the enforcement system, not merely in terms of established legal norms. For example, given the importance being attached to technological issues in the Justice Department and the FTC, it is critical to follow carefully developments in thinking there in order to assess whether "essential facilities"-type concerns may gain in strength. I say "essential facilities-type concerns" because enforcement officials may seek to avoid that label in fashioning strategies for dealing with their concerns.

A focus should also be on the likelihood that a US plaintiff may be willing to incur the expenses of private litigation to test the possibility of being successful with essential facilities-based arguments. This will depend in part on assessment by counsel of the likelihood that a court might apply the essential facilities doctrine. It need not be a certainty or even a near certainty, especially given the possibility, as noted above, that the process of discovery may yield tactical advantages or highly useful information, regardless of whether the suit is successful or not.

V Conclusions

By way of conclusion, therefore, the concerns that have been expressed in Europe about the potential impact of the essential facilities doctrine on intellectual property holders draw little support from the situation in the US. Current law does not view intellectual property rights as facilities for purposes of applying that doctrine. This means that owners of intellectual property rights operating in the United States can generally assume that the doctrine will not cause the mere holding of those rights to generate an obligation either to divulge information about the covered technology or to license the rights themselves. Moreover, courts and administrative officials outside the USA that look to that experience will find a pattern of refusal to apply the doctrine in these circumstances.

On the other hand, caution is advisable. A major monopolist such as Microsoft controlling a technology access to which may be necessary for there to be competition in a particular market appeals to the same general concerns as those to which the essential facilities doctrine is directed. Consequently, it is far from inconceivable that government officials, courts and/or commentators might call for the application of the essential facilities doctrine in that situation and require the monopolist to provide information to competitors or even license rights to competitors.

7

PATENTS AND ANTITRUST

*Valentine Korah**

I Policy Issue

I want to raise an issue of policy about the relationship between antitrust and intellectual property rights, especially patents. I look forward to hearing your views today. It seems fairly clear that, very occasionally, some patents are being granted that are wider than necessary to induce the original investment, which delay incremental r & d and lead to high prices.

This is probably important only in relation to a few industries. In the last century, the internal combustion engine gave rise to some very wide patents. Computers might have done so, but at first, everyone thought about copyright, so when patents were thought relevant, the basic ideas were no longer novel. More recent problems have arisen in biotechnology, where some very wide patents are being granted to the first person to identify the polypeptide chain for a virus, although the very basic ideas were published by a university and are in the public domain.[1]

Should the law be changed to make the conditions of patentability stricter? Should inventions have to be closer to the market to be protected by patent? Should competition authorities be consulted before intellectual property legislation is enacted or changed? Should any legislative changes be limited to biotechnology where the current problems are arising?[2] Doubtless, over the next century, there will be some other sector where wide products emerge.

Where patents are unduly wide, are the current remedies appropriate? The

* Professor Emeritus of Competition Law at University College London, Author of several books including: *EC Competition Law and Practice* (6th edn., Hart Publishing, Oxford, 1997); *Technology Transfer and the EC Competition Rules* (Oxford University Press, 1996); *Cases and Materials on EC Competition Law* (Sweet and Maxwell, 1996), slightly revised version reprinted by Hart Publishing 1998.

Since the AIPPI Forum in 1996, the OECD invited talks on the incentives for follow up inventions by Nancy Gallini of the University of Toronto, John Barton of Stanford University, Willard Tom of the Federal Trade Commission and myself. They are to be published and placed on the internet in the Autumn of 1998.

[1] I am grateful to John Richards of Ladas and Parry for conversations on the topic. He has not seen even a draft of this paper, so can not be blamed for my mistakes.

[2] In many industries, newcomers can invent around the patent, but this is not true of a polypeptide chain. The holder of the first patent may be able to control both tests and cures for an important disease for 25 years and remove the incentives to further innovation by others.

scope of patent protection may be challenged first by opposition proceedings in the patent office and later in the courts, but challenge is very expensive, may take years and the outcome is often unpredictable, so often not feasible for smaller firms.

Should compulsory licences at a reasonable royalty and on other reasonable terms also be required on antitrust grounds on an *ad hoc* basis, at least where a subsequent inventor has made an important development? What terms are reasonable: the cost of issuing the licence or also a significant contribution to the cost and risk of the underlying basic r & d, or something in between?

I shall consider some of the case law in the European Community on the grant of compulsory licences on competition grounds after raising the other issues, and hope that you, who know far more about patents than I do, will consider the policy of limiting the grounds of patentability.

Those in favour of strong patent protection argue that upholding the exclusive right under very broad patents increases the incentive to the investment that led to the original invention, and also that the hope of obtaining an important exclusive right leads to investments in many other aspects of r & d which may happen to result in less important innovations. To reduce the width of the patent protection or to compel licensing would marginally reduce the incentives, and might lead to less investment in basic research and to fewer inventions, basic and otherwise.

Those favouring intervention argue that maintaining the exclusive right in extreme cases may delay research into developments from the basic innovation for many years, as the incentives are lacking. The holder may have no further need to invest in innovation, and third parties would not be able to exploit the results of their investment without a licence under the basic patent. Any monopoly profit resulting from the subsequent investment would have to be shared with the holder of the basic patent. Consequently, less than the optimal amount of investment might be expected. In some cases none.

The difficulty for policy makers is that it is not possible to quantify the value of the results that will be lost either if compulsory licences are not granted or if they are. The Federal Trade Commission in the USA held some fascinating hearings into the desirability of the antitrust agencies intervening in these and other situations. Very able economists, business managers and lawyers contributed to the discussions in November 1995.[3]

My immediate reaction was that the width of the claims would be better dealt with by patent offices as this would lead to greater certainty earlier and to less litigation than *ad hoc* intervention case by case through antitrust

[3] Summaries of the evidence were published in 69 Antitrust and Trade Regulation Report, 670. The full paper and oral discussion were also placed on the internet. In May 1996, the staff of the FTC published a summary, *Anticipating the 21st Century: Competition Policy in the New High-Tech, Global Market Place,* especially chapters 7–9.

proceedings. Patent examiners are likely to have more of the relevant skills relating both to patent law and the particular technology than competition authorities. The difficulty is that patent offices, faced with a block-busting innovation, may not realise how wide the claims are. Consequently, the issue remains whether antitrust or competition law should act as a backstop to require licensing after the event, when a third party wants to exploit a very important innovation protected by patent or whether provision should be made for the patent office to grant compulsory licenses in extreme cases.

A The FTC hearings

In Autumn 1995, the Federal Trade Commission in the USA held some hearings and devoted a day to the issue of compulsory licensing. Marshall Phelps and some of the foremost economists, lawyers and businesmen presented papers and answered questions from the Chairman and his officials.

John Barton[4] raised the question of very broad patents, such as one granted in the USA for "all transgenic rice" and another for "all human genetic therapy in which the actual genetic transformation of the cells is done outside the human body". As a result of a small survey he conducted, he thought these were not exceptional, although I am told that such wide patents might not be granted in Europe. The decision what to do was difficult because the original innovation may be very important and have cost a lot. Yet the width of the protection may reduce the incentives to incremental and follow on research.

Wide patents may lead to cross licensing and patent pools limiting access by third parties even if the cross-licenses are not expressed to be exclusive. An inner group of firms may form with access through cross-licensing, and a new entrant needs a sufficiently important improvement to balance the aggregate technology of the group to join it. This weakens the incentives of the inner group to invest in invention. The need for third parties to negotiate a cross-licence adds an additional uncertainty to the outcome of its research. Moreover, there will be only one monopoly profit for the third party to earn and it will have to share it with the holder of the basic patent. Consequently less than the optimal amount of investment in subsequent R & D is to be expected.

He went on to consider possible remedies under patent law to increase the incentives for a subsequent inventor: expanding the experimental use exemption, limiting patent protection to inventions closer to the market, or requiring a compulsory licence to be given to the subsequent inventor of a very important development. The alternative remedy is to invoke antitrust, and treat the refusal to license a very basic or very broad patent as monopolisation even in the absence of any other kind of fault.

[4] George E. Osborne Professor of Law at Stanford University.

Douglas Rosenthal stressed the importance of antitrust specialists contributing to the decision how wide intellectual property rights should be. He also raised the need to consider antitrust considerations in trade negotiations.

F.M. Scherer[5] suggested that it was only in the pharmaceutical and agricultural chemical fields that the possibility of gaining a patent operated as one of the most important incentives to investment in innovation. He gave some examples of situations where he thought that patent protection deserved scrutiny: where an idea was being widely discussed and one firm won the race to the patent office[6]; when a firm acquired a patent from a competitor in order to prolong the protection when its own patents had expired, and where there was exclusive licensing from the only two innovating firms upstream. One might expect most systems of antitrust to intervene in the last two situations.[7]

In answer to a question, he advocated some form of mandatory licensing where there was a genuine bottleneck situation and a very strong public interest in breaking it. He advised reticence in doing so, because of the reduction of incentives.

During the question session, several people stressed that some of the questions should be answered when establishing or interpreting the criteria for obtaining an intellectual property right. They advocated that the competition and intellectual property people concerned in legislation should enter into a dialogue. This might reduce the extent of intellectual property rights and would have the advantage of laying down rules in advance rather than intervening ad hoc after the event. This would result in greater certainty. The consensus seems to have been that compulsory licences should be rare but that it might be appropriate to narrow the scope of patents.

I shall now turn to the possibility of *ad hoc* intervention under antitrust.

[5] Larsen Professor of Public Policy at the John F. Kennedy School of Government at Harvard University, at the FTC hearing on 29 Nov.

[6] He gave an example where the invention had actually been published, but this was not noticed when the patent was granted.

[7] The first is a horizontal agreement between competitors adding to the market power of the acquirer. It would probably be appraised under a rule of reason in the USA. In the EC, bringing together the two sources of technology might be attacked under Art 85 or Art 86. See *IGR Stereo Television*, *Commission's Eleventh Report on Competition Policy,* point 63, *Commission's Fourteenth Report on Competition Policy,* point 76; and *Tetra Pak I (BTG licence)* (88/501/EEC), 26 July 1988 [1988] OJ L272/27 [1990] 4 CMLR 47 and, on appeal, *Tetra Pak Rausing SA* v. *Commission* (T–51/89), 10 July 1990, [1990] ECR II–309, [1991] 4 CMLR 334, [1990] 2 CEC 409.

In the second example, the second exclusive licence to a firm that already had one from the only other innovator would also be a horizontal, also bringing together the only sources of technology. The same problem is raised.

II The Case Law May Require Compulsory Licences from Dominant Firms

As David Gerber has explained, section 2 of the Sherman Act prohibits monopolisation and there is a doctrine resulting from case law of essential facilities—the owners of an essential facility may monopolise unless they make the facility available to outsiders. Philip Areeda of Harvard, however, concerned about reducing incentives to investment in creating the essential facility, has pressed for this doctrine to be applied very rarely, mainly in cases where a group of competitors has acquired a bottle neck facility that they did not have to create.[8] The holder of a vital patent is likely to be at the other end of the spectrum of possibilities. One of Professor Barton's concerns, the insiders who cross-license each other, comes at least in the middle of spectrum. The incumbents have made important contributions to technology, but it is the aggregate value of all their research that the newcomer may have to match to join the pool and compete.

In the European Communities, there is no need to invoke a doctrine of essential facilities to require a firm with far less market power than those to which section 2 of the Sherman Act applies to supply third parties, although the doctrine has been invoked by the Commission in several cases relating to transport.[9]

Article 86 EC forbids, as incompatible with the common market, the abuse of a dominant position within the common market. This has been construed far more broadly that section 2 in the USA. Firms with no power over price have been held to be dominant over very narrow markets, such as bananas to the exclusion of summer fruits,[10] or the supply of tyres for heavy vehicles, to the exclusion of retreads, to retailers in the Netherlands.[11]

The Community Court has frequently held that a firm enjoying a dominant position may be required to supply former customers,[12] and the

[8] "Essential Facilities: An Epithet in Need of Limiting Principles", 58 *Antitrust Law Journal* 841.

[9] E.g., *British Midland* [1992] OJ, L96/34, [1993] 4 CMLR 596, [1992] 1 CEC 2261, *French African Shipping* [1992] OJ, L121/45, [1993] 5 CMLR 632, [1992] 1 CEC 2297, paras 68–69; *Rodby* [1994] OJ, L55/52, para 12. See John Temple Lang, "Defining Legitimate Competition: Companies' Duties to Supply Competitors, and Access to Essential Facilities", [1994] *Fordham Corporate Law Institute* 245, and reply by James S. Venit, and John J. Kallaugher, "Essential Facilities: A Comparative Law Approach", *ibid.* 315.

[10] *United Brands Co. and United Brands Continental BV* v. *Commission* (27/76), 14 Feb 1978, [1978] ECR 207, [1978] 1 CMLR 429, CMR 8429.

[11] *Michelin—Nederlandsche Banden-Industrie Michelin* v. *Commission* (322/81), 9 Nov 1983, [1983] ECR 3461, [1985] 1 CMLR 282, CMR 14031. The retailers' customers were users of heavy trucks, and could have picked up a supply of the appropriate tyres when returning from making a delivery in other countries.

[12] In *United Brands Co. and United Brands Continental BV* v. *Commission* (27/76), 14 Feb 1978, [1978] ECR 207, [1978] 1 CMLR 429, CMR 8429, the Community Court said:

doctrine was applied to new customers in *GVL*.[13] EC competition law, being far more desirous than US antitrust of enabling smaller firms to enter a market, is more likely to require the grant of a licence.

In the European Communities, the Court has been hostile to patents and other intellectual property rights and reduced their value very considerably in the 1970s.[14] They were perceived as barriers to entry depriving undertakings of their natural right to enter markets. In the 1980s, the Community Court became rather more sympathetic towards intellectual property rights and began to mention the need for rewards and incentives if investment were to be made.

In 1995, however, it confirmed the views of the Commission and Court of First Instance that in exceptional circumstances the television companies which held copyright in their individual listings might be required to supply the information to a third party and license publication in a comprehensive guide. The refusal to supply the information amounted to the abuse of a

"182. In view of these conflicting arguments it is advisable to assert positively from the outset that an undertaking in a dominant position for the purpose of marketing a product—which cashes in on the reputation of a brand name known and valued by customers—cannot stop supplying a long standing customer who abides by regular commercial practice, if the orders placed by this customer are in no way out of the ordinary.

183. Such conduct is inconsistent with the objectives laid down in Article 3(f) of the Treaty, which are set out in detail in Article 86, especially in paragraphs (b) and (c), since the refusal to sell would amount to discrimination which might in the end eliminate a trading party from the relevant market.

184. It is therefore necessary to ascertain whether the discontinuance of supplies by UBC in October 1973 was justified . . ."

[13] (7/82) [1983] ECR 483, [1983] 3 CMLR 645, CMR 8910.

[14] In an annex I have described briefly the doctrine of exhaustion and possible changes advocated by Fennelly AG in *Merck* v. *Primecrown*. The Court held in 1974 that once a product has been sold in one Member State by or with the consent of the holder of an intellectual property right, he could not exercise that right to restrain its commercial import into another Member State, even if the product was not capable of patent protection in the country of export—*Merck & Co. Inc.* v. *Stephar BV* (187/80), [1981] ECR 2063, [1981] 3 CMLR 463, CMR 8707. This doctrine prevented a holder from earning the reward of a discriminating monopolist.

The doctrine is particularly serious for the pharmaceutical industry, as the price of drugs is controlled in different ways and at different levels in many Member States, in order to keep the cost of health care low. At the moment there is a flood of imports of pharmaceutical products from Spain and Portugal. Until they joined the European Patent Convention, it was not possible to obtain product patents in those countries and maximum prices were controlled at very low levels. By the time they had joined the EPO, many inventions, protected by patents in the older Member States were no longer novel and had been sold in Iberia at very low prices making parallel trade very popular.

Parallel trade from France where prices for pharmaceutical products are still controlled at low levels is also profitable and proliferating.

For the national controls affecting patented medicines, see Derek Ridyard and David Lewis, "Parallel Trade in Patented Medicines—Economics in Defence of Market Segmentation" [1998] Int. TLR 14.

dominant position contrary to Article 86 of the EC Treaty.[15] The judgment is controversial and it is not clear whether it applies also to patents.

Although the Community authorities are more likely to intervene under Article 86, actions in national courts have not been frequent. Community law does not provide for multiple damages and there is even a scintilla of doubt whether even single damages can be obtained under the Community competition rules, although they do have direct effect in the courts of Member States. Procedure is governed by national law. The common law countries do not permit the massive discovery known in the USA, most of which we would call a "fishing expedition" and the civil law jurisdictions have nothing like it. In the common law jurisdictions, class actions are far more limited and contingency fees are not permitted. Nevertheless, there have been several cases arising out of Community competition law in England over the last year.

A *Volvo and Renault*

When faced with a claim for a compulsory licence under Article 86 EC in *Volvo*,[16] the Court ruled that the exclusive right was part of the very subject

[15] *Magill TV Guide (Re the): ITP, BBC and RTE* v. *Commission* (89/205/EEC), 21 Dec 1988, [1989] OJ, L78/43, [1989] 4 CMLR 757, [1989] 1 CEC 2223; on appeal, *Radio Telefis Eireann and Others* v. *Commission* (T–69, 70, 76–77 & 91/89), 10 July 1991, [1991] ECR II–485 *et seq.*, [1991] 4 CMLR 586 *et seq.*, [1991] 2 CEC 114, 147 & 174 (CFI); *Radio Telefis Eireann and Others* v. *Commission* (C–241 & 242/91P), 6 April 1995, [1995] ECR I–743, [1995] 4 CMLR 718, [1995] 1 CEC 400 (ECJ).

[16] *Volvo AB* v. *Erik Veng (U.K.) Ltd.* (238/87), [1988] ECR 6211, [1989] 4 CMLR 122, CMR 14498, the Court said:

7. It must first be observed, as the Court held in its judgement (*Keurkoop* v. *Nancy Keen Gifts* [1992] ECR 2853) with respect to the production of designs and models, that, as Community law stands at present and in the absence of Community standardization and harmonization of laws, the determination of the conditions and procedures under which protection of designs and models is granted is a matter for national rules. It is thus for the national legislature to determine which products are to benefit from protection, even where they form part of a unit which is already protected as such.

8. It must also be emphasized that the right of the proprietor of a protected design to prevent third parties from manufacturing and selling or importing, without its consent, products incorporating the design constitutes the very subject-matter of his exclusive right. It follows that an obligation imposed upon the proprietor of a protected design to grant to third parties, even in return for a reasonable royalty, a license for the supply of products incorporating the design would lead to the proprietor thereof being deprived of the substance of his exclusive right, and that a refusal to grant such a license cannot in itself constitute an abuse of a dominant position.

9. It must however be noted that the exercise of an exclusive right by the proprietor of a registered design in respect of car body panels may be prohibited by Article 86 if it involves, on the part of an undertaking holding a dominant position, certain abusive conduct such as the arbitrary refusal to supply spare parts to independent repairers, the fixing of prices for spare parts at an unfair level or a decision no longer to produce spare parts for a particular model even though may cars of that model are still in circulation, provided that such conduct is liable to affect trade between member states"

matter of a design right and that to require a compulsory licence even for a reasonable royalty would deprive the holder of the very substance of his intellectual property right. It added, however, that a holder enjoying a dominant position who refused to license might be abusing that position in three situations: (1) where he refused to supply spare parts to independent repairers, (2) where he charged too high a price for those spare parts, and (3) where he ceased making spare parts for a particular model, when there were many cars still on the road.

These examples were suggested by Counsel during oral argument and since there was no reason to think that Volvo was doing these things, no-one had any reason to dispute that they would amount to an abuse. Article 86 lists specific examples of an abuse, including unfair pricing, so it would be difficult to argue that the second example was wrong, although it is not easy to apply[17] and Advocate General Mischo said at paragraph 32 that it, the holder, might charge a sum covering not only production costs and profit margin, but also a sum to cover a contribution to the original R & D. The other two examples seem to me to be far more questionable.

In *Renault*[18] the Court gave a virtually identical ruling.

Business was delighted, but the three examples came back to haunt it in the next case. Clearly, they are not exhaustive.

B The Magill Litigation[19]

Under the law of the UK (until 1988) and Ireland, television companies were held to have copyright in the listings for their programmes. Each of the three companies that transmitted television programmes that could be received in Ireland and Northern Ireland published a weekly guide to its own programmes. Each also provided lists to daily and periodical newspapers on request and licensed them without charge to publish daily and weekend lists as well as weekly highlights.

When Magill first published a comprehensive weekly guide to the programmes of all three stations, each of the television companies sued it successfully for copyright infringement and restrained publication. Magill made a complaint to the EEC Commission which decided that the refusal to license amounted to an abuse of a dominant position contrary to Article 86

[17] The Commission usually avoids the difficulty by leaving the appraisal to a national competition authority or a national court.

[18] *Consorzio Italiano della Componentistica di Ricambio per Autoveicoli et Maxicar* v. *Régie Nationale des Usines Renault* (53/87), 5 Oct 1988, [1988] ECR 6039, [1990] 4 CMLR 265, [1990] 1 CEC 59.

[19] *Telefis Eireann (RTE) & Anor* v. *Commission* (C–241 & 242/91P), 6 April 1995, [1995] ECR I–743, [1995] 4 CMLR 718, [1995] 1 CEC 400; appeal from the Commission decision, *Magill*, (89/205/EEC), 21 Dec 1988, [1989] OJ L78/43, [1989] 4 CMLR 757, [1989] 1 CEC 2223.

of the EEC Treaty and ordered the three television companies to terminate the infringement:

"by supplying . . . third parties on request and on a non-discriminatory basis with their individual advance weekly program listings and by permitting reproduction of those listing by such parties."

This was confirmed by the Court of First Instance and, on points of law, by the Community Court.[20] At paragraph 46 the Community Court confirmed its earlier rulings that "mere ownership of an intellectual property right cannot confer" a dominant position. It added, however, that the three television companies enjoyed:

"a *de facto* monopoly over the information used to compile listings for the television programs received in most households in Ireland and 30% to 40% of the households in Northern Ireland. The appellants are thus in a position to prevent effective competition on the market in weekly television magazines. The Court of First Instance was therefore right in confirming the Commission's assessment that the appellants occupied a dominant position . . ."

This was a narrow market, far narrower than the broad patents which Professor Barton discussed at the FTC hearings, but there is case law in the EC treating a firm on whom other undertakings are dependent as dominant.[21] The Court went on to say that there were no substitutes for the information, and the unusual copyright operated as a barrier to entry.

At paragraph 49 it confirmed that in the absence standardisation or harmonisation it was for national law to define the scope of intellectual property law, and that a refusal to license did not necessarily amount to an abuse.[22]

It added at paragraph 50 that the exercise of the exclusive right might however amount to abusive conduct in exceptional circumstances and referred to the circumstances relied on by the Court of First Instance: (1) that there was no substitutes for the information (paragraph 52),[22a] (2) that there was a specific constant and regular potential demand for a comprehensive

[20] By this time, Magill had gone out of business and the only issue in the end was who was liable for the costs of the litigation.

[21] The Commission has issued a notice on the definition of the relevant market OJ C372/5, [1998] 4 CMLR 177 based on whether a hypothetical increase of price of between 5 and 10 % would be profitable. It is not entirely consistant with the case law of the Community Courts, and although it represents the current practice of the Commission it remains to be seen whether the courts follow it. The notion of dependence is not consistent with the new test.

[22] "In the absence of Community standardization or harmonization of laws, determination of the conditions and procedures for granting protection of an intellectual property right is a matter for national rules. Further, the exclusive right of reproduction forms part of the author's rights, so that the refusal to grant a license, even if it is the act of an undertaking holding a dominant position, cannot in itself constitute abuse of a dominant position".

The court referred to the passage from *Volvo* cited in n. 16 above.

[22a] The court mentioned 5 circumstances in what it called its first point.

guide,[23] (3) the refusal deprived consumers of the choice of a comprehensive guide,[24] (4) that the refusal prevented a third party from introducing a new product for which there was a potential demand and (5) which the television companies did not offer (paragraph 54).[25]

Second, the refusal was not justified (paragraph 55),[26] and third, the appellants thereby reserved to themselves a secondary market in weekly TV guides (paragraph 56):[27]

"57. In the light of all those circumstances, the Court of First Instance did not err in law in holding that the appellants' conduct was an abuse of a dominant position within he meaning of Article 86 of the treaty. . . ."

The judgment has been highly controversial, but might have been expected. Few countries in Europe or the USA grant copyright to protect information.[28]

[23] "50. However, it is also clear from that judgment (para. 9) that the exercise of an exclusive right by the proprietor may, in exceptional circumstances involve abusive conduct . . .

52. Among the circumstances taken in account by the Court of First Instance in concluding that such conduct was abusive was, first, the fact that there was, according to the findings of the Court of First Instance, no actual or potential substitute for a weekly television guide offering information on the programs for the week ahead. On this point, the Court of First Instance confirmed the Commission's finding that the complete list of programs for a 24-hour period—and for a 48-hour period at week-ends and before public holidays—published in certain daily and Sunday newspapers and the television sections of certain magazines covering in addition, 'highlights' of the week's programs, were only to a limited extend substitutable for advance information to viewers on all the week's programs. Only weekly television guides containing comprehensive listings for the week ahead would enable users to decide in advance which programs they wished to follow and arrange their leisure activities for the week accordingly. The court of First Instance also established that there was a specific constant and regular potential demand on the part of consumers . . ."

[24] "53. Thus the appellants—who were, by force of circumstance, the only sources of the basic information on program scheduling which is the indispensable raw material for compiling a weekly television guide—gave viewers wishing to obtain information on the choice of programmes for the week ahead no choice but to buy the weekly guides for each station and draw from each of them the information they needed to make comparisons".

[25] "54. The appellants' refusal to provide basic information by relying on national copyright provisions thus prevented the appearance of a new product, a comprehensive weekly guide to television programs which the appellants did not offer and for which there was a potential consumer demand. Such refusal constitutes an abuse under heading (b) of the second paragraph of Article 86 of the Treaty".

[26] "55. Second, there was no justification for such refusal either in the activity of television broadcasting or in that of publishing television magazines . . ."

[27] "56. Third, and finally, as the Court of First Instance also held, the appellants, by their conduct, reserved to themselves the secondary market of weekly television guides by excluding all competition on that market [The Court cited *Commercial Solvents*, para. 25] since they denied access to the basic information which is the raw material indispensable for the compilation of such a guide."

[28] The draft directive in the EC on databases, provided that information not otherwise available should not be the subject of an intellectual property right. Since the judgment in *Magill*, however, this provision has been deleted from the version of the database directive adopted: Dir. 96/)/EC, 11 Mar 1996, [1996] OJ L77/20. Some say this is because reliance can be placed on *Magill*, others to meet the objections of industry.

Any court would hesitate to enable the holder of such a disreputable right to prevent the activities of an entrant to a market downstream as a matter of policy.

The controversial questions are whether the precedent extends beyond unmeritorious copyright to respectable but broad patents that may have resulted from massive investment in R & D, whether, and if so when, is the holder of an improvement patent protecting a new product entitled to a compulsory licence under the basic patent and on what terms? The wording of the judgment of the Community Court seems to affirm that the precedent may extend beyond copyright[29] and require a compulsory licence in exceptional circumstances, but in other respects it is narrow and closely tied to the facts of the case.

The Commission's legal service is construing the precedent narrowly[30] but some officials in the Commission's department dealing with intellectual property are concerned that legal advisers may construe it widely.[31] It is very much shorter than the opinion of Advocate General Gulmann and it is thought that where it does not expressly overrule his opinion, the latter retains some authority.[32]

I would be concerned if the precedent were extended to other intellectual property rights that are intended to induce investment in innovation unless

[29] At paras 49 and 50, the Court refers to intellectual property rights generally and not just to copyright. At para. 50 it asserts that each television company was dominant over the information, not that it had copyright in it.

[30] In *PMI-DSV*, [1995] OJ. L221/34, [1996] 5 CMLR 320, the Commission rejected the complaint made to it by Ladbroke Racing Deutschland that the direct and indirect refusals to grant it a licence for Germany infringed Art. 86. In T–504/93 *Tiercé Ladbroke* v. *Commission* [1997] 5 CMLR 309, 12 June 1997, an appeal from a different decision that consisted of an unpublished letter rejecting Ladbroke's complaint that the holders of copyright in French horse race films had refused to license it, the C.F.I. confirmed that even if the copyright holders were dominant, there was no duty to license Ladbroke which was already dominant in the Belgian market for betting shops. A new entrant was not being kept out. There are several cases of *Ladbroke* v. *Commission.* It is important to check the Court's file number. The judgment has been appealed, C–300/97P. I published a critical note for [1998] ECLR. Advocate General Jacobs has also interpreted the judgment narrowly *in Oscar Bronner GmbH & Co. KG* v. *Mediaprint Zeitungs- und Zeitschriftenverlag GmbH & Co. KG and Others,* (C–7/97) opinion 28 May 1998, judgment 26 November 1998.

[31] Paul Waterschoot said that *Magill* cannot be limited to its facts: "Recent Developments in Intellectual Property", to be published in Hugh Hanson (ed.); *III International Intellectual Property Law and Policy* (Juris Publications and Sweet & Maxwell). See also the views of the Counsel to the Commission in the case, Ian Forrester, "A Famous Victory?" *II International Intellectual Property Law and Policy*, chap. 35. He said "the impact of the *Magill* judgment cannot easily be limited to these rare circumstances 'and' a refusal to license in order to prevent the emergence of a new product has become an independently identifiable case of abuse; and ,this judgment is a very potent weapon".

[32] He referred to the specific subject matter of the copyright right which would include the right to refuse a licence, and its specific functions: moral rights and a reward. Where a licence would interfere with that function, he considered that intervention under the competition rules should be very limited.

there is a real bottle neck and the new entrant has something really novel and valuable to offer.

Taken literally, the judgment could result in the holder of a basic patent in an invention for which there is no substitute, being under a duty to license the holder of an improvement patent which protects a new product.[33] The holder of the basic patent is restrained by the improvement patent from producing the improved product to satisfy demand. So all the conditions set out in paragraphs 52–57 of the *Magill* judgment would be fulfilled.

This must be wrong. It would reduce the incentive to the investment leading to the basic patent. Copyright in information is most unusual. Civil lawyers tend to think of copyright primarily as protecting moral rights, and even common law jurisdictions have limited copyright in listings. They are not protected in the USA since the judgment in *Feist*,[34] nor since the Act of 1988 in the UK.

I regret the Court's repetition in paragraph 49 of its earlier rulings that, in the absence of harmonisation or standardisation at a Community level, it is for national law to decide the limits of intellectual property. I would have preferred the Court to have held that there must be some limitations to the national intellectual property rights which can be invoked by dominant firms. One can sympathise with the gut reaction that there was no justification for copyright in the listings. It was not needed to encourage investment either in compiling the listings or in developing the programmes, but by leaving the scope of intellectual property rights to national law, the Court may have created a precedent that might later be extended to more respectable intellectual property rights for requiring compulsory licences.

The reference to the role of national law, however, does make it easier to say that it is only rarely that Community law will interfere with it and require a compulsory licence.

The Court emphasised in paragraph 50 that it is only in "exceptional circumstances" that the exercise of an exclusive right is abusive. The lack of substitutes mentioned in paragraph 52[35] was a question of fact of which the Court of First Instance was the final arbiter.

As Professor H. Hansen of Fordham University observes in a forthcoming contribution to *European Competition Law Yearbook*,[36] the Court's language is narrow in several respects. It is tied closely to the unusual facts of the case. The conditions for its application described in paragraph 53 include not only that the appellants were the "only source" of the information, but

[33] The meaning of 'new' is discussed below.

[34] *Feist Publications* v. *Rural Telephone Service*, 499 US 340 (1991).

[35] It seems to me that there were substitutes both from the limited licences given royalty-free to newspaper and from the individual guides. The comprehensive guide was not very "new". See below text to n. 37.

[36] To be published by Sweet & Maxwell, probably in 1998.

also that the information was "indispensable" to create the product downstream, not merely helpful or better than anything else available.

The Court held, also at paragraph 53, that it was the basic information rather than the copyright over which the companies were dominant. Professor Hansen thinks that this enables one to argue that when copyright is more meritorious the answer would be different because information would not be being withheld.

The Court suggested at paragraph 54 that when the third party wants to produce a new product he can claim damages or a compulsory licence. How "new" must it be? It is hoped that this condition may be tightened, especially if the precedent be applied to patents. It is only when the new product amounts to an important innovation that Professor Barton and other witnesses at the FTC hearings advocated the possibility of a compulsory licence. Most of those bearing witness were wary of reducing the incentives to the basic R & D and advocated that intervention should be very restrained.

Professor Hansen suggests that the comprehensive guide Magill tried to publish was only an improvement and not a new product. The distinction must be one of degree and hard to draw.[37] It may be drawn at different places for different purposes. It is important that whoever draws it recognises the importance of incentives being in the right place to induce the right amount of investment in innovation. On that basis, compulsory licences should be rare.

Where a firm spends a fortune on developing the cure for a serious and widespread disease and obtains a patent, the circumstances might be thought not to be sufficiently exceptional within the meaning of paragraph 50 of the judgment in *Magill* to warrant intervention with the exclusive right. Moreover, there might also be a justification within the meaning of paragraph 55. It may be argued that the intellectual property right is not the justification of the exclusive right, but that the inducement of significant investment may be. It was not the copyright, but the information, over which the television companies were held to be dominant.

I am not happy with *ad hoc* consideration of the inducement needed to the investment leading to a particular invention. Some important and valuable inventions may come cheaply, as one runs for a bus, or is relaxing in the bath. Usually, they result from thinking about the problem first, but this investment may be impossible to quantify. Developing the idea to the stage of applying for a patent may be expensive, but some firms choose to patent

[37] In *Maize Seed*—Breeders' rights/Maize Seed (78/823/EEC), 21 Sept 1978, [1978] OJ L286/23, [1978] 3 CMLR 434, CMR 10,083, the Commission said that maize seed was not a new product warranting an exclusive licence. On appeal however, in *Nungesser (L.G.) KG and Kurt Eisele* v. *Commission* (258/78), [1982] ECR 2015, [1983] 1 CMLR 278, CMR 8805, the Court referred to the variety of maize "newly developed" by Mr Eisele which could be grown in the cold clays of Northern Europe and was a major innovation justifying an open exclusive licence. In Ladbroke, cited note 30 above, the CFI construed the concept of newness strictly.

at an early stage of development. I have been happy with the rule that one does not have to establish the cost of developing an invention to obtain a patent. The market decides on the value of the invention, rather than an official or judge deciding the merits of the inventor or firm paying for his services and equipment.

I hope that compulsory licensing from an individual firm required on grounds of competition by a competition authority or a civil court, neither of them likely to be expert in either the technology or patent philosophy, should be rare. There may be reason to intervene *ad hoc* on antitrust grounds when competing firms come together in patent pools.[38]

One of the problems of requiring compulsory licences is that lawyers are usually brought up to think *ex post,* once the technology has been developed it would clearly be more competitive to have more firms using it. Production would probably be greater and prices lower. More use would be made of the invention. Perceived *ex ante*, however, as is habitual for businessmen and economists, the possibility of compulsory licensing reduces the incentives for investment in innovation. Unless a firm can reap where it has sown—can appropriate the benefit of its investment—it is less likely to make it.

No one knows what is the optimal incentive to produce the best level of investment in innovation. The great benefit of patent law as it has developed is that the market decides how investment is directed. Governments and research institutes do not make these decisions free from market constraints.

If the *Magill* judgment does apply beyond unmeritorious copyright to breakthrough patents, it is very important that the qualifying licensee should be limited to one able to provide an important innovation.

1 Terms of Any Compulsory Licence

Where compulsory or statutory licensing of intellectual property rights is required, for instance for records, the royalty that may be required is usually far below the value of the licence. If compulsory licences are to be required for breakthrough patents, should the holder be entitled to hold out for the value of the licence: for the cost of the opportunity? Its value would not be easy to determine, but such a test would reduce the incentive to innovation very much less than an arbitrary 5 or 10 per cent of the price obtained for the products made by use of the invention. At the other end of the spectrum, should the fee be the cost of drafting the licence plus a profit margin? That

[38] These may provide positive benefits by enabling the parties to carry on with R & D and production without having to check whether some operation is restrained by intellectual property rights. Patent pools may also enable incumbents to amass patents which they refuse to license to outsiders, who are thereby prevented from competing unless they can buy their way in or have patents as useful as the aggregate owned by all the incumbents. See n. 5 above and text thereto. In the USA they are analysed under the rule of reason and exclusive licensing between the members of a patent or know-how pool is excepted from the EC automatic block exemption for technology licensing agreements.

would remove much of the incentive to the original investment and might lead to a proliferation of applications for minor patents in the hope of obtaining a compulsory licence.

In *Volvo*, Advocate General Mischo said that the holder should be able to recover the cost of developing the innovation. That is helpful as far as it goes, but perceives the issue *ex post*, after the investment has been made. I would add that he should also be allowed at least to multiply this figure by a factor representing the risk of the investment.[39]

One of the terms that should be required by the holder of the basic patent if he be required to license should be a cross-licence under any existing or future improvement patents or developments in the know-how, otherwise the holder, who took the risk of the basic research, would be at a competitive disadvantage to his compulsory licensee who probably accepted far less risk.

C Article 90 in Combination with Article 86

Another legal pathway for the Commission to require a compulsory licence in the European Communities would be Article 90 of the EC Treaty. It forbids Member States from enacting or maintaining in force measures contrary to the rules of the Treaty in the case of undertakings to which they grant special or exclusive rights and, subject to an exception that has been narrowly construed, enables the Commission to address directives or decisions to Member States which infringe the Article.[40]

Intellectual property rights are exclusive, and there was some concern that the case law under Article 90 in combination with article 86, which has been expansive, might result in the evaporation of the intellectual property right if the patentee were unable, or chose not, to meet demand[41] or, indeed, even if there were a danger that it might fail to meet demand.[42]

[39] The risk of designing a vehicle may not have been as great as that accepted when conducting the R & D that leads to a break-through patent.

[40] There is no right for third parties to require the Commission to adopt such an act. It retains discretion, T--548/93 *Ladbroke Racing Ltd.,* v. *Commission* [1995] ECR II–2565. Nevertheless, the question might come before the Community Court on a reference from a national court asked to enforce the exclusive right as in the cases cited in the next two footnotes.

[41] See Nicolas Green, "Intellectual Property and the Abuse of a Dominant Position under European Union Law: Existence, Exercise and the Evaporation of Rights" (1993) XX *Brooklyn Journal of International Law* 141, after considering the AG's opinion in (C–41/90) *Höfner* v. *Macrotron GmbH* [1991] ECR I–1979, [1993] 4 CMLR 303. I replied critically *ibid.* at 161 and in particular, at 168. One of the problems is that exclusive rights are given to enable holders to reap monopoly profits. It is presupposed that a patentee will produce less and obtain a higher price—in other words, that he will not supply the demand that would exist in a more competitive market. This sort of consideration was not spelled out in the Court's judgment on Art. 90 in combination with Art. 86 where the exclusive right was normally not granted to encourage investment in innovation.

[42] See Green's reference at 151 to the Court's judgment in (C–260/89) *ERT* v. *DEP* [1991] ECR I–2925.

So far, neither Court nor Commission has shown any inclination to invoke Article 90 to limit intellectual property rights. I fervently hope that this continues. Any other view would be difficult to reconcile with the Court's case law where it recognises that the existence of national intellectual property rights is protected by Article 222 of the Treaty[43] and that the their exercise may be justified under Article 36.

The purpose of patent and copyright law is to enable those devoting resources to innovation to obtain a reward as an incentive to creative activity. This can only be done by enabling them to raise price, i.e. not supplying those who are unwilling to pay the higher price made possible by the exclusive right.

D Conclusion

Currently, there is pretty wide agreement that *Magill* should be construed narrowly.[44] It is important that it should be. As Hugh Hansen says[45]:

> "*Magill* is *sui generis* and will have little effect of future EC competition-law judgments of the Court of Justice. There remains the danger that cautious attorneys will counsel clients in a way that gives broad effect to *Magill*, thus giving it a life not intended by the Court."

In 1988, we thought we could ignore the three examples given in *Volvo*, but they came back to haunt us in *Magill*. As the composition of the Court changes frequently, there is danger that the Community Court may construe *Magill* more widely to extend to patents, designs and meritorious copyright. It is thought that there is little likelihood of Article 90 being used by the Commission to require access by third parties, but the Commission might be by-passed by a request for a preliminary ruling under Article 177 from a national court asked to enforce the right.

In many decisions, the Commission has treated as restricting competition contrary to Article 85(1) any restriction of conduct that is important on the market, even if necessary to encourage investment by conferring protection against third party free riders.[46] It has invoked Article 86 against a firm with no power over price[47] for any conduct that excludes others otherwise than

[43] *Consten SA and Grundig-Verkaufs GmbH* v. *Commission* (56 & 58/64), [1966] ECR 299, [1966] CMLR 418, CMR 8046; *Volvo AB* v. *Erik Veng (U.K.) Ltd.* (238/87), [1988] ECR 6211, [1989] 4 CMLR 122, CMR 14498, and most of the cases on exhaustion.

[44] Immediately after the judgment, the Court's information service provided a summary of the judgment stressing that the circumstances were exceptional.

[45] Note 36 above.

[46] *Davidson Rubber Company (Re the Agreement of)* (72/237/EEC), 9 June 1972, [1972] JO L143/31, [1972] CMLR D52, CMR 9512.

[47] *United Brands Co. and United Brands Continental BV* v. *Commission* (27/76), [1978] ECR 207, [1978] 1 CMLR 429, CMR 8429.

on the basis of performance and has not been very articulate in distinguishing competition on the merits from other exclusionary practices.

The antitrust agencies in the USA are familiar with more sophisticated economic analysis and I would be less concerned if they were, very occasionally, to grant compulsory licences. I would, however, be concerned if the Commission or Court took power from the *Magill* judgment to intervene with the validity of patents even if they be too wide. I suspect that patent examiners would be more familiar with the technology and with the criteria of patentability and I would prefer the possibility of compulsory licenses to be appraised by patent experts rather than by the European Competition Department. Currently, there is the possibility of challenging the validity of wide patents in the courts. I do think, however, that even in Europe competition authorities should make their view known and enter into debate with the intellectual property people whenever intellectual property law is being revised.[48] It may be appropriate to provide for compulsory licences to be granted by the patent offices of the world, at least for biotechnology, but this would require legislation.

III Annex on the Protection of Pharmaceutical Products from the Principle of Free Movement

I have been asked also to mention some of the EC developments on intellectual property and the free movement of goods where in the past the Court has been unsympathetic to the holders of intellectual property rights. There will not be time to speak to this part of my paper, as we want to focus on the interface between intellectual property rights and competition rather than between intellectual property rights and free movement, which is a peculiarly European problem.

In the Community, there has been concern that pharmaceutical patents do not give adequate protection to induce investment in R & D in Europe. Sometimes as much as 12 years of the 20-year life of the patent is taken up with clinical tests required to satisfy the regulations for safety. So, the supplementary protection certificate for medicinal products has been introduced by legislation[49] to confer, usually, about an additional five years of protection. It would be very serious if the protection of the patent and

[48] Some of the Community directives requiring Member States to expand the scope of their intellectual property rights have been absurdly wide and ill considered. Council Dir. 93/98 has extended the term of copyright to the life of the author plus 70 years, merely because this was the term protected in Germany, without any consideration of whether this was sensible for the many works now protected by copyright, such as computer software, nor that should happen to works that are already entered the public domain.

[49] Council Reg. 1768/92 [1992] OJ L182/1.

supplementary protection certificate were seriously undermined by compulsory licensing under the competition rules.

In the 1970s, the Community Court drastically reduced the value of pharmaceutical patents through its development of the doctrine of Community exhaustion. In numerous judgments it has ruled that once a product has been put on the market by the holder of a patent or other intellectual property right or with its consent, the holder cannot exercise its right to restrain commercial import to another Member State.

This has proved particularly serious in relation to medicines where some Member States impose maximum price control, or reimburse prescription charges only for a list of cures selected, amongst other criteria, for their cheapness,[50] or do not grant process patents. Different Member States have used different means to reduce the costs of health care and medicines are sold at widely different prices in different Member States. This makes parallel trade particularly profitable.

In *Merck & Co. Inc.* v. *Stephar BV*,[51] the Court applied the doctrine of exhaustion, so prevented the exercise of patent rights in the country of import, even though it accepted that Merck could not have obtained a patent for its drug in Italy where Merck had placed it on the market at the time when the invention was still novel. The Community Court was asked to reverse that judgment in *Merck & Co. Inc. and others* v. *Primecrown Ltd. and others*, but refused to do so.[52]

Some countries which seek to join the Common Market do not grant product patents for pharmaceutical products. When Spain and Portugal joined, this was considered so serious that they were required to join the European Patent Convention, and until three years after that date, there was no free movement of goods for pharmaceutical products between Spain and Portugal on the one hand and the rest of the Common Market on the other. This period is now over, but the Commission has rejected the applications of France and Belgium to adopt safeguard measures to restrain imports from Spain to other Member States.[53]

Merck and Beecham have been trying to exercise their UK patent rights to restrain imports from Spain and Portugal into the UK and Jacob J invited the Community Court to rule that *Merck* v. *Stephar* is no longer good law. The problem may seem to be temporary in that Spain and Portugal now enforce

[50] See, e.g., Mr. Van Miert's answer to the Parliamentary question of Amedeo Amedeo [1996] OJ C161/59, [1996] 5 CMLR 22 about Adalat that was coming into the UK from France, where prices are controlled, and Spain, where product patents could not be obtained at the time the drug remained novel.

[51] (187/80), [1981] ECR 2063, [1981] 3 CMLR 463, CMR 8707.

[52] Despite the contrary opinion of Fennelly AG, *Merck & Co Inc.* v. *Primecrown Limited* (C–267 & 268/95), 5 December 1996, [1996] ECR I–6285, [1997] 1 CMLR 83, [1997] 1 CEC 261.

[53] [1996] OJ, L122/20 and 21. Merck has appealed against these decisions: *Merck & Co. & others* v. *Commission* (T–60/96).

product patents granted by the EPO for Spain, but the problem may continue for nearly 17 more years, and indeed, another five thereafter with supplementary protection certificates. As new countries join the Common Market from Eastern Europe, the problem will have to be addressed, I hope by more enduring provisions in their Acts of Accession.

The *Primecrown* case was excellently argued and Advocate General Fennelly has asked the Court to rule that a patent may be used to restrain imports where there was no opportunity to obtain a product patent when the invention was still novel, but he was not prepared to go further and state that when the price of a product capable of patent protection is reduced by stringent control of maximum prices free movement should be restricted. I would like the Community Court to rule that such price control distorts competition and is contrary to Articles 3(g) and 5(2) of the EC Treaty. This radical solution would have had the advantage of not requiring an arbitrary decision as to which prices were too low, or what control of prices is excessively strict. Unfortunately, however, the Court refused to alter its earlier precedent.

In *MPA Pharma GmbH* v. *Rhône-Poulenc Pharma GmbH*[54] at paragraph 19 the Court said:

> "distortions caused by divergent pricing rules in one Member State must be remedied by measures of the Community authorities and not by another Member State introducing measures which are incompatible with the rules for the free movement of goods."

Unfortunately, it did not say which Community authorities, or include itself in the description.

The laws and customs of the various Member States require differing numbers of doses to be packed in a blister pack or other container, and the pharmaceutical companies comply with these differing traditions. Consequently, a parallel trader may have to cut open a blister pack and repackage the drug to correspond to the tradition in the country of import. This may well amount to an infringement of national trade mark law.

The Court ruled in *Bristol-Myers Squibb and others* v. *Paranova*[55] and in *Eurim-Pharm Arzneimittel GmbH and Biersdorf and others*[56] that trade marks cannot be exercised when this has the effect[57] of restraining imports from Spain if:

[54] C–232/94, 11 July 1996 [1996] ECR 1–3671.

[55] C–427, 429 & 436/93, 11 July 1996, [1996] ECR 1–3457.

[56] C–71–73/94, 11 July 1996, [1996] ECR 1–3603. See also *MPA Pharma GmbH* v. *Rhône-Poulenc Pharma GmbH,* cited in note 54 above.

[57] Note that the Court has returned to the criterion of "effect" it had adopted in *Hoffmann-La Roche & Co. AG* v. *Centrafarm Vertriebsgesellschaft Pharmazeutischer Erzeugnisse GmbH* (102/77), [1978] ECR 1139, [1978] 3 CMLR 217, CMR 8466, rather that of "intention" which it used shortly afterwards in *Centrafarm BV* v. *American Home Products Corp.* (3/78), [1978] ECR 1823, [1978] 1 CMLR 326, CMR 8475.

- the repackaging could not affect the original condition of the product,
- the packaging clearly states who repacked the product,
- the presentation of the repackaging is not such as to be liable to damage the reputation of the mark and
- notice be given to the trade mark holder before the product was put on sale.

It is for the national court to decide whether cutting the blister packs so as to provide the number of doses required or traditional in the country of import would meet the first condition.

The Court considered the justifications for using trade mark law under Article 36 EC in the judgment in *Eurim-Pharm* and under the trade mark directive in *Bristol-Myers Squibb*. The function of marks has not been held by the Community Court to include the maintenance of high prices, so these cases give little indication of the Court's attitude to *Primecrown*.

The Commission imposed a fine on Bayer for an alleged concerted practice between Bayer and its dealers in Spain and France restraining them from exporting Adalat to other Member States.[58] Bayer denied any such concerted practice, although it accepted that it had decided to supply only 10 per cent more Adalat than had been ordered in the previous period in the hope that this might limit the parallel trade. It appealed to the Court of First Instance,[59]and asked for an order suspending the decision in so far as it might be construed as requiring Bayer to supply unlimited amount to its Spanish dealers. It claimed (paragraph 18) that its decision was a unilateral act and not collusive. The President of the Court granted that order, but judgment is unlikely to be delivered before 1999.

[58] *ADALAT*, (IV/34.279/F3) [1996] OJ, L201/1.

[59] Order in *Bayer AG* v. *Commission*, T–41/96 R, 3 June 1996, [1996] ECR II–383, [1996] 5 CMLR 290.

8

INDUSTRIAL PROPERTY MANAGEMENT IN A MULTINATIONAL CORPORATION

*Marshall C. Phelps, Jr.**

I will speak about industrial property management largely from a business perspective; first because relevant legal concerns will be more than adequately covered by my co-panelists and other experts throughout the week and, secondly, because the business aspects of intellectual property management are often overlooked.

My business perspective comes from managing IBM's world-wide intellectual property portfolio. It is extensive. IBM has:

- over 12,000 US patents,
- over 30,000 patents world-wide,
- an equal number of pending applications,
- over 8,500 trade marks world-wide,
- a vast portfolio of copyrighted software, manuals, other product-oriented materials and business tools,
- and of course, unquantifiable repositories of trade secrets.

And, in spite of IBM's perhaps over-documented financial difficulties in the recent past, we continue to build our intellectual property portfolio. We spend billions annually on R&D. Arising from that investment, IBM has received more US patents than any other company, three years running. IBM has recently made a conscious decision to accelerate and expand our patent filings to ensure the fruits of our R&D investment are firmly established. Similarly, for the years for which we have data, IBM received more Japanese patents than any other non-Japanese company and more EC patents than any other non-European firm. This is not an image exercise or done just for protective or defensive purposes. My job description, in a few words, is to *optimise* the return on IBM's intellectual property.

Any company blessed with even a modicum of industrial or intellectual property, especially a large, high-tech, multinational firm, faces a fundamental choice; retain intellectual property for its exclusive use or adopt some form of licensing. There is not a "one size fits all" answer; it will vary by industry and by company. In those situations where the patent equals the

* IBM Corporation, Vice President, Intellectual Property and Licensing Services, New York, USA

product, perhaps most applicable to pharmaceutical and chemical companies, the general motivation will tend toward exclusive use of intellectual property. In those situations where legal necessity dictates or companies have needs from each other, the arrow moves toward some form of licensing. IBM is firmly in the latter camp for both reasons. While IBM came to open licensing perhaps reluctantly, we have, in the vernacular, managed to make "lemonade out of lemons"; so that today, our licensing programme is of substantial benefit to the company.

IBM was introduced to open licensing through legal pressures. Pursuant to a *consent decree* entered into with the United States Department of Justice in 1956, IBM agreed, *inter alia*, to implement open and non-discriminatory licensing. We were to get a lot of practice under this particular provision as the last patent subject to the *decree's* provisions expired only a few years ago in 1991. By then, of course, IBM had entered into hundreds of licensing arrangements, which, if IBM were to do an about face, would have taken years and years to unwind.

Moreover, by then IBM had begun to use other avenues for enabling the I/T industry to use our technology: through training of competitive maintenance providers (also required by the *consent decree*), providing selective attachment or interface information (*EC undertaking*), as agreed to in world-wide standards deliberations, or as part of alliance and joint venture activities—something now common in our industry.

Even so, IBM has periodically re-examined its licensing practices. Each time, the results have been the same. We have come down squarely on the side of open licensing. For IBM, this practice has resulted in new products reaching markets faster, open systems better meeting customer needs, interoperability (a customer dictate), evolution of new markets, acceleration of the creation of intellectual property, and development of important business relationships. And, since "open" does not mean "free", the generation of substantial revenues.

Even absent legal pressures, IBM would be following a similar path. IBM, and the electronics industry writ large, are driven to open licensing largely because we cannot prosper without each other. The accelerating pace of product development coupled with boundless capital requirements define our environment.

Let me offer an example of this interdependency. As many of you know, the architecture of the IBM PC is, to a great extent, a *de facto* standard in the industry. It is also an area where IBM has the pre-eminent patent portfolio because of our early invention and leadership. Even so, an IBM PC cannot be built without using the patents of a substantial number of other companies, proof positive that, in complex electronics, companies in the arena rely heavily on the combined invention of the world-wide industry. No company can go it alone and few attempt to do so.

IBM and others are framing this environment in a positive fashion by licensing our rivals under reasonable and largely non-restrictive and non-discriminatory terms. In our case, this has resulted in over 1,200 licensees world-wide—companies now with varying degrees of access to IBM's patented technologies. And, obviously, IBM has access to theirs. The point is, licensing is not a zero-sum game. Both sides benefit.

Moreover, because of the generally disparate size and value of the respective portfolios, IBM is able to generate substantial income in the process—even though our royalty rates (1–5 per cent) are reasonable by any standard. Our revenues from this active licensing programme are growing dramatically. While I cannot publicly estimate where we will be for 1996, we expect a dramatic improvement year-on-year over 1995. In that year, our intellectual property licensing activities took in some $650 million.

This turns out to be rather special income for three reasons. First, it is income largely ignored by IBM in the past, so in that sense, it is "found money". Secondly, it comes from our competitors. Thirdly, it goes right to the bottom line. And, on a personal note, it has had the second order effect of making our little department pretty popular within IBM.

There are two other benefits I would like to touch on briefly before I get to the other side of the coin.

The first is something we tend to discount but it is probably worth more than all else combined. We call it "freedom of action". What it really means is that because IBM now has licences with so many of our competitors, our developers can go about their work without an inordinate concern that the fruits of their labour will likely result in an infringement challenge resulting in product delay or substantial monetary harm. We know that without our licensing portfolio, IBM would be paying tens of millions in litigation expenses and hundreds of millions in royalties annually, assuming we were able to obtain licences, when needed, under reasonable terms and conditions.

Secondly, because of the benefit that extends to both sides as a result of licensing arrangements, strong relationships often develop between companies, relationships which commonly expand into other areas of technical co-operation. It is difficult to conceive of a major technical partnership in our industry which can exist without some form of intellectual property licensing between the parties.

Conversely, I believe a "closed" strategy is a less efficacious one in today's high-tech world for three reasons.

First, at least in our industry, it is difficult to dominate an environment for long due to this need to interface to the offerings of others. Secondly, as you will hear all week, there are real limitations on the ability to refuse to license others, whether imposed by legal or quasi-legal initiatives. "Essential facilities" doctrines, compulsory licensing initiatives (whether government mandated or judicially imposed), or standards/consortia driven initiatives all exist on the landscape to bound anti-competitive activity. Thirdly, as noted earlier, the pace and scope of technology advances work to make such practices self-defeating.

Of course, there are and have been cases of over-reaching. The trick, and it is a hard one for governments everywhere, is to correct discontinuities by addressing individual situations, not by penalising all participants. This problem is compounded by the pace of change making it difficult for regulators to keep up and making it often the case that they have fought the previous war by the time a situation is resolved. Thus, antitrust agencies, such as the US Federal Trade Commission, are struggling to set an appropriate agenda in this environment.

In 1995, the US FTC held a lengthy series of hearings in an attempt to wrestle these issues to the ground and create an overarching agenda. I do not have time now to reprise IBM's testimony in those hearings. But I would like to repeat a few points many of the participants made.

We exist in an enormously complex industry. It is an industry which redefines itself constantly. It is relatively young and it is growing fast. International Data Corporation, an outfit that chronicles our industry, listed over 70,000 companies in the I/T industry in 1995, and we are only just beginning to enter a new world of network computing, a world that seems to be producing new competitors by the hour.

In this world, innovation is the pre-eminent component of competitiveness. No matter which aspect of the industry one looks at—microprocessors, storage devices, displays, memory, etc.—the price/performance ratio is improving by 30-40 per cent annually as it has since the dawn of the industry. And it shows no signs of letting up. To bring this point home on a personal level, the PC you are likely to spend US $2,000 to buy this year will have 50 per cent more disk storage and double the raw computing power of last year's model.

In my view, the I/T industry is a case study in free enterprise, marked by competition, innovation and lower prices for the consumer, precisely the values antitrust laws should encourage. And, because courts and governments must exercise deliberation and caution in reaching decisions, the industry characteristics are likely to change in the interim to nullify the antitrust consequences initially predicted. Our industry has a built-in remedial force. Thus it is unlike other industries such as steel, vehicles, banking and pharmaceuticals, to name a few, which have a greater incidence of political, regulatory, environmental or other limitations. The I/T industry is constrained mainly by human intelligence and imagination. It is precisely this paucity of artificial limitations that has fostered the innovation that is the hallmark of the industry. The important role for antitrust enforcement agencies in this environment is to ensure that this atmosphere, shown to be largely conducive to competition, is preserved.

Of course, there will be instances where responsible governments must act to correct individual situations. But in doing so, I would caution against excessive regulation and generally ill-advised schemes such as compulsory licensing. Regulation is a blunt instrument, not useful when surgery is called for.

To come full circle, I hope I have made the case for open licensing from a business and legal perspective. There is so much to gain: improved image, close alliances, enhanced technical competence, better products for our customers, additional revenues *and* a more benign legal environment. Given the nature of our industry and the needs we have from each other, there is little to lose. It is just good business.

Panel IV
Strategies of Dispute Settlement in Industrial Property

9
THE EMPLOYMENT OF EXPERTS IN MEDIATING AND ARBITRATING INTELLECTUAL PROPERTY DISPUTES

*Robert Goldscheider**

With the rise of intellectual property litigation in the United States—a phenomenon which has also affected many foreign-based companies doing business in America—a professional sub-speciality has arisen which plays a significant role in these conflicts. This is the appearance of a cadre of experts who regularly assist litigating attorneys and the judiciary on various issues, including:

- analysing technology, particularly relating to patent infringement, and the availability of non-infringing alternatives;
- projecting the financial dimensions of patent, trade mark and copyright infringements, as well as the misappropriation of trade secrets and know-how, usually in the form of lost profits;
- providing opinions as to damages, frequently expressed as "reasonable royalties", that should be paid to the proprietors of such intellectual property rights as a result of such infringements and misappropriations; these exercises often involve simulating negotiations between the proprietor and accused infringers; and
- commenting about standard industry attitudes and practices which could provide better understanding of the disputes that inspired the legal proceedings.

The range of experienced input which these experts bring to the resolution efforts can help clarify and focus several issues. Indeed, the employment of experts is expressly sanctioned in certain statutory provisions[1] and key

* Chairman, The International Licensing Network, Ltd. New York, USA.

[1] In 35 USC §284 (1987) which relates to damages resulting from patent litigation, it is stated that "the Court may receive expert testimony as an aid to the determination of damages or of what royalty would be reasonable under the circumstances".

decisions.[2] If such contributions are carefully regulated by the judicial authorities in these cases, hearings can be expedited and the interests of the parties in obtaining a fair and effective hearing should be well served.

The employment of expertise on the noted issues is not limited to formal court cases, and has become well accepted in ADR proceedings, including mediation and arbitration.[3] The realism, based on actual experience, that truly qualified experts can contribute often provides useful guidance in the adjudicating process. This is especially true in ADR hearings, which tend to be more informal and free-ranging than court proceedings, because the mediators and arbitrators and other judicial figures are in a good position to ask penetrating questions of experts that can illuminate the real issues.

It usually happens that each side will offer its own team of experts who may be expected to espouse the respective positions of the parties that have retained them. This is not surprising, since no party may logically be expected to offer an expert whose views differ from the party's allegations. Moreover, this consistency is not bad, nor need it create unnecessary delay in the resolution of a conflict, particularly if it can help to illustrate the realities. Opposing experts, particularly if they are articulate as well as experienced, can theoretically present more objective analyses of the issues about which they testify than can employees or principals of the parties. This is the adversarial approach to dispute resolution at its best.

As with most other things in life and business, there can be abuses in the use of expertise in the course of litigation and ADR. Without resolute case management by a judicial officer, experts, whose remuneration is usually based on the amount of professional time expended, can inappropriately expand their roles by submitting overly lengthy reports, or by straying to side issues that can broaden the dispute unnecessarily.

This writer has seen such results avoided by the setting of clear-cut terms of reference for expert and other types of testimony, including carefully moderated time limits.[4]

When the interpretation of a licensing agreement or other contract involving intellectual property is the subject of litigation or an ADR proceeding, the use of experts to comment about contractual language may be questioned, and indeed excluded. If an expert, however eminently qualified, is introduced to

[2] In the leading US case on the subject of patent infringement damages: *Georgia-Pacific Corp.* v. *United States Plywood Corp.*, 318 F Supp. 1116 (SDNY 1970), 15 factors deemed relevant to the measure of damages are listed, the 14th of which is "the opinion testimony of qualified experts".

[3] See Robert Goldscheider, "The Use of Reasonable Royalties as the Measure of Damages in Arbitration and Other ADR Proceedings that Adjudicated Intellectual Property Disputes" 6(1) *The American Review of International Arbitration* (1995).

[4] An eloquent and lively commentary on case management and related issues is "Delay and Cost Booby Traps in Arbitration and How to Avoid Them", a paper presented by Tom Arnold (of Arnold, White & Durkee in Houston, Texas) to several functions and publications of The Licensing Executives Society.

assist the judge(s), mediator(s) or arbitrator(s) to interpret the specific terms of an agreement, this may be considered as usurping the responsibilities of the judicial authority or neutral professional. If, however, the expert can shed light upon the tradition or environment in which the parties were performing, that can contribute to a more realistic decision in the case.

An example of this occurred in a dispute between two multinational companies which had simultaneously developed a powerful new agricultural chemical ("A"). One of the companies ("X") had succeeded in getting the pre-eminent patent position relating to A in the United States, while the other company ("Y") obtained a stronger patent portfolio covering A in the most important foreign jurisdictions. The two companies decided to cross-licence each other. It was very important to X, however, that the players in this market for A be limited to the two companies. A clause was therefore included in the cross-licence agreement prohibiting either party from granting any sublicences, except to controlled subsidiaries.

A few years later, Y decided to curtail its activities in the relevant market, and was even interested to close or sell its production plants. At about the same time another large multinational company ("Z") completed development of a new agricultural chemical product that included A as a major ingredient. Because Z had high hopes for its new product, it was anxious to secure a reliable source of A, and was even prepared to purchase or lease Y's A production plants.

X became aware of this and reminded Y about the sublicensing prohibition. Indeed, X was looking forward to the time when it would be the sole production source of A. Z, on the other hand, was reluctant to be in a position where it would have no alternative but to purchase all of its requirements of A from its competitor, X.

In an attempt to solve this problem, Y and Z sought the advice of a prominent and creative firm of attorneys. They recommended that Y and Z enter into an agreement whereby Z would manufacture 100 per cent of Y's requirement of A for Y. It so happened that this quantity of A would be precisely equal to Z's requirement of A. Y agreed to purchase this production at an agreed price, P, and then agreed to resell all of such A to Z at the price of Q, which was 10 per cent higher than P. Q, however, was cheaper than the price at which Z could purchase A from X. The net result of this legal sleight of hand was that title to a 55-gallon drum of A would change from Z to Y to Z without the drum changing its physical location at all; it would be made by Z, and consumed by Z, with the full acquiescence of Y.

Upon learning of this envisaged arrangement, X sought a declaratory judgment against Y in the Superior Court of Delaware, alleging breach of the contractual prohibition against sublicensing. Both X and Y retained the services of experts to help resolve the issue whether a sublicence from Y to Z had occurred.

The expert for Y explained the legal theory of licensing as a proprietor's covenant not to sue another party that "uses" one or more of the proprietor's intellectual property rights. The described transaction did not, strictly speaking, involve "use" of such rights by Z, since it was merely performing services *for hire*, in producing A "for" Y. Z's subsequent purchases of A from Y would be "merely as a customer". Thus, licensing (and hence sublicensing) was not involved.

The expert for X criticiced this approach as a sophisticated legalistic manoeuvre to defeat the clear original intent of the parties to prohibit sublicensing. Such expert stressed the fact that technology licensing agreements usually involve long time relationships, based on mutual trust, as distinguished from a single purchase and sale transaction in which the doctrine of *caveat emptor* may be said to prevail. Because of this tradition, X's expert declared the "loophole mentality" manifested by Y and Z, and their reliance on the fruits of "clever lawyering", inappropriate in a licensing environment.

There was no real dispute regarding the facts at issue, and the case turned on the different conclusions of the experts. The trial judge expressed admiration for the creative attorneys retained by Y and decided in Y's favour. He was promptly, and emphatically, reversed by the Supreme Court of Delaware that decided, by a 5–0 decision, that a "loophole mentality" had no respectable place in licensing. This is still good law in the State of Delaware.[5]

This case could just as easily have been submitted to mediation, arbitration or some other form of ADR. Had this occurred, the value of opposing experts to expand the scope of judicial analysis would have been equally important and, in the opinion of this writer, would have improved both the efficiency of the proceedings and the quality of the outcome.

This effective employment of experts may be compared to an experience in a recent ICC-administered arbitration between a large European pharmaceutical company ("E") and a smaller, California-based, biotech company, ("C"). The parties had entered into a long-term relationship whereby E made a minority investment in C, funded a multi-year development programme to be executed by C, with E being supportive in various technical and marketing aspects of the work and also being periodically informed of progress. The objective was to create carefully defined products ("LPs") for E, with E then obtaining an exclusive world-wide licence to manufacture, have manufactured, use and sell LPs, paying an agreed royalty to C, upon E's acceptance of C's results.

One of the crucial issues raised by E was whether the relationship between E and C was a "joint venture". If so, E alleged that C would be deemed to have certain fiduciary duties to E that could impact on interpretation of the contractual language in the agreement between E and C. Experts for both sides were prepared to testify about "real world" conditions surrounding joint ventures, to assist the arbitrators to decide that point.

[5] See *DuPont* v. *Shell*, 498 A 2 1108 (1985).

The chairman of the arbitral tribunal, while acknowledging the impressive qualifications of both experts, stated that such testimony was essentially irrelevant. He indicated that there was a basic dispute about the meaning of the contract, that these opposing views had been ably briefed by the attorneys for E and C, and that further expert commentary was essentially redundant. Such expertise could not relieve the tribunal from its responsibility to interpret the language of a complex agreement. Accordingly, this was deemed to be an inappropriate venue in which to employ expertise in dispute resolution. It was clear that the proffered testimony of E's expert was treated as essentially irrelevant, and C's expert never took the witness stand, as a result of this "signal".

The two cases may be distinguished, in that the first involved an explanation of special circumstances in a specific area of law and business, while the second essentially dealt with the definition of a legal concept, a task which the arbitrators considered themselves to be equally capable of performing.

This does not detract from the principle, however, that experts can make valuable contributions to the quality and efficiency of ADR proceedings provided that their input reflects special skills and experience that add increased understanding of the issues involved.

The following example[6] illustrates how the input of an expert impressed the parties to a dispute sufficiently to precipitate a settlement, the ultimate size and substance of which had previously escaped the imagination of both parties. G and H were direct and fierce competitors in a regional market in the USA. They both owned and operated chains of retail stores that sold larger household appliances—refrigerators, stoves, freezers, washing machines, air conditioners and major electronic products. They sold the same types of products and even carried numerous items bearing the same brand names and model numbers. Each advertised extensively, with G always featuring its red house logo and H prominently displaying its gold house logo.

One holiday season, H took an aggressive initiative of questionable taste and placed G's logo on all garbage cans in numerous places inside and at the entrance to H's stores. The implication was that any of G's sales brochures could be disposed of there and that, generally, G could be equated with garbage. News of this "prank" by H was rapidly spread by word of mouth throughout the area in which the two companies competed, and provided considerable amusement among the consuming public. It was not necessary actually to have seen the "offending" garbage cans to be able to envisage exactly what was done.

G threatened immediate litigation, including a declaratory judgment action based on the theory of malicious damage to G's reputation and

[6] Taken from the actual case with the names of the parties an certain key circumstances of the dispute changed in order to preserve anonymity.

valuable logo. Senior management of H, which was unaware of the "prank" being instituted by some of its junior executives, intervened. The "offending" logos were immediately removed from the garbage cans in H's stores and H offered to submit to mediation the issue of the amount of damages that G had suffered. G agreed to this procedure, especially since it would be relatively confidential and would hopefully not provoke further satire in the press. Following a lengthy mediation session, however, the parties could not agree on the amount of damages. Since both G and H were anxious to put the matter behind them, they requested the services of a neutral expert who was experienced in valuing intellectual property rights, including trade marks.

The expert's approach was to place a value on G's logo before and after the prank. In this regard, he elicited the following information:

- in each of the past ten years, G had maintained an annual advertising budget that averaged $ 20 million; this covered newspaper advertisements as well as radio and television commercials, all of which featured G's red logo;
- all of the signage in G's 55 stores prominently displayed the red logo, and a hang tag consisting of the logo and indicating the price was attached to each item sold by G;
- sales by G during the same ten years totaled over $3 billion, and annual sales had steadily increased;
- G enjoyed a good reputation for integrity in the communities it served, and regularly contributed to local charities.

On the basis of these data, the expert opined that the value of G's universally used and widely recognised red logo was at least $100 million. The next issue was to determine how much this value had been diminished by the behaviour of H, especially since the general public tends to remember acts of ridicule long after the acts themselves cease. The expert stated that such decreased value was at least 1 per cent, and could be as much as 5 per cent—meaning a range of damages from $1–5 million.

At this point the mediator stepped in and observed to both parties that the principle of a sincere apology was more important than a sum of money that might change hands, since the two families that respectively controlled G and H were extremely wealthy. In fact, the mediator suggested that the repair to the reputation of G was the really central issue. With the combined inputs of the expert and the mediator, the following settlement was then reached by the parties:

- H would place a tasteful sign on every garbage can to which the G logo had been previously affixed, stating that H apologised to G for its error in judgement by H's unauthorised use of the G logo. These signs were to be removed after one month.

– H would contribute $1 million in G's name to charities of G's choice, and would pass along the charitable tax deduction to G.

The parties agreed that this mutually acceptable result could not have been achieved without the insights and inputs from the expert and the mediator. The extra dimensions they provided helped to resolve a conflict that could have had many negative results for both G and H.

The case that I have selected for special scrutiny in this paper involved a situation that is no longer uncommon. It was an action brought by a client against its former patent law firm in which, through negligence, a foreign patent application had failed to be filed in time. In this situation, the plaintiff was a medium-sized biotech company, "M". M had developed a new screening methodology that greatly increased the speed and efficiency with which researchers could explore a promising new area of gene therapy. It was expected that compounds to be identified utilising this methodology could prove useful in the treatment of Parkinson's Disease and Alzheimer's Disease. Such identified compounds would eventually be the subject of separate patent applications, to be filed by M in the future.

The patent law firm had been instructed by M to file foreign patent applications, based on a pending US patent application relating to the same methodology that the lawyers had previously filed. The jurisdictions selected were those deemed to have a "critical mass" of experienced researchers and equipment to be able to carry out the contemplated research. They included several European countries, Israel, Canada and Japan. Through a clerical error, the Japanese patent application had been misdirected and temporarily misplaced. As a result, the critical filing deadline passed, and the possibility of obtaining a Japanese patent on this invention was lost.

The original attempt to resolve this matter was via mediation between M and the patent lawyers. The facts were not in dispute, but the parties disagreed on the economic significance of the patent, and hence the amount of damage, sustained by the plaintiff. The defendant patent law firm was represented by attorneys engaged by its malpractice insurance company. They took a hard line, offered only a minimum settlement amount, and the parties remained far apart.

Two experts accompanied the plaintiff to the mediation hearing. One was an investment banker who had organised numerous strategic alliances between large pharmaceutical companies ("Big Pharmas") and small biotech companies, similar to the previously described relationship between E and C. This expert explained the considerable dimensions of those deals as well as their speculative nature. He opined that the technology developed by this plaintiff appeared to be very promising but that the lack of a Japanese patent, which would enable an unlicensed research team in Japan to benefit from this accelerated researching methodology (described as a "highlighted road map") would almost certainly make it impossible for M to close a strategic alliance in the usual pattern and value with a Big Pharma.

The second expert retained by the plaintiff was a professional negotiator of licensing agreements, who had worked in the pharmaceutical and biotech industries, among others. He had been informed by M that a major American Big Pharma, ("B") was known to be interested in this specific area of biotechnology. B was therefore a very logical potential strategic alliance partner to be approached by M.

This expert was also aware that B enjoyed a long-standing working relationship with a leading Japanese biotech research laboratory. Thus, if B were to learn the teachings of M's methodology invention, because of the issue of the US patent or one of the foreign patent applications for which applications had been timely filed, and also become aware of the absence of an equivalent Japanese patent—referred to by the expert as "a hole in the bucket"—B's behaviour would be very predictable. It would instruct its associated Japanese biotech laboratory to employ M's "unpatented" methodology in Japan, possibly financing such research. The chances of this being successful were reasonably good because the Japanese researchers will have been provided with H's highlighted road map. If this resulted in the identification of any new patentable compounds in the field of inquiry, B would presumably obtain separate international patent portfolios on each such compound deemed to be of serious potential value. M would not be able to oppose the issue or commercialisation of such compound patents.

The expert then proceeded to structure two hypothetical negotiations between M and B. The first placed a value on a strategic alliance between M and B assuming an intact patent portfolio covering the methodology invention, and the second taking into account the "hole in the bucket" created by the absence of a Japanese patent on such invention. The expert had a realistic yardstick for the first analysis, because M had recently concluded other strategic alliances with two other Big Pharmas, each relating to distinctly different genetic foundations, but both of which might yield compounds which could theoretically also be effective against the same diseases.

The expert's analysis also contained realistic cost and profitability figures based on credible historical data and other precedents. From this, he was able to project sales volumes, determine royalty rates and calculate the net present values of both scenarios. The difference in the two results constituted the expert's opinion of the amount of damage theoretically sustained by M from its lack of a Japanese patent. In the spirit of conservatism, and acknowledging that certain aspects of the analysis were speculative, the expert then halved the figure arrived at and adopted that as his position on the amount of damages sustained by M.

This presentation was carefully and clearly set forth by the expert to the mediator. This was initially done *ex parte*, i.e. not in the presence of the representatives of the patent attorneys. At the conclusion, the mediator stated that he was strongly impressed. The "bottom line" was a damage figure of several million dollars. In his effort to persuade the parties to settle the matter, the mediator then informed the representatives of the patent attorneys about the results of the expert analysis, including the strong impression it had made.

This indication nevertheless failed to elicit a substantial change of position by the insurance lawyers representing the patent attorneys. The mediation therefore failed and was broken off.

Instead of proceeding to arbitration, however, this particular matter then went to trial in a state court before a jury. After presenting the undisputed facts exposing the negligence of the patent attorneys, M called upon the same two experts to explain their analyses and conclusions to the jury. The lawyers for the patent attorneys (i.e. the defendants) observed that these presentations were apparently having a favourable impact upon the jury similar to that which had previously been experienced and explained by the mediator. As a result, the defendant requested an adjournment, and the case was promptly settled in the judge's chambers for several million dollars. This was consistent with the mediator's earlier "advice", based on the combined input of M's two experts. When questioned about the result, the lawyers for the defendant admitted that the similarity in the reactions by the mediator and the "body language" of the jury had motivated them to settle the case on the agreed terms.

Conclusions

- The widely advertised advantages of ADR are speed of resolution, avoiding appeals, lower cost and greater potential efficiency in reaching a pragmatic solution.
- These are laudable goals that require adroit and firm administration of the proceedings by able judicial officers if they are to be achieved, especially in large, complex ADR proceedings.
- The involvement of truly qualified experts, whose contributions can be focused on issues where they can credibly provide added insights and information, constitutes a valuable aid to achieve those desirable results.

10

IMPLICATIONS OF THE TRIPS AGREEMENT FOR DISPUTE SETTLEMENT IN INDUSTRIAL PROPERTY

*Adrian Otten**

One of the major innovations of the Agreement on Trade-Related Aspects of Intellectual Property Rights (the "TRIPS Agreement"),[1] compared to the pre-existing international intellectual property conventions, is the attention it gives to procedures and remedies for the resolution of disputes about intellectual property rights, both those between private parties and those between Member States of the Agreement. The purpose of this presentation is to explore the implications of the TRIPS Agreement for the resolution of disputes in industrial property, including those which involve an interface between domestic legal proceedings about private rights and international dispute settlement proceedings between states about treaty rights.

I Brief Introduction to the Trips Agreement

The TRIPS Agreement is an integral part of the Agreement establishing the World Trade Organisation which came into effect on 1 January 1995. Any country which wishes to be a Member of the WTO is obliged to accept the TRIPS Agreement; there are presently 133 Members with an additional 20 countries in the process of negotiating their accession. The Agreement covers the main categories of intellectual property rights: copyright and related rights; trade marks including service marks; geographical indications including appellations of origin; industrial designs; patents including the protection of new varieties of plants; the layout-design of integrated circuits; and undisclosed information including trade secrets. In respect of each of these categories of intellectual property, it requires application of national and MFN treatment, establishes minimum substantive standards of protection that must be provided in the national law of each Member, specifies

* Director, Intellectual Property and Investment Division, World Trade Organization, Secretariat, Geneva, Switzerland.

[1] *The Results of the Uruguay Round of Multinational Trade Negotiations: The Legal Texts* (WTO Secretariat, Geneva, 1994).

procedures and remedies that must be available under national law so that right-holders can effectively enforce their rights and provides for the application of the WTO dispute settlement mechanism to resolve disputes between Member States. Transitional periods are allowed to give Members time to make the necessary changes to law and practice. The transitional period of developed countries ended at the beginning of this year and, in the main, developing countries have the option of delaying application until the beginning of 2000 and least-developed countries until the beginning of 2006.

II Minimum Substantive Standards and Procedures for the Acquisition and Maintenance of Rights

Before addressing in more detail the TRIPS provisions on domestic enforcement and international dispute settlement, let me say a word about the TRIPS obligations on the scope and availability of intellectual property rights (Part II of the Agreement), since they are relevant to the substantive content of industrial property disputes. The minimum substantive standards for each of the categories of intellectual property covered are set at a level broadly comparable with that in the main industrial countries today. Each of the main elements of protection is defined, namely the subject matter to be protected, the rights to be conferred and permissible exceptions to those rights, and the minimum duration of protection. The Agreement sets these standards by requiring, first, that the substantive obligations of the main conventions of the WIPO, the Paris Convention and the Berne Convention, in their most recent versions, must be complied with. Secondly, the TRIPS Agreement adds a substantial number of additional obligations on matters where the pre-existing conventions are silent or were seen as being inadequate.

The TRIPS Agreement does not go into detail on procedures for the acquisition and maintenance of intellectual property rights and related *inter partes* procedures. In the one Article on this matter (Article 62), the main aim is to ensure that unwarranted procedural difficulties do not impair the basic protection that should be available under the Agreement. For the purposes of this presentation, it is particularly relevant to note that paragraphs 4 and 5 of the Article require procedures for the acquisition or maintenance of rights and, where applicable, for administrative revocation and *inter partes* procedures such as opposition, revocation and cancellation to be governed by a number of principles of fairness, equity and due process laid down in the Agreement.

III Enforcement of Intellectual Property Rights

High substantive standards of protection of intellectual property are of little use if rights cannot be effectively enforced. Thus, a major set of obligations in the TRIPS Agreement (its Part III) requires Members to provide domestic procedures and remedies so that private right-holders can take effective action against any act of infringement of intellectual property rights covered by the Agreement. While recognising basic differences between national legal systems, these provisions aim to ensure that each Member's legal system will contain the elements considered essential for effective and fair enforcement of intellectual property rights and that the system will work in practice. These rules constitute, to my knowledge, the first time in any area of international public law that such rules on domestic enforcement procedures and remedies have been negotiated.

I will only summarise very briefly the provisions on enforcement, which cover some ten pages of the text of the Agreement. The basic features of civil judicial procedures that must be available to right-holders to challenge any infringement are described, as are the remedies that it must be within the power of judicial authorities to order, including injunctions, damages and, in certain situations, forfeiture of infringing goods and implements to produce them. Prompt and effective provisional measures, including where necessary *ex parte* measures, must be available to judicial authorities to prevent infringement or to preserve relevant evidence. In respect of at least imports of counterfeit trade mark and pirated copyright goods, there must be a means by which right-holders can obtain the assistance of customs administrations to prevent the release of such goods into free circulation. Finally, it is required that criminal procedures be applied at least in cases of wilful trade mark counterfeiting or copyright piracy on a commercial scale and that the consequent penalties must be sufficient to provide a deterrent consistent with the level of penalties applied to crimes of a corresponding gravity.

IV Direct Applicability in National Legal Proceedings

The basic obligation in the TRIPS Agreement is to ensure that national law and practice are consistent with the provisions of the Agreement. There is no requirement to make provisions of the TRIPS Agreement directly applicable as part of national law. Provided a Member gives effect to the provisions of the Agreement, the way it does so is left to it, within its own legal system and practice. Thus, the situation concerning direct applicability of TRIPS obligations will differ between countries.

There is in some countries a long tradition of direct applicability of the main intellectual property conventions, and it is clear that in many of these countries, especially in Continental Europe and in South America, provisions of the TRIPS Agreement form part of national law and are thus directly applicable by national courts. Of course, such courts will have to determine which provisions are sufficiently precise and mandatory in nature to be construed as capable of direct application.

Even in countries where the provisions of the TRIPS Agreement are not considered capable of direct application, they may be invocable in national legal proceedings. Where national law permits more than one interpretation, national courts may be expected to prefer an interpretation which is consistent with that country's international obligations in the TRIPS Agreement over one that is not. Moreover, there are cases where national intellectual property laws in dualist countries, which do not admit direct applicability of international treaties, nonetheless specifically provide for international obligations to prevail.

V Dispute Settlement

One of the major innovations in the international intellectual property system is that obligations between States under the TRIPS Agreement will be subject to a functioning dispute settlement system. This is the integrated dispute-settlement system of the WTO, a reinforced version of the earlier GATT mechanism.[2] In fact, there have already been several TRIPS complaints by WTO Member States under the dispute settlement system—complaints by both the United States and European Community against Japan in regard to the protection of existing sound recordings, a complaint by the United States against Portugal in regard to the term of protection for existing patents, and complaints by the United States against Pakistan and India in regard to the so-called "mailbox" provisions of Article 70.8 and the exclusive marketing rights provisions of Article 70.9 relevant to the areas of pharmaceuticals and agricultural chemicals etc.While some of the issues remain unresolved, most of the cases were settled by consultation and will lead to the adjustment of national provisions under the systematic monitoring activities of the TRIPS Council by the Dispute Settlement Council upon dispute settlement. In 1997, a panel and the Appellate Body held in India—Pharmaceutical and Agricultural Products (International Trade Law Reports vol. 2 at p. 621, 687)—that India has not lived up to its obligations under the TRIPS Agreement in order to provide adequate means to bring about so called pipe-line protection for patentable innovations which are subject to future patent protection in India. This was the very first case on the TRIPS agreement, and it is likely that others will follow in coming years.

[2] Understanding on Rules and Procedures Governing the Settlement of Disputes, *ibid.*

Most GATT and now WTO disputes between States originate in representations from a private party to its government alleging that its commercial interests in another WTO Member are being damaged as a result of a failure of that Member to meet its GATT/WTO obligations. It is virtually unknown for the system to be employed for reasons purely of principle and without a real commercial interest at stake. Some complaints result from an alleged unsatisfactory domestic legal proceeding, for example about anti-dumping or intellectual property. Some others relate to an allegedly inconsistent law or regulation of general application. Often the complaints involve a mixture of the two elements.

To illustrate the workings of the WTO dispute settlement system and, in particular, the interface between disputes between private parties under national legal procedures on the one hand and disputes between States under the WTO on the other, the GATT case relating to section 337 of the United States Tariff Act and the patent dispute between Du Pont Nemours and Akzo over certain aramid fibres is of interest. In 1984, Du Pont filed a complaint with the United States International Trade Commission (USITC) under section 337 alleging the importation, sale and marketing in the United States without its authorisation of certain aramid fibre produced by Akzo in the Netherlands by a process for which Du Pont had received a patent in the United States. In November 1985, the USITC, holding that Du Pont's process patent was valid and infringed, issued a limited exclusion order limiting the entry of certain forms of aramid fibre made abroad by Akzo using the process in question for the remaining life of the patent. Akzo unsuccessfully appealed the USITC determination to the Court of Appeals for the Federal Circuit and was also unsuccessful in seeking review by the Supreme Court in the United States.

In December 1985, Akzo filed a complaint under the New Commercial Policy Instrument of the European Communities alleging that the procedures under section 337 of the US Tariff Act, which only apply to unfair imports, are discriminatory against imported goods and therefore inconsistent with the United States' obligations. The European Communities, after investigating, found grounds for a justifiable complaint, and in April 1987 requested bilateral consultations with the United States under Article XXIII:1 of the GATT, the first step in the GATT dispute-settlement process. In July 1987, the Community informed the GATT Council that the consultations had not led to a satisfactory solution and requested the establishment of a panel, an *ad hoc* group of experts that would hear the parties to the case and make findings and recommendations. In October 1987, the GATT Council agreed to establish a panel. After consultations with the parties to the dispute, the terms of reference and the composition of the panel were determined in January 1988. The terms of reference, which were standard ones, were "to examine, in the light of the relevant GATT provisions, the matter referred to the CONTRACTING PARTIES by the European

Economic Community in document L/6198, and to make such findings as will assist the CONTRACTING PARTIES in making the recommendations or rulings provided for in paragraph 2 of Article XXIII". The panel consisted of three people, the usual number, nominated by the Secretariat and agreed by the parties. It was chaired by Graham Fortune, the Ambassador to the GATT of New Zealand, the other two Members being Professor Lowenfeld of the New York University School of Law and Mr Pierre Pescatore, a former judge of the European Court of Justice.

After determining its working procedures, the Panel received written initial submissions and rebuttals from the parties to the dispute and held oral hearings with the parties in March and May 1988. A number of other GATT Member States which had registered an interest in the case were also given the opportunity to make presentations. GATT/WTO dispute settlement hearings are not held in public, and private interested parties do not have a right of access to them, although often those directly interested will be consulted by and lend assistance to their governments when those governments are parties to the dispute. While, as the European Community made clear, its complaint was prompted by the examination of a specific case, that between Du Pont and Akzo, it originally requested the panel to make findings concerning the compatibility with the United States GATT obligations of the application of section 337 not only in the *Certain Aramid Fibre* case but also in general. In May 1988, Du Pont and Akzo executed a settlement agreement on aramid fibre. The Community then withdrew its request to the panel to make specific findings on that matter.

In January 1989, the panel submitted its report to the GATT Council.[3] The panel found that on six counts section 337 accorded less favourable treatment to imported products alleged to infringe United States patents than that accorded under United States Federal District Court procedures to like products of United States origin, and that most of these inconsistencies with the national treatment provision of Article III of the GATT would not be justified under the general exceptions clause contained in GATT Article XX(d). After initial reticence on the part of the United States, the panel report was adopted by the GATT Council by consensus in December 1989. The United States said it would make changes to its legislation to bring itself into conformity with the panel findings in conjunction with its implementing legislation for the Uruguay Round, then scheduled to end in 1990. As you know, the Uruguay Round was not concluded until 1994. Changes to section 337 were adopted by the United States Congress later in 1994.

The section 337 case illustrates well the interface between domestic proceedings about private rights and international proceedings about treaty rights that may well arise in the TRIPS area. It is noteworthy that the European Community, although prompted to take action by the specific

[3] United States, s 337 of the Tariff Act of 1930, *Basic Instruments & Selected Documents*, 36th Suppl., GATT 1990.

aramid fibre case, generalised its complaint to the application of section 337 in patent cases as a whole. In this regard, it is important to note that, in GATT/WTO jurisprudence, only laws which mandatorily require action inconsistent with GATT/WTO obligation can be successfully challenged as such; where a law leaves the executive discretion to act consistently or inconsistently, only a specific measure under that law can be challenged.

There are of course major differences between dispute resolution on intellectual property matters under the WTO compared to that which I have described under the GATT:

- One concerns the substantive law applicable. The relatively few disputes about intellectual property matters under the GATT, for example the cases relating to section 337 of the United States Tariff Act and the Manufacturing Clause of the United States Copyright Act, were about discrimination against imported goods, not about protection of intellectual property. Now with the TRIPS Agreement, disputes will also be about protection, in terms of conformity with the obligations regarding both minimum substantive standards and domestic enforcement procedures.
- A second difference concerns the improvement to the dispute settlement procedures under the WTO compared to those under the GATT which I outlined in the description of the section 337 case. The major element of strengthening that has been introduced is the elimination of the means by which it has been possible for defending or losing parties to be able to delay or block the dispute-settlement process. This has been done, on the one hand, by the introduction of stricter time-limits for the different stages of the dispute-settlement process, and, on the other hand, by reversing the consensus rule required for decisions by the Dispute Settlement Body (DSB) on the adoption of panel reports and on any eventual suspension of concessions. Previously, such decisions required a positive consensus, which meant the acquiescence of the losing party. This often took some time to obtain and, in a few cases, was withheld altogether. Under the new system, panel reports and decisions on eventual retaliation will be considered adopted unless there is a consensus against their adoption. Thus, the system has become considerably more juridical in nature than hitherto. In the light of this more binding and automatic nature of panel findings, provision has been made for recourse to a standing Appellate Body whose findings, once adopted by the DSB according to the same decision-making rule, would be final.

The interface between domestic legal proceedings about private rights and international dispute settlement proceedings about treaty rights is likely to give rise to a number of issues that will require careful handling. One which has already arisen, in the area of anti-dumping, is the standard of review of the findings resulting from domestic legal proceedings to be employed by panels. Article 17.6 of the WTO Agreement on Anti-Dumping[4] provides that:

"(i) in its assessment of the facts of the matter, the panel shall determine whether the authorities' establishment of the facts was proper and whether their evaluation of those facts was unbiased and objective. If the establishment of the facts was proper and the evaluation was unbiased and objective, even though the panel might have reached a different conclusion, the evaluation shall not be over-turned;

(ii) the panel shall interpret the relevant provisions of the Agreement in accordance with customary rules of interpretation of public international law. Where the panel finds that a relevant provision of the Agreement admits of more than one permissible interpretation, the panel shall find the authorities' measure to be in conformity with the Agreement if it rests upon one of those permissible interpretations."

In the final stage of the Uruguay Round, there was considerable controversy as to whether these provisions should also be applicable to disputes in other areas, notably TRIPS. The outcome was a decision of the Uruguay Round Trade Negotiation Committee that this standard of review shall be reviewed after three years with a view to considering the question of whether it is capable of general application.[5]

VI Concluding Remarks

The purpose of this presentation has been to attempt to describe the implications that the TRIPS Agreement will have for the resolution of disputes in and between WTO Members on industrial property, including those between private parties. These implications can be summarised as follows:

- the substantive intellectual property law that is at stake in national proceedings will have to conform with the minimum requirements of the TRIPS Agreement, often involving a considerable increase in the level of protection;
- domestic enforcement proceedings and also proceedings before industrial property offices will have to provide for the procedures and remedies set out in the TRIPS provisions in Parts III and IV of the Agreement;
- in some countries, TRIPS provisions, whether on substantive standards or on enforcement, will be directly applicable by national courts. In some others, national courts may wish to take them into account in interpreting national law;

[4] *Agreement on Implementation of Art. VI of the General Agreement on Tariffs and Trade 1994, The Results of the Uruguay Round, The Legal Texts* (WTO, June 1991).

[5] Decision on Review of Art. 17.6 of the Agreement on Implementation of Art. VI of the General Agreement on Tariffs and Trade 1994; *ibid.*

- dispute settlement proceedings between WTO Members on intellectual property will often be prompted by specific difficulties brought to the attention of governments by private parties. In some cases these difficulties may result from domestic legal proceedings, which are considered to have been procedurally defective in relation to TRIPS obligations or which have interpreted national law in a way considered to be TRIPS inconsistent.

11
THE ROLE OF LITIGATION IN CORPORATE INTELLECTUAL PROPERTY STRATEGY

*Melvin Sharp**

For the past ten years it seems to me that I have been continuously involved in some form of patent litigation, although I am not a litigation attorney. Principally, I have been involved in licensing that seems to have led to litigation on a continuing basis. I consider litigation to be a last resort—one in which the results do not always work out for the most meritorious side. It is a 50–50 proposition, as most trial lawyers advise their clients.

I would like to break my experience into two time frames. The first, 1985–90 where I was chief patent counsel of Texas Instruments and was a principal party in evolving the architecture of a licensing programme to bring in very substantial sums of money for Texas Instruments. And in the period thereafter when I took early retirement from TI and joined the Board of Directors of Cyrix Corporation who were at the time defending patent lawsuits from Intel Corporation when Cyrix tried to enter the microprocessor market. So in the first time period, I was a patent plaintiff asserting patents for value in order to generate a royalty income, and in the second period of time I was involved in defending against patents for the survival of the defendant company.

At TI in 1985, I was very familiar with the licensing practices in the semiconductor and electronics fields and such practices through the 1970s until 1985. At that time, I worked on the architecture of a licensing policy that contributed to changing the attitude toward intellectual property in the electronics field (some would call the change a revolution in thinking about IP).

In 1985, in the semiconductor industry, the dominant licensing theme was freedom of action. What that meant was that companies wanted to ensure freedom to operate in a given market or markets—at the lowest possible risk of patent litigation. This attitude was in part due to the legal environment at that time in which the courts generally held patents in disfavour. The business environment also contributed to the defensive view towards patents. This was a period of rapid growth in the semiconductor

* Attorney-at-Law and Counselor in Intellectual Property Law and Related Matters (former Chief Patent Counsel of Texas Instruments), Dallas, Texas, USA.

industry, and patents were seen as a barrier to that growth that had to be overcome.

In the face of this backdrop, we sought to introduce a shift in thinking about intellectual property rights. We had two primary goals in mind. Our long-term goal was to increase recognition of the value of intellectual property in the electronics field. Our short-term goal was to obtain increased recognition of TI's patent portfolio and the technology underlying it.

Of course, to bring about a fundamental change in people's thinking you have to get their attention.

In January 1986, TI filed lawsuits against a total of nine Japanese and Korean defendants alleging the unlicensed importation of semiconductor memory devices known as DRAMs into the United States. We brought claims in federal district court for infringement of ten of TI's patents covering four generations of the defendants' memory products. Additionally, we took advantage of section 337 of the International Trade Commission (ITC) Statutes and brought a claim of unfair competition against the defendants before the International Trade Commission, alleging the defendants were introducing DRAMs into the US in violation of TI's patents.

We caught their attention. Our initial litigation spawned other lawsuits in the USA and Japan. Hitachi sued TI in the Eastern District of Virginia—the so-called Rocket Docket—where they presumably sought an early disposition of their action prior to the cases TI brought. Patent infringement lawsuits were filed in Japan seeking, in addition to damages, a preliminary injunction to shut down TI's Japanese subsidiary.

The staff of the International Trade Commission called TI's action, the largest in the ITC's history. It has been reported that TI spent more than ten million dollars and the defendants collectively spent over 100 million dollars in legal fees on the various actions before the dust settled.

To put another perspective on the scope of the litigation: one document filed with the court was a Protective Order which outlined the terms of protecting confidential information that was produced during litigation. Such a document typically contains the names of the lawyers involved in the litigation who will have access to the information. In this case, over 150 lawyers were named as being associated with the litigation.

At the ITC, the case was broken into four trials covering various groupings of the ten TI patents involved. Massive as the litigation appeared, it was relatively short-lived. Shortly after the first trial in August of 1986, various defendant companies began reaching settlements with TI. Ultimately, TI settled with all the defendants. TI settled because it had reached its goals. The defendant companies agreed to pay royalties to TI that were commensurate with the newly recognised value of TI's patent portfolio and underlying technology. Royalties were paid on a unit basis for every DRAM made or sold in the United States throughout the lives of the settlements—which were typically five years through 1990. The agreements have been re-negotiated and renewed since then.

Clearly, the value base of intellectual property has changed dramatically since 1985. To understand how that occurred, let me provide a little more background regarding the legal and international trade environments and the licensing precedents prior to 1985, and the shifts that were occurring around that time.

In the late 1970s and early 1980s, America was undergoing a profound loss of international competitiveness. America's productivity was deteriorating. Foreign nations were entering into and succeeding in the lucrative high-technology markets and America's economy was suffering as a result. As part of its investigation into the worsening international trade picture, Congress scrutinised the US Patent System. The Office of Technology Assessment (OTA) of the Commerce Department investigated the patent system to provide recommendations. The key conclusion was that America needed increased research and development spending to remain competitive and that a more reliable patent system was needed to encourage American companies to make the investment in R&D.

At the time, however, the legal environment regarding patents was weak. Patents were routinely held invalid or non-infringed by the courts, and defendants often successfully threatened anti-trust defences when faced with actual or threatened patent litigation. Simply put, patents were unreliable as a means to protect research and development.

The licensing environment of the 1970s reflected the way we viewed the strength of the patent system, so licences were available to all comers on reasonable non-discriminatory terms. Typical agreements involved broad cross-licences with surviving rights for the terms of the covered patents with only nominal royalty payments being expected or received. The emphasis was on freedom to operate and the seemingly unlimited growth that lay ahead in the electronics field. The goal was simply to eliminate what were seen as barriers to market entry in the electronics field. In those days, licensing executives did not have a lot of influence or a lot of fun. All that started to change, however, in the early 1980s.

First, a dramatic shift in the legal environment began in 1982 with the formation of the Court of Appeals for the Federal Circuit, which was given exclusive jurisdiction over appeals of all patent litigation. The CAFC heralded in a time of renewed judicial respect for patents. The various remedies that were nominally available to patentees became reality—even when a clash of titans was involved. In *Polaroid* v. *Kodak* we learned that injunctive relief was for real. The courts began granting substantial damages for lost profits. Damages were trebled for wilful infringement. Preliminary injunctions were granted. Patentees began having valuable, substantial remedies with which to enforce their patent rights.

America's rediscovered respect for patents took on international significance as well. In 1988, the International Trade Commission became a more important patent forum. The US patent law was amended in 1988 to allow US process patents to reach foreign practised processes when the resulting product was imported into the United States, thus closing a loophole in US patent law that had had a serious impact in the semiconductor industry.

These were the changes that were evolving in July 1985 when the then chairman of Texas Instruments pulled together a team to review TI's licensing policies and practices. The team reviewed all aspects of TI's business, the legal environment and the political environment. There were no sacred cows. Our charter was to take more risks and obtain greater results.

A lot of major events were happening at that time. First, the CAFC was three years old by then, and the legal environment looked very encouraging. On the market front, dumping of DRAMs was rampant. Some manufacturers were dumping 64K DRAMs—chips capable of storing 64,000 bits of information—at $.90 per unit; about the price of a box from the 1970s. Old ideas regarding competitiveness and intellectual property were giving way to new, more aggressive ones.

Let me talk a little more about the DRAM market for a moment. Although American companies were instrumental in the development of the DRAM, by 1985 most American companies had pulled out of the market. Key players such as Motorola, Intel, and Mostek had stopped producing DRAMs commercially. Only Micron and Texas Instruments remained as American commercial DRAM manufacturers. Many felt that foreign importers were unfairly stacking the deck by dumping DRAMs at below cost to drive out competition. Micron initiated an action against Japanese importers for dumping 64K DRAMs. Shortly thereafter, the US government also initiated a dumping action against Japanese importers covering 256K DRAM products. About the same time, Intel brought its own dumping action for another type of memory product known as EPROMs.

The Reagan administration announced that year that intellectual property would be an important part of US trade policy. The over-arching attitude emerging amongst US business and government was that adequate intellectual property laws and their enforcement were needed on an international scale so as to give the innovators of technology proper rewards. This policy of providing rewards to the inventors would ultimately benefit the US it was thought.

You may be wondering why all the fuss was made about DRAMs. DRAM, which stands for Dynamic Random Access Memory—is probably the most advanced type of microchip with well over one million transistors on a single chip that is about the size of a fingernail. DRAM technology drives the semiconductor industry forward. Once new processes are learned and developed for DRAMs, other products benefit from the new processes as well. And, as many of you are no doubt aware, DRAMs are an essential component for the computer industry. The four, eight, or 16 megabytes of

RAM commonly referred to in the personal computer industry refers to the amount of DRAM memory the computer contains.

So, to summarise how things looked to the team in 1985, at stake was the DRAM market, a key component in the electronics industry. The market-place was awash with losses, driving out key players. Internationally, the trade environment with Japan was tense. The US government stepped in the place was awash with losses, driving out key players. Internationally, the trade environment with Japan was tense. The US government stepped in to support US industry. On the legal front, the outlook was encouraging to intellectual property owners for the first time in quite a while.

In addition to trying to determine TI's best course of action, given the current conditions, we formed several teams to come up with counter-moves that might be taken by foreign governments or companies based on various scenarios of TI actions. There was a host of issues to be addressed and responses to be anticipated.

For example, we agonised over issues such as the ramifications of filing a lawsuit against our own customers (the targeted companies represented about 70 per cent of TI Japan's business). We considered the impact on TI's US customers in the computer industry who needed the imports of the defendants. We also worried what would be the response of the foreign governments and how it would affect TI's overseas activities and about the publicity that TI would receive in Japan and Korea and at home in the US.

The analysis of all this involved months of effort by so-called red tag teams of TI experts such as lawyers, public relations personnel, marketing and operations managers who needed to deal with the foreign governments involved and so on. We tried to look at every possible issue that could impact on our position and to test the reasons underlying our proposed actions. When we put it all together, there was one recurring realisation that drove our decision. And it was this: the originators of technology disappear while those who did not share in the original development concentrate on lower costs and emerge as the victors. Intellectual property must have a value sufficiently high for the originator of technology to be able to look forward to profits that justify its R&D expenditures.

In this way, research and development spawns new products and new intellectual property. By realising value for intellectual property, greater incentive for additional research and development is realised, resulting in more new products to market and still more intellectual property. The resulting synergy of intellectual property complementing and supporting business objectives can keep a company competitive in tough markets and in times of rapid change.

Having made this commitment to intellectual property values, the next step was to put together a licensing programme that included litigation as an essential element. Let me add a disclaimer here that litigation is a last resort for dispute resolution. But, at the level of obtaining competitive advantage, it is a practical reality.

So why did we chose to litigate? Primarily, because litigation posed a sufficient threat to the defendants to force settlement at a high enough level to reward the originator and justify the R&D costs. Litigation provides the risk of large damages awards and, in some cases more significantly, the very real threat of an injunction after verdict, if not a preliminary injunction at the outset. Also, litigation requires a response—it is compulsory once a defendant is served that it respond and defend itself, or risk having a judgment with *res* judicative effect entered against it.

Arbitration and mediation do not provide the same leverage against infringers as litigation remedies do, although mediation may be desirable after a lawsuit has been filed and the plaintiff has brought his case to bear upon the defendant.

I have stated that litigation is the choice of last resort, and yet I provide a case study in which TI's opening salvo was to litigate. In general, there may be strategic advantages to bringing litigation early on. First, subsequent to filing a lawsuit, arbitration and mediation still remain options, whereas the reverse is not normally true. Secondly, for the reasons I have just stated, litigation puts the plaintiff in a position of strength, with a real threat of damages and injunction. Additionally, the first to the courthouse usually chooses the forum and venue for the lawsuit. The forum in the USA is still very important. Any earnest negotiations regarding patent licensing are likely to open the door for a pre-emptive declaratory judgment lawsuit if the patentee is not careful. And, of course, litigation provides the opportunity to obtain discovery regarding infringement, wilfulness, and the like.

In the case of TI in 1985, there was another reason for going straight to the courthouse. We were breaking new ground in intellectual property licensing. The programme was designed to bring about, to force if you will, a new way of thinking about the value of TI's patents. We knew that crucial competitive advantages would be won and lost based upon the outcome of the programme and that the only way to bring about such a fundamental shift in thinking was to bring the full coercive powers of legal action against the defendants.

The results for TI have been impressive. In 1986 and 1987, TI reported 211 million dollars in royalty income. In 1988, royalty income was 152 million dollars, while the entire company's net income was 366 million dollars. Cumulatively, TI has generated approximately 3.3 billion dollars on royalty income since 1986. These amounts are net of the outflow for patents of others and are for bare patent licences.

So, to pull this all together, TI's approach was to use litigation in order to enhance corporate profits. Like any good licensing programme, the effort involved the integration of three elements: the business objective, which in this case was to enhance corporate profits; the patent enforcement strategy—this requires determining the value of your portfolio, identifying infringers, and acting appropriately; and finally the litigation strategy, which I outlined in some detail just a moment ago.

There are, of course, other business obiectives that can drive a company's IP strategy. Three main business objective are freedom of action, income generation and obtaining market share. You will note that most of these strategies do not involve a high risk of litigation. Even income generation, when it is at or below historical levels, or precedent, does not involve a high degree of risk of litigation.

When a company seeks to generate income above traditional levels, however, as TI sought in 1985, litigation becomes a very real, in fact a likely possibility. Under those circumstances, a company is wise to adopt litigation as part of its initial strategy rather than react to the inevitable lawsuit that the targeted licensee is likely to bring.

Another business objective that carries with it a high risk of litigation is what I have noted as the market share strategy. This refers to the role of patents as barriers to entry into a field. Litigation is typically the result in this type of programme when the patentee does not want additional competition in the field, and the newcomer is usually in a do-or-die situation in which compromise is not a viable option.

I would like to share with you my experiences with Cyrix Corporation and the role of patent litigation in Cyrix's attempt to enter the microprocessor market. In the early 1990s, Cyrix Corporation was a start-up company entering into the microprocessor market, which was, and still is, dominated by Intel. Sales were about 25 million the first year, and are now over 250 million per year.

Cyrix's business objective was to gain entry into the market and gain market share. Cyrix's patent strategy was to develop a patent portfolio for bargaining positions. Although the company has developed a lot of innovative technology relating to microprocessors, there is typically a three- to five-year lead-time between innovation and obtaining a patent. In the meantime, Cyrix needed to sell product. That drove the litigation strategy.

As soon as Cyrix entered the market, patent lawsuits arose, some filed by Cyrix Corporation, some filed by Intel. Intel sought injunctions preventing Cyrix from selling product—damages were not the issue. At stake for Intel was protecting its market dominance against all comers. At stake for Cyrix was the company's very existence. It was a harsh lesson for a very young company of the importance of intellectual property.

Under those circumstances, there was no opportunity for mediation or arbitration. Cyrix had no room for negotiation and Intel had no incentive to reach a compromise or settlement position. That is typically the case when intellectual property is employed toward a business objective of obtaining or defending market share. The risk of litigation is very high. The patent enforcement strategy and litigation strategy must be considered an integral part of any such business plan.

Likewise, when a company embarks on an income-producing strategy such as TI's, the rewards can be high, but the risk of litigation is also high. That does not mean these business objectives should not be considered and pursued. It does mean, however, that a realistic assessment of the pros and cons of litigation must be part of the overall strategy.

I have explained the potential benefits of a litigation strategy. Let me briefly touch upon the possible down-side. First of all, unlike mediation and arbitration, a company really puts its patents on the line with litigation. A finding of non-infringement is one possible outcome. A finding of invalidity may also result. An interesting twist of the judicial system is that a finding of patent validity in one litigation does not bind another separate defendant from challenging the validity of that patent, whereas a finding of non-validity has *res* judicative effect on the patentee, such that the patent is no longer enforceable against anyone.

Circumstances can change with time, such that a one-time dominant force in the industry finds itself subsequently weak in relation to its competitors. New companies that start with little or no patent position can develop or acquire a strong portfolio. Or several weak companies might combine forces against a common strong competitor or form a common defence fund. The legal or political environment may change suddenly. All of these are real possibilities that can significantly change the strength of one's litigation strategy and its integration with the overall business objectives.

I believe, however, that the advantages that can be obtained by integrating a litigation strategy into the overall business objective, and the potential for high rewards if successful make the risk worthwhile. Especially under those circumstances as I have discussed, when the goal is to generate substantial income or to gain or defend market share, the risk of litigation is very high and should be anticipated from the outset.

In summary, then, the first step in using intellectual property to achieve corporate goals is to establish what specifically the business objective is. Recognise that some business objectives carry a higher risk of litigation then others. A patent enforcement strategy and a litigation strategy should be considered an integral part of the overall business plan. This means assessing the strength and scope of your own patents and what may be asserted against you. It also means evaluating the legal, business, and political environment in which you are operating with the understanding that the current environment may shift.

Finally, I would note, pick your targets carefully. Using intellectual property as a strategic asset, even today, is still a fairly bold proposition. A long-drawn-out battle with entrenched positions can sap a company's enthusiasm for the overall plan. Management support is strengthened when you win the first battle and a snowball effect is created by one victory feeding into and paving the way for the next. Your competition will also be keeping an eye on your progress and will likely adjust its thinking when you demonstrate a winning position early on in the programme.

By carefully integrating a cogent patent enforcement strategy litigation strategy, and business plan, a company can find its intellectual property to be a valuable asset in obtaining corporate goals.

Panel V

Ethical and Ecological Aspects of Industrial Property Rights

12

REWARDING CREATIVITY FOR CONSERVING DIVERSITY IN THE THIRD WORLD: CAN IPR REGIME SERVE THE NEEDS OF CONTEMPORARY AND TRADITIONAL KNOWLEDGE EXPERTS AND COMMUNITIES IN THIRD WORLD?

*Anil K. Gupta**

The debate on the relevance and appropriateness of the conventional IPR regime for plant varieties, products based on knowledge of local communities and individual informal experts and the use of local bio-diversity even without the use of associated knowledge systems has become very emotive in recent years. Many NGOs and activists see no merit in the IPRs regime for providing incentives to local communities and creative individuals. They term the attempts of the large corporations (generally MNCs) to access bio-diversity without sharing any benefits with local communities as "biopiracy". Many others oppose the IPRs because these are supposed to commoditise knowledge which reportedly was always in the common domain for universal/local benefit. The high cost of hiring patent attorneys is supposed to make the present patent system out of reach of grassroots innovators. The absence of any institutional set up in most developing countries to (1) provide information about IPRs, (2) extend help to obtain patents for individuals or communities and (3) oppose the patents by others on the knowledge traditionally known to local communities, have further alienated the moderates and hardened the attitudes of the conventional opponents.

* Co-ordinator, SRISTI and Professor, Indian Institute of Management, Ahmedabad, India.

The arguments of those who do not see any hope in the provisions of TRIPs can be summarised as:

- All the knowledge held by people about use of bio-diversity for treating various ailments of human and animals, producing vegetative dyes, developing local land races etc., is held in common by the local communities. This knowledge is supposed to have been transferred by one generation to another over very long period of time with (or without) some value addition by successive generations.
- The knowledge must be held in the common domain and should not be allowed to be monopolised by MNCs (though the behaviour of public sector and private but national drug companies is no different from the MNCs[1]).
- The intellectual property right regime has evolved for protecting industrial designs and processes and is not suitable for biological processes and products.[2]
- Since the knowledge of various plants has been developed over several

[1] We have made this unpopular argument for last several years through the columns of the *Honey Bee* newsletter and otherwise that southern governments should not discriminate among national and international companies/organisations regarding (1) the threat to the environment from unrestrained exploitation of germ plasm or bio-diversity without replacing or repairing disturbance to natural habitats, (2) the exploitation of local or traditional or contemporary knowledge of people without prior informed consent, and ensuring an equitable sharing of benefits, (3) contributions to national capacity building in negotiating fair and reasonable contracts among people and the bio-diversity prospectors.

Some exceptions may be made in the case of those NGOs or civil society organisations which are explicitly accountable to people and are experimenting to evolve models of rewarding creativity through material and non-material incentives for individuals and communities.

[2] The concept of inventiveness in biological materials has remained very contentious. Merely attaching a codon before and after a genetic sequence confers a protection on naturally produced diversity. Similarly, purifying a microbial culture confers similar advantage, since in nature these cultures will be mixed with many other cultures.

The argument of the industry has been that if benefits commensurate with the investments are not ensured, nobody will invest in the research and the product development. Perhaps if part of these benefits were to be spent for conservation of habitats and cultural practices which contribute to conservation of microbial diversity, the popular perception may change. Maybe a major Colombo Plan kind of initiative is required for building infrastructural and human capacity in developing countries in this field through partnership of the corporations and research institutions benefiting from this diversity.

SRISTI undertook a comprehensive survey of soil microbial diversity in 80 villages of Gujarat sampled from eight agro-ecological regions to map diversity from cultivated and uncultivated fields to distinguish chemical intensive and organic farms and also to see whether this diversity could be screened for useful purposes. So far we could analyse only about 60 samples out of 720 collected at great cost. Incentives for conservation can indeed be generated if more that 1,900 bacterial, fungal and acrinomycetes cultures isolated so far are properly identified and screened (SRISTI, 1996).

generations, why should the present generation be entitled to reap all the rewards if any?[3]
- Why should governments be entitled to any benefits from the commercialisation of patented products when the resource and the knowledge were actually provided by individuals or communities?[4]
- While process patents can be provided, the product patents impede research, generate excessive monopoly to one or few inventors, make the technology or products out of reach of the common people due to price increases, and discourage expertise of successful reverse engineering in the third world.

There are many other arguments on ethical and efficiency grounds against the patenting of life forms[5] and also against the products derived from common knowledge without any reciprocity towards knowledge generators or providers in one or more countries in the region.[6] I propose to dispel many of these myths, acknowledge where there is a genuine case for

[3] It should be noted that as against fewer than 2,000 medicinal plants mentioned in the classical Aryurvedic texts, uses of about 7,000 plants are already documented in the folk oral tradition (Dr. Pushpangandan, 1996). We have ourselves identified many plants for which either no use is mentioned in the NAPRALERT database at the University of Chicago (it has comprehensive information about 40,000 species published in more than 125,000 papers/books and 500 journals screened every month) or the use mentioned is different from or opposite to the one found in the Honey Bee survey of farmers' innovations.

Large number of innovation for herbal pesticides or veterinary medicines were in fact developed only recently by individuals. One of my students, *viz.* Astad Pastakia, recently finished his doctorate research on heuristics of 20 such innovators who had developed new uses of biodiversity for sustainable pest management. Two heuristics had not been reported in formal scientific literature before including the one dealing with combining plant and insect to produce a pest repellent.

[4] This argument has arisen in the context of Art. 15.5 as well as Arts. 8 j and 10 c of Convention of Biological Diversity (CBD). Prior informed consent is required only of parties to the Convention i.e. the contracting Nation States, and not of the knowledge- and resource-providing communities. Under Art. 8 j, however, the approval and involvement of local communities and Individuals is required for ensuring equitable sharing of the benefits. Whether, that happens will of course depend upon the legislative environment and local institutional capacity in each country. The institutions which deprive knowledge-rich, economically poor people of their basic rights and needs would let any benefits trickle down to them will depend upon the access of such people to alternative frameworks of negotiation and mutually agreeable contracts.

[5] The campaign against life forms in Europe and many other parts of the world is based essentially on the notion that tinkering with life forms through trans-genic animals or genetically engineering animals may threaten the very existence of life on this planet.

[6] The ethical issues in accessing bio-diversity were articulated in an issue paper (Gupta, 1994) which led to the development of ethical guidelines by a group of Pew Conservation scholars and later endorsed by a larger community of Pew Scholars in principle (Ethical guidelines, 1994, Honey Bee, 1995, Eubios, 1995). It was recognised that the relationship of the outsiders with local bio-diversity and related knowledge could be guided by extractive and non-extractive modes for commercial and non-commercial purposes. It was also stressed that negotiations for benefit sharing should take place at different stages of value addition.

reforms of patent regime and finally suggest an alternative framework which may be needed to help achieve the goals of IPRs i.e. rewarding inventive and creative activities in society. It is acknowledged that encouragement to creative and innovative spirit at grassroots level will not be possible only through IPR regimes.[7]

My case is:

(a) Not all the knowledge held by people in bio-diversity-rich, economically poor regions and communities is (1) traditional, (2) carried forward in fossilised form from one generation to another but has been improvised by successive generations, (3) collective in nature, and (4) even if known to communities, is reproduced by everybody.[8]
(b) Considerable knowledge of economic importance is produced by individuals and also in recent times i.e. through contemporary innovations.
(c) Even the traditional knowledge should receive a certain kind of protection if incentives have to be generated to conserve not only the knowledge but also the institutions of its reproduction and intergenerational transfer. We should not kill the goose which has laid the golden eggs for so long.
(d) Given the high hit rate in formal research around locally identified uses of plants and other kinds of bio-diversity, transaction costs of formal R & D systems in private and public systems are reduced considerably.[9] They should in turn share the benefits that may accrue from commercialisation of such protected products. In some cases local communities or individuals, as the case may be, should be considered co-inventors of the new-value added products.
(e) The newness and non-obviousness of traditional knowledge should be

[7] It is for this reason that we have been arguing since 1989 that various models of reward involving material and non-material incentives for individual and communities applicable in the short and long term should be explored. One of the material individual ways of rewarding creativity can be patenting and other such forms of protection of intellectual property (Gupta, 1989, 1990, 1991, 1995, Honey Bee 1989–95).

[8] There are many herbalists who provide service to everybody in the community even without charge. However, the beneficiaries of this knowledge contribute to this knowledge to the same extent as do students in a class to the knowledge of the teacher. There is a lot a teacher learns from some students. Do students become co-author of all publications of their knowledge? In any case why are not all the books and papers published by critiques of IPRs anonymous or co-authored by everyone with whom they have discussed the ideas ever. In fact I noticed that the contribution of personal communications in the writing of such critics may be more or less than in others.

[9] It should be remembered that out of 114 plant-derived drugs, more than 70 % are used for the same purpose for which the native people discovered their use (Farnsworth, 1988). This proves that basic research linking cause and effect had been done successfully by the people in the majority of cases. Modern science and technology could supplement the efforts of the people, improve the efficiency of the extraction of the active ingredient or synthesise analogue of the same, thereby improving effectiveness (Gupta, 1991).

seen in the light of the available repertoire for that particular purpose.[10]

(f) The local knowledge should qualify to be considered new for the purposes of prior art, since outside communities/companies may not have had access otherwise. The norms regarding exhaustion of the rights due to publication of local knowledge should be reconsidered and modified so that incentives to share the knowledge by local communities with outsiders are not affected adversely.[11]

(g) The argument that all the knowledge should be treated as common property is not tenable because large number of local experts we have met so far are extremely knowledgeable though very poor. They know far more than anybody else in the village and have the expertise to prepare various solutions. Others may know about it but they may not have contributed to it except by giving an opportunity for testing. To that extent they should have a small share in the entitlements. But the entitlements of an expert could not be on a par with those of the rest of the community. Local communities have not provided them with any significant incentives, such that either their children or other younger people should try to learn their skills. It should also be noted that secrecy is not a gift of the modern patent regime. Lots of traditional knowledge has already been lost or is in the process of being lost because the expert concerned did not ever share the innovation with any one.

[10] This is a rather complicated issue given the differences in the US and European patent norms. Shayan Kadilal suggests that the USPTO norms have not undergone change in this regard for almost 100 years and require publications accessible in USA to claim prior art. Also given the very limited time that is spent by examiners (often only few hours and generally not more than 20–30 references), the prior art examination creates situations like the one witnessed in the patent on turmeric powder applications for oral and external application for wound healing. This patent should never have been granted and makes a mockery of inventiveness as well as non obviousness.

Chris Blanc had given an example in personal communication of a patent that was opposed on account of a third party thesis reporting the results which had been patented. However, the patent was upheld because the thesis had not been catalogued and thus was not easily or reasonably accessible to the patentee. This ground can be used to patent any traditional knowledge of the third world by any one in the USA.

[11] Further to the previous n., the norms of protection being granted to an applicant if applications are made within one year of publication may have to be modified in the case of people's knowledge. We have to consider the fact that the Government of India has already prohibited, and for good reason, the publication of results of the All India Co-ordinated Project on Ethnobiology administered by the Ministry of the Environment. This could become a trend all over the world. Further, this policy also comes in the way of sharing of this knowledge back with the people (not that this knowledge was ever shared back with people even without this restriction). The Honey Bee network faces this dilemma every day. Since our major aim is to empower the creativity of local communities and individuals without impairing their IPRs, we have to decide how much detail to publish even in the local language. But we have erred on the side of sharing whenever there was some knowledge that could help small farmers reduce their costs and replace or reduce chemical inputs.

(h) Every patent office in a western country should insist that a patent applicant declares that the knowledge and resources used in a patent have been obtained lawfully and legally.

This implies the need for regulations in developed countries requiring full disclosure by any corporation or an individual seeking patent protection on a plant based drug or any other natural product. The disclosure should provide that the source material has been rightfully and lawfully acquired. "Rightful" acquisition would involve moral as well as ethical issues in access to bio-diversity. For instance even if a local community has not asked for any price for sharing the material or the knowledge about it, is the corporation bound by ethical conduct to set up trust funds and other forms of reciprocity for local communities? Is it incumbent upon it to ensure that the superior ethics of local communities remaining poor despite conserving biological diversity and the knowledge around it does not become a reason for perpetuating their poverty, and thus endangering the survival of diversity itself?

The "lawful" acquisition will imply that prior informed consent and approval and the involvement of local communities and creative individuals has been ensured provided that the bio-diversity donor country has laws requiring such consent and approval. If a country does not have any such laws, as for instance India, then acquiring any material will be lawful or legal but may not be rightful.

(i) The publication of local knowledge deprives on one hand any benefit that may arise from value addition in local knowledge to the individual or community or nation concerned and, on the other, makes it possible for people struggling with similar problem to learn from it. This happens through publication in local languages as attempted by Honey Bee. However, the challenge is to marry two goals of easy and quick opportunity for lateral learning (through local language publication) and sharing of benefits through value addition in the same knowledge. Giving legitimacy to databases like Honey Bee and a registration system of innovations, as proposed in the next point below, may provide the answer. Honey Bee will then make its databases accessible to all patent offices in lieu of the protection provided to the communities and individuals whose knowledge is catalogued in it. The alternative of greater secrecy and withholding of knowledge will make everyone a loser through (1) greater erosion of oral knowledge, (2) continued unwillingness of the younger generation to learn the knowledge, innovations and practices developed over a long period of time, (3) depriving knowledge holders as well as those dependent upon them any opportunity to improve their livelihood prospects through sharing of possible benefits, (4) lack of material incentives for the conservation of endangered species, (5) knowledge-rich poor communities may migrate out due to low opportunities for subsistence and employment and not take care of local resource or over-exploit the resource itself, netting very little value in a short period of time, and (6) stifling the very creative and buoyant laboratory of innovations at the grassroots by denying any social esteem for such knowledge through material as well as non-material incentives and general neglect.

(j) Since it will be very difficult for any and every community to seek protection of its knowledge and inventive recipes for various purposes such as herbal pesticides, human or veterinary medicines, vegetative dyes, etc., a registration system should be developed as explained below.

SRISTI and the Honey Bee network have been pleading for a global system of registration for grassroots innovations. The Honey Bee database has more than 2,300 innovations with the names and addresses of the innovative/creative community and/or individuals along with the names of the communicators through whom we have learned these innovations.

Such a registry will prevent any firm or individual seeking a patent on community knowledge as well as on knowledge and innovations produced by individuals without some kind of cross licensing.

It will be possible to achieve the following results from such a registry:

(a) Acknowledgement of individual and collective creativity.
(b) Grant entitlements to grassroots innovators for receiving a share of any returns that may arise from commercial applications of their knowledge, innovations or practices with or without value addition secondary entitlements.
(c) Linking the golden triangle of entrepreneurship by linking investments, enterprise and innovations. Small-scale investors in the North and South cannot afford to go to various countries, scan diversity of knowledge and resources, negotiate contracts and invest up front huge investments for value addition. If they do not participate, then the field will remain dominated by only large corporations. This register will help small-scale investors seek opportunities of communication with communities and individual innovators and explore opportunities of investment. A large number of potential negotiations will take place, increasing the opportunities for innovative communities and individuals. The competition among the investors tempered by competition among potential suppliers of various kinds of knowledge as well as diversity will moderate expectations on both the sides.
(d) An autonomous authority of which local community representatives will be the majority members could be entrusted with the responsibilities of having access to all the contracts. A copy of the contracts may have to be deposited with this Authority so as to avoid short changing of the communities. These contracts will also be scrutinised to see whether management plans for sustainable extraction of diversity have

been drawn in a scientifically appropriate manner or not. Penalties may have to be imposed for non-sustainable extraction of herbs by domestic as well as external extractors.

(e) Each entry in the register will be coded according to a universal system like ISBN. The postal pin code of the habitat of the community or individuals registering innovations will be incorporated in the indexation system so that geo-referencing of innovations can be done. In due course the contextual information of innovations can also be incorporated in the system so that this systems of innovations can help cross connect the communities having similar ecological situations or facing similar constraints or challenges.

(f) The entry in the register will at the first stage be mere acknowledgement of creativity and innovation at grassroots level. But later some of the innovations will be considered appropriate for the award of inventors' certificates or a kind of petty patent which is a limited purpose and limited duration protection. The essential purpose of this innovation is also to enable the potential investors (a co-operative of consumers, producers, an entrepreneur, or a large firm in the private or public sector).

(g) The award of a certificate will also increase the entitlement of the innovator/s to access to concessional credit and risk cover so that the transition from collector, or producer of herbs to developer and marketeer of value added products can take place in cases where innovators deem that fit.

(h) The registration system will also be part of the knowledge network linking problem-solving people across the world at the grassroots level (see the discussion on the knowledge network in the later section). This will promote people to people learning and serve as a multi-language, multi-level, multi-media (oral, textual, electronic) clearing house for local and indigenous communities. Wherever necessary and possible, formal scientific institutions will be linked up in the network.

Apart from the registration system a large number of specific incentives would need to be developed for different categories of knowledge, innovations and practices. Similarly the incentives for preservation of sustainable lifestyles of indigenous communities would also be different.

We realise that most governments in developing countries do not have the resources even to pay the salaries of public administrators, to expect them to provide benefits to conservators of diversity and developers of innovations is not a realistic goal. If the private or public or co-operative sector has to share the benefits, they should obviously make profits. IPRs do play a significant role in generating these profits. However, very broad patents like the one in the case of transgenic cotton (which was later rescinded) are in the interest neither of science nor business efficiency in the long term.

So far as sustainable technologies are concerned, such as herbal pesticides, growth regulators, vegetative dyes etc., the South can provide technologies to the North. But if such innovations are used without appropriate reciprocities, then the knowledge systems which produced these innovations will not last very long. It is true that poor people in the third world may be creative and innovative, but they cannot afford costly attorneys. A system has to be evolved to provide this help through public-interest institutions or initiatives. Inventor assistance programmes like the ones tried by the Franklin Law Pierce Center should be tried out on a global scale and in many countries immediately.

The patentees in the case of innovations like the ones based on neem trees should agree to share part of their profits with an international innovations support and bio-diversity conservation fund. After all they did not stumble upon neem tree-based knowledge randomly. The contributions of local communities in several countries made the innovation possible.

The paper makes a case for adapting patent systems not only to accommodate the creative urges of local communities but also to ensure that this vibrant and dynamic laboratory for developing sustainable technologies and products does not die down just because a community of IPR experts could not fathom its long-term potential.

Selected Papers from the SRISTI Group on the Subject

Gupta, Anil K., *Survival Under Stress: Socio-Ecological Perspective on Farmers' Innovation and Risk Adjustments*, W.P. No. 738, 1988, International Congress on Plant Physiology, New Delhi, 1988., revised version published in *Capitalism, Nature and Socialism*, 5, 1990, 79–96.

Scientific Perception of Farmers' Innovations in Dry Regions: Barriers to Scientific Curiosity, September 1987, IIM Working Paper No. 699, presented at International Conference on Farmer Participatory Research at IDS, Sussex, July 1987.

The Right to Resource: Peasant Knowledge, Protocol of its "Extraction" and Ethics of Collaboration In Extractions, W.P. no-851, January 1990, 12. Also published in brief as "Peasant Knowledge—Who has Rights To Use It?" ILEIA, News Letter, Mar. 1990. 24–5.

Why Does Poverty Persist in Regions of High Biodiversity?: A Case for Indigenous Property Right System, Paper invited for the International conference on Property Rights and Genetic Resources sponsored by IUCN, UNEP and ACTS at Kenya, 10–16 June 1991.

(With Kirit K. Patel and B.L. Patil), *Conserving Diversity For Sustainable Development, The Case of Plants of Insecticidal and Veterinary Medicine Importance*, Presented at Project Design Workshop on Genetic Resources for Sustainable Agriculture, convened by M.S. Swaminathan Research Foundation, Madras, 22–3 November 1991. IIMA Working Paper No. 1003.

Sustainability Through Biodiversity: Designing Crucible of Culture, Creativity and Conscience, Presented at International Conference on Biodiversity and

Conservation held at Danish Parliament, Copenhagen, 8 November 1991. IIMA Working Paper No. 1005.

Biodiversity and Poverty vis-à-vis Biotechnology and Prosperity, IIMA Working Paper No. 954., August 1991.

Biodiversity, Poverty and Intellectual Property Rights of Third World Peasants: A Case for Renegotiating Global Understanding, The paper is an invited contribution for Project Design Workshop on Genetic Resources For Sustainable Agriculture, M S Swaminathan Research Foundation, Madras, 22–3 November 1991, Published in "Biodiversity: Implications for Global Food Security" (eds. M.S. Swaminathan, and S. Jana).

Biotechnology and Intellectual Property Rights: Protecting the Iinterests of Third World Farmers and Scientists, IIMA Working Paper No. 1057., published in *Commercialization of Biotechnologies for Agriculture and Aquaculture: Status and Constraints in India* (eds., U.K. Srivastava, S. Chandrasekhar) (New Delhi, Oxford, IBH Publishing Co. Pvt. Ltd.), 31–56.

Biotechnology for Lifestock Improvement: Some Issues and Perspectives, published in *Commercialization of Biotechnologies for Agriculture and Aquaculture: Status and Constraints in India* (eds., U.K. Srivastava, S. Chandrasekhar) (New Delhi, Oxford, IBH Publishing Co. Pvt. Ltd.), 117–26.

Developing Technologies for Sustainable Resource Management: Eating your Cake and Having it Too!, paper presented at an International Course on Technology Triangle-linking scientists, extension workers and farmers at Royal Agri. and Vety. Univ., Denmark, 6–10 April 1992.

Eco-Institutional Perspective on Maintaining Diversity, presented at the Second Conference of the International Society of Ecological Economics on Investing in Natural Capital, Stockholm, August 1992, IIMA W.P No. 1060, 1992.

Environmental Policy Analysis for Maintaining Diversity, presented in AASREC Seminar on Environment and Sustainable Development, organized by ICSSR, at IDS, Jaipur, during 4–5 January 1993.

(With Aseem Prakash), *On Internalization of Externalities*, IIMA WP No. 1126, August 1993.

Biotechnology and IPR: Third World Issues for Farmers and Scientists, published in Biotechnology Monographs: Focus on Third World Issues, Series 1, Number 1, May 1993.

Compensating Local Communities for Conserving Biodiversity: Shall We Save the Goose that Laid the Golden Eggs So Long, IIMA Working Paper No. 1206, August 1994.

Ethical Issues in Prospecting Biodiversity, IIMA Working Paper No. 1205, August 1994.

Dilemma in Conservation of Biodiversity: Ethical, Equity and Moral Issues—a Review, prepared for a workshop of Pew Conservation Scholars on Developing Ethical Guidelines for Accessing Biodiversity, Arizona, October, 1994, published under the title, "Ethical Dilemmas in Conservation of Biodiversity: Towards Developing Global Acceptable Ethical Guidelines" in Eubios Journal of Asian and International Bioethics 5 (Japan), March 1995, 40–6.

Social and Ethical Dimensions of Ecological Economics, Key Note Paper invited presentation at the Conference, Down To Earth International Society of Ecological Economies, Costa Rica, October 1994.

Suggested Ethical Guidelines for Accessing and Exploring Biodiversity—A Pew Conservation Scholars Initiative, 21 October 1994 (a collective effort of Pew Conservation Scholars based on three background notes including G 16 and G 17), published in *Eubios Journal of Asian and International Bioethics* 5 (Japan), March 1995, 38–40.

Secular Basis of Sustainable Spirit: Understanding Roots of Creativity and Innovations at Grassroots Level, SRISTI/IIMA Discussion Paper No. 2, November 1993.

(With Vijaya Sherry Chand), *Alternatives for Action: SRISTI's Vision on Prioritization of Investments under Biodiversity Convention—A Submission to Global Biodiversity Forum*, Bahamas, 26–9 November 1994.

Conservation Through Competitions: Global Campaign for Biodiversity Contests.

Crossroads of Creativity: Building upon People's Knowledge, background paper for a Workshop organised for the Top Management of International Fund for Agricultural Development (IFAD), Rome, April, 1995.

Misinformation on Neem: What Could be the Motive?, a shorter version published in *Down To Earth*, 1994.

Commercialization of Agricultural Technologies, a note prepared for discussion at ICAR on the subject, 1994.

Compensating Local Communities for Conserving Biodiversity: How Much, Who Will, How and When, (ed. L. Guruswamy and Jeff McNeely), Seeds They Preserve, Arizona: University of Tulsa, forthcoming.

People's Knowledge for Survival: Grassroot Innovations for Sustainable Natural Resource Management.

Knowledge Centre: Building Upon What People Know, presented at the IFAD's International Conference on Hunger & Poverty in Brussels during 16–23 November 1995.

Neem-mania, What Else?, published in Down to Earth, November 1995, 52–3.

Patents on Neem: Will They Deprive Indian Farmers of Their Rights to Use it as a Pesticide, Published in Biotechnology Law Report, Volume 15, Number 1, January–February 1996, 6–14.

Farmers' Innovations for Sustainable Resource Management and Conservation of Biological Diversity, presented as invited paper in the International Symposium on Food Security & Innovations: Successes and Lessons Learned at University of Hohenheim, 12–15 March 1996.

(With Chokkakula Srinivas), *Knowledge Centers/Networks for Empowering Knowledge-Rich-Economically Poor Communities and Innovators*: DSS for Solution Augmentation for Sustainable Development, presented as invited paper in the Workshop on DSS organized by The United Nations University in Macau, 26 February–8 March 1996.

Crops, Creativity and Compensation: Honey Bee Network Approach to Participatory Breeding, Diversity, 1996, forthcoming.

The Honey Bee Network: Voices from Grassroots Innovators, Cultural Survival Quarterly, Spring 1996, 57–60.

Aseem Prakash and Anil K. Gupta, 1994, "Institutions and Environmental Sustainability", in Willem A. Hamel (ed.) *Proceedings of the Ecol-Environmangement Group*, 39–49, The Association of Management, 12th Annual Conference, Dallas, Texas, 10–13 August.

13

ETHICAL AND ECOLOGICAL ASPECTS OF INDUSTRIAL PROPERTY RIGHTS IN THE CONTEXT OF GENETIC ENGINEERING AND BIOTECHNOLOGY

*Klaus M. Leisinger**

I Introduction

Genetic engineering and biotechnology[1] are considered to be amongst the most powerful and economically promising technological means for use in many areas. To discuss "Ethical and Ecological Aspects of Intellectual Property Rights in the Context of Genetic Engineering and Biotechnology" in a meaningful way is as impossible as to analyse the benefits and risks of genetic engineering and biotechnology in general. One would have to refer to health, agricultural and industrial as well as environmental problems, look at things from a biological, economic and social, as well as cultural, point of view and, last but not least, discuss every issue involved in the context of

* Executive Director and Delegate of the Board of Trustee of Novartis for Sustainable Development, formerly Ciba-Geigy Foundation for Co-operation with Developing Countries, and Professor of development sociology on the philosophical-historical faculty of the University of Basel, Switzerland.

[1] In this paper *genetic engineering (recombinant DNA technology)* means "the calculated modification of hereditary genetic material in living organisms by the addition, removal or exchange of one or more genes, resulting in the passing on of this altered genetic information to descendants": cf. K. Dohmen (ed.), *Gentechnologie—die andere Schöpfung?* (Metzler, Stuttgartt, 1988), 5. *Biotechnology* is "the integrated application of biochemistry, microbiology and process technology with the objective of turning to technical use the potential of micro-organisms and cell and tissue cultures as well as parts thereof": cf. H. Dellweg, *Biotechnologie, Grundlagen und Verfahren.* (VCH, Weinheim, 1987, 1. Biotechnology therefore deals with the utilisation of biological processes in technical operations and industrial production. Genetic engineering is a means to an end, inasmuch as it allows the properties of micro-organisms to be modified in such a way that a desired effect is brought about in biological processes, among others. *Three different generations* of biotechnology can be distinguished. In the first, bacteria or yeast, for example, were used in making cheese or beer. In the second, micro-organisms were used to produce antibiotics and molecular biology was further developed. In the third generation, finally, it has become possible to alter the genetic material of an individual cell directly. The term "agricultural biotechnology" encompasses well established techniques, such as those used in biological pest control and the production of vaccines and bio-fertilisers, but also recombinant DNA technology, monoclonal antibodies, and new cell and tissue culture techniques.

industrialised and developing countries and against background of disparate value premises. Each one of these different aspects raises highly controversial issues for the discussion of which one would have to organise whole seminars—and still depart with divergent views.

Even a discussion limited to one particular aspect, e.g. the *ethical* aspects of intellectual[2] property rights in the context of genetic engineering and biotechnology *for developing countries*, touches on too many highly complex issues to allow a meaningful conclusion in today's lecture. The collective term "developing countries" is itself already too sweeping: it takes in countries so different in economic and social terms and neglects such important specific political and cultural circumstances as to preclude generalisations.

Hence, focusing becomes an absolute necessity for any fruitful discussion.

A Circumscribing our Focus

We will focus our discussion on the ethical aspects of intellectual property rights in the context of genetic engineering and biotechnology in food crops of developing countries.

This focus is warranted by the fact, that after 40 years of national and international development endeavours, hunger is still a reality for over 800 million poor people and food security still remains one of the most desirable objectives of sustainable development.[3] The United Nations Food and Agriculture Organisation (FAO) has estimated that it will be necessary to double overall agricultural production (i.e. not only food output) by the year 2000 in order to meet the needs of growing populations. According to FAO, this will require a virtual "agricultural revolution" through massive investments in new technologies and inputs as well as an increased awareness of the need to preserve resources.[4]

The World Food Summit in Rome in November 1996 concluded that sustained improvements in the area of food security necessitates poverty-oriented development policy, social reforms and *appropriate technological innovation*. Of course, appropriate technological innovation comprises much more than just genetic engineering and biotechnology, but in the opinion of an international conference of experts convened by the World Bank, UNDP and FAO, a solution to the problem of securing world food supplies while preserving the environment is today inconceivable without recombinant genetics and biotechnology.[5]

[2] To give the discussion wider scope, we will argue for "intellectual" rather than "industrial" property rights.

[3] FAO, Food Security Assessment. (WFS 96/Tech/7), Rome, Jan. 1996.

[4] FAO, Agriculture: Toward 2000, Rome, 1981, 57.

[5] See CGIAR Highlights: Feeding the World—Protecting the Environment, UN briefing co-sponsored by World Bank, UNDP and FAO. (Washington, DC, May 1992); see also A.S. Moffat, "Improving Plant Disease Resistance", in *Science*, Vol. 257, 24 July 1992.

Before we start our discussion, one principal question has to be answered: are intellectual property rights in the context of genetic engineering and biotechnology in food crops of developing countries so unique and distinctive as to necessitate an ethical analysis which is different from that of one of other technologies?

B Intellectual Property Rights in the Context of Genetic Engineering and Biotechnology: A Unique Subject for Moral Reasoning?

If one excludes human genes and human gene therapy, there are—at least in my judgement—no distinctive and unique ethical aspects of intellectual property rights in the context of genetic engineering and biotechnology and their application on food crops in developing countries.

With regard to technical safety issues as well as to the impact on the common good, the ethical analysis of genetic engineering and biotechnology is comparable to that applicable to other potent technologies and their transfer to developing countries. The questions that must be asked are therefore the same as with other technologies and their implementation in poor societies.

What are the risks and what the benefits of genetic engineering and biotechnology in food crops of developing countries, and what is the role and weight of intellectual property rights in this context? Who can derive advantage from the benefits and who bears the risks? What are the moral responsibilities accruing to the different stakeholders?

Having identified the issues and the prospective controversies, we will suggest ways and means to minimise ethical conflicts and maximise social compatibility and recommend models for co-operation between the different stakeholders.

II Benefits and Risks of Genetic Engineering and Biotechnology

Neither intellectual property rights nor genetic engineering and biotechnology are ends in themselves—they are tools to accomplish particular economic and social ends. Ethics in the sense of moral philosophy analyse practices and activities with a view to their morality. Questions raised in the moral context concern the consequences for the common good as well as for the duties and obligations incumbent on the different stakeholders. The precepts deriving from moral reasoning differ between ethical schools. However, there is a broad common denominator, namely of doing things in ways that neither intend nor do direct or indirect harm to others.

In order to form an opinion on whether a technology promises on balance to contribute to the common good or whether it may inflict significant harm on society and its members, one must first analyse that technology's potential and real benefits and risks.

Where do intellectual property rights come in? Intellectual property rights such as patents are statutory rights which prevent imitation for a limited time. They are thus a legal instrument to protect an inventor's investments in his or her innovation. One of the requirements for patenting is public disclosure of the invention—a procedure which serves to increase the availability of scientific and technical knowledge. Such information may also be used by others for further inventions.

The protection of an inventor's investment in innovation promotes scientific progress and innovation by abetting the quest for better answers to given problems in the health, agricultural and industrial sectors. Comparing nations with and without intellectual property rights, there is no doubt that not only the inventor but also society at large benefits from patents. In the long run consumers tend to be the major beneficiaries. Intellectual property rights in the context of genetic engineering and biotechnology for food crops in developing countries do not differ basically from patents in other areas.[6] So if the issue of compensatory justice can be decided affirmatively, the outcome of an ethical analysis of intellectual property rights will mainly depend on a benefit-risk-analysis of genetic engineering and biotechnology.

Not surprisingly in light of the issue's complexity, our benefit-risk-analysis will not provide simplistic black-and-white answers. We shall discover that there are benefits *and* risks, and these have to be weighed against each other in order to determine whether the positive or the negative impact is more pronounced. If the benefits accrue to different societal groups than do the risks, we will have to make explicit whose benefits and whose risks carry what weight for the ethical analysis. This cannot be done without explicit individual valuations. As Willy Brandt once said, "development will never be, and never can be, defined to universal satisfaction. It refers, broadly speaking, to desirable social and economic progress, and people will always have different views about what is desirable."[7]

The social and economic progress that I consider desirable has the following characteristics:

(a) it contributes to the satisfaction of basic needs and increases the economic productivity of all members of a society;
(b) in pursuing economic efficiency and growth, the preservation of natural resources (land, air, water, raw materials, species) remains an explicit and valuable policy objective;
(c) It—at least in the long run—helps to reduce social inequalities with respect to income, property and opportunities. In the short run, the

[6] There are few exceptions: see J. Van Wijk, J.I. Cohen and J.Komen, *Intellectual Property Rights for Agricultural Biotechnology*. (ISNAR, The Hague, 1993).

[7] Independent Commission on International Development Issues (ed.), North–South: *A Programme for Survival* (Pan Books, London 1980), 48.

minimum condition is that if the "rich" get richer, the "poor" get less poor.[8]

It is against this background that the risks and benefits of genetic engineering and biotechnology in food crops of developing countries, as well as the role of intellectual property rights, will be weighed.

A Benefits

1 The Theory

The spectrum of potential benefits from the application of genetic engineering and biotechnology to food crops in developing countries ranges from diagnostic aids, for example in plant diseases, through to gene mapping, where the genetic characteristics of plants are visibly cartographed, enabling speedier identification of interesting genetic material for every kind of plant usable in agriculture.[9] The main objective is to find improved seed varieties, i.e. varieties with properties such as resistance to or tolerance of plant diseases (fungi, bacteria, viruses) and animal pests (insects, mites, nematodes) as well as to so-called stress factors such as climatic variation or aridity, poor soil quality, crop rotation practices and others. The idea of genetic engineering, then, is not to invent freakish hybrids but rather to improve certain properties of important cultivated plants.

An equally important goal of research is the transfer of genes with nitrogen-fixing capacity onto grain. Ideally, seed varieties which result from such research endeavours should lead to the cultivation of plants which fit into the concept of "sustainable" agriculture, i.e. they should not abet erosion or leaching of the soil. To complete the packet of *desiderata*, a variety should afford dependable or even high yields at low production costs.

The big edge that recombinant genetics has over conventional breeding is that the desired properties can be systematically sought, identified, extracted ("snipped") from a plant or almost any other organism, and within a relatively short time transferred ("spliced") to another plant. The result is the same as that achieved with conventional methods, but without the costly and time-consuming cross-breeding they involve.

In addition, gene technology has the capability to provide growers with a greater diversity of hardy plant varieties by transposing properties from one

[8] There are other desirable and indispensable characteristics such as peace, respect for human rights and the preservation of human dignity. These, in turn, make a reduction of the prosperity gap between the world's rich and poor countries necessary, as well as a peaceful resolution of diverse political, economic, religious, ethnic and other competing interests. In the present context, these "macro-level goals" will be neglected, as they depend on different variables from a successful implementation of genetic engineering and biotechnology in the agriculture of poor countries.

[9] See OECD, *Biotechnology, Agriculture and Food* (Paris, 1992); see also C. De Groot, "Forestry Biotechnology" in *Biotechnology and Development Monitor*, No. 5, Dec. 1990, 20 ff.

species to another—a further advantage it has over conventional methods. For example, the resistance to such and such a pest possessed by a variety of bean can be built into maize. To a substantial number of researchers, biotechnology - especially agricultural biotechnology—presents huge opportunities for international development.[10] It is obvious that the realisation of these possibilities is expected to be of substantial advantage to the farmers and hence to the rural communities as a whole.[11]

2 *The Reality*

Today a significant part of this theoretical potential is on its way to practical realisation. Some potentialities have already been realised: Several case studies show that over the years biotechnology and—so far only to a lesser extent—genetic engineering have made possible marked concrete advances in the direction of higher food security, be it through resistance to fungal and viral diseases in major food crops or through improved plant properties.[12] The development of new plant protection techniques with the aid of genetic engineering and biotechnology (primarily transposing selected traits of *Bacillus thuringiensis* into crops) has already led to noteworthy progress in respect of the environment and lessened dependence on chemical weapons.[13]

Particularly where arable land is getting to be scarce and the use of fertilisers and plant protection agents is nearing the ecologically tolerable limit, genetic engineering and biotechnology, by providing novel products and mechanisms of action, can indeed bring farmers closer to solving some of the current agricultural problems[14]—problems either not solvable with traditional technologies or else only with a far greater expenditure of time.[15] No one can add to the area of arable land available on earth. But with the aid

[10] See e.g. G.J. Persley (ed.), *Agricultural Biotechnology: Opportunities for International Development* (CAB International/World Bank, Oxford, 1990); see also G.H. Toenniessen, "Plant Biotechnology and Developing countries" in *TIBTECH*, Vol. 13, Sept. 1995, 404–9.

[11] See e.g. J.F.G. Bunders (ed.). *Biotechnology for Small-scale Farmers in Developing Countries. Analysis and Assessment Procedures* (VU university Press, Amsterdam 1990); B.J. Miflin, "Plant biotechnology: Aspects of its application to Industry" in *Proceedings of the Royal Society of Edinburgh*, Vol. 99b, No.3 1992, 153–63.

[12] See I. Potrykus (ed.), *New Horizons in Swiss Plant Biotechnology—from the Laboratory to the Field.* Proceedings of a Symposium organised at the ETH Zürich on the occasion of the 125th anniversary of the Department of Agronomy and Food Science, (Zürich, 1996); see also A.F. Krattiger and A. Rosemarin, (eds.), *Biosafety for Sustainable Agriculture*, (Stockholm Environment Institute, Stockholm, 1994), s. 1.

[13] See P. Commandeur and J. Komen "Biopesticides: Options for Biological Pest Control Increase" in *Biotechnology and Development Monitor*, No. 14, Mar. 1993, 3 ff.

[14] See Bunders and Miflinn. 11 above, 153–63; see also J.M. Walker and E.B. Gingold *Molecular Biology and Biotechnology* (The Royal Society of Chemistry,. Reprint, 2nd ed., Cambridge, 1992).

[15] See e.g. for China Z. Chen and H. Gu, "Plant Biotechnology in China" in *Science*, Vol. 262, 15 Oct. 1993, 377 ff.

of new plants "made to measure" using gene technology and with biotechnological methods it is possible to wrest more food from the land we have with less energy input (fertilisers) and less problematic plant protection.

Based on the empirical evidence already compiled by the International Labour Organisation (ILO) on the effects of biotechnological and gene-technological interventions in Third World agriculture, the ILO draws the conclusion that the positive impact could prove more far-reaching than that resulting from the application of present-day mechanical and chemical technologies.[16]

In spite of the widely uncontested favourable potential of genetic engineering and biotechnology, the climate of opinion in the industrial countries remains sceptical, even to the point of rejection. This has to do with the following perceived social and ecological/biological risks:

- Dangers to public health and environmental safety;
- Aggravation of the prosperity gap between North and South, and
- Growing disparities in the distribution of income and wealth within poor societies, as well as
- Loss of biological diversity.

All of these risks have ethical relevance.

B The Risks

There is a wealth of scientific and popular discussion concerning the risks of genetic engineering and biotechnology.[17] To a great extent, it can be compared to the earlier discussion about the "green revolution", an agricultural technology consisting of high yielding varieties, fertilisers, irrigation, pest control and mechanisation.[18] The improved seeds of the green revolution

[16] See ILO (Technology and Employment Program)—e.g. P. Bifan, *New Biotechnologies for Rural Development*, (Geneva 1989); see also International Service for National Agricultural Research (ISNAR)—e.g. J. Komen and G. Persley, Agricultural Biotechnology in Developing Countries, ISNAR Research Report 2, The Hague, Sept. 1993, as well as International Rice Research Institute (IRRI): *Sharing Resposabilities: IRRI 1991—1992*, (Los Baños, 1992) and IRRI, *Rice Research in a Time Change* (Los Baños, 1993).

[17] For critical views of gene technology and biotechnology in relation to the Third World see: G. Altner, W. Krauth, I. Lünzer and H. Vogtmann (eds.), *Gentechnik und Landwirtschaft* (2nd edn, C.F. Müller, Karlsruhe, 1990; A. Studier (ed.), *Biotechnologie: Mittel gegen den Welthunger? Schriften des Deutschen Übersee-Instituts*, No. 8 (Hamburg, 1991); R. Walgate, *Miracle of Menace Biotechnology and the Third World* (Panos Dossier, London, 1990); H. Hobbelink, *Biotechnology and the Future of World Agriculture* (Zed Books, London, 1991); C. Fowler and P. Mooney, *Shattering—Food, Politics, and the Loss of Genetic Diversity* (University of Arizona Press, Tucson, 1990).

[18] For a short overview see K.M. Leisinger, "Toward a Green Evolution", *United Nations Development Forum*, New York, Mar. 1987, 8f. There is, however, one major difference between the old fashioned "green" and the incoming "gene" revolution: whereas the former had its origins in publicly funded plant-breeding institutions, the biotechnological advances are firmly in the hands of the private sector.

of the 1950s and 1960s were developed through systematic selection and crossing (hybridisation) with the objective of increasing the production volume and averting famines, particularly in Asia.[19] Despite undisputed successes in achieving a much higher volume of food production and the overall positive employment effect,[20] there was (and sometimes still is) vociferous criticism, making the green revolution responsible for growing disparities in poor societies and for the loss of biological diversity.[21]

The current public debate on the "gene revolution" often suffers—like that centred on the "green revolution"—from a failure to differentiate between the risks *inherent* in a technology and those that *transcend* it. This differentiation is of utmost importance in any attempt to reason out the matter on moral grounds.

1 Technology-inherent Risks

Technology-inherent risks arise when a technical action plan is designed to improve an existing situation, but then during the research or implementation phase unforeseeable problems and unwanted "side effects" crop up. Technology-inherent risks related to genetic engineering and biotechnology in food crops of developing countries would arise if genetically engineered organisms interacted differently from expected in the new environment and caused biological damage or put human life or health in jeopardy. The extend of such risks would be incalculable, were the interactions to prove irreversible and cumulative. Specialists refer to this category of risk as the risks to biosafety.[22]

Technology-transcending risks are of an altogether different nature.

2 Technology-transcending Risks

Technology-transcending risks emanate from the application of a technology in certain political and social circumstances. In developing countries these risks spring from both the course the global economy is taking and country-specific political and social configurations. The most critical fears in this connection have to do with three socio-political and ecological concerns:

[19] L. Brown, *Seeds in Change. The Green Revolution and Development in the 1970s* (London, 1970); S. Sen, *Reaping the Green Revolution* (New Delhi, 1975).

[20] See R. Baker, R.W. Herdt and B. Rose, *The Rice Economy of Asia. Resources for the Future* (Washington, DC, 1985); see also P.B.R. Hazell, C. Ramasamy, *The Green Revolution Reconsidered* (Johns Hopkins University Press, Baltimore, 1991).

[21] E.g. P.R. Mooney, *Seeds of the Earth* (Ottawa, 1980); also E.C. Wolf, "Beyond the Green Revolution. New Approaches for Third World Agriculture", in *Worldwatch Paper* No. 73. Washington DC, Oct. 1986.

[22] See A.F. Krattiger, A. Rosemarin (eds.), *Biosafety for Sustainable Agriculture* (Stockholm Environment Institute, Stockholm, 1994). See also G.J. Persley, L.V. Giddings, C. Juma, *Biosafety. The Safe Application of Biotechnology in Agriculture and the Environment*, ISNAR Research Report No.5, The Hague, 1993.

- Aggravation of the prosperity gap between North and South, e.g. through possible substitution of tropical agricultural exports with genetically engineered products, as well as the exploitation of indigenous genetic resources of the South without appropriate compensation by the North.
- *Growing disparities in the distribution of income and wealth within poor societies* because the privileged classes (by dint of better education or stronger financial position) profits earlier and more from the introduction of powerful technologies than do the socially disadvantaged. This problem accompanies every innovation, of course, but the high potency of genetic engineering and biotechnology stirs fears that the negative effects on development may prove specially severe.
- *Loss of biodiversity*, as farmers will increasingly use the small number of more productive genetically engineered varieties instead of the many thousands of traditional local varieties they have previously used.

In light of the growing disparities within specific poor societies or between developed and developing countries,[23] the dwindling competitiveness of a great many poor countries and the ongoing loss of biological diversity,[24] very serious heed must be paid to these concerns. Global sustainable development cannot be achieved with growing social disparities and a shrinking ecological foundation.

3 Technology-inherent Risks: Dangers to Public Health and Environmental Safety

A number of scientists and laymen perceive the risk that genetically engineered organisms could interact in the foreign environment into which they are released (by accident, for field-testing or production) other than theoretically expected by mainstream scientists and cause incalculable biological damage, including harm to human life or health. This perception depends on the hypothesis that genetically engineered organisms entail problems that are structurally different from conventionally altered organisms, a difference that could lead to an irreversible vicious circle. This *issue of biosafety* is a biological sub-issue of the common good discussion, as ecological and health harm of such magnitude would undoubtedly have negative economic and social consequences.

The evaluation of biosafety risks is normally done by science specialists and controlled by good scientific practices and an appropriate regulatory framework. There is a wealth of scientific literature on the deliberate release

[23] See for these issues *UNDP, Human Development Report 1996, 1994 and 1992* (Oxford University Press, New York, 1996, 1994 and 1992).

[24] For an introduction to this complicated problem area, see P.R. Ehrlich, "The Loss of Biodiversity. Causes and Consequences", in E.O. Wilson (ed.), *Biodiversity* (National Academy Press, Washington, DC., 1988), 21 ff. also the special ed. of *Ambio* (Journal of the Human Environment): Economics of Biodiversity Loss. Vol. XXI, No. 3, May 1992.

of plant pathogens, soil microbes and plant and animal symbionts either into new habitats or into areas where the potential for significant harm exists. Yet no major disasters have occurred, and today there is a broad consensus amongst scientists that much of the concern about the release of recombinant organisms is unwarranted.[25]

Their judgement supports the early principle of the US National Academy of Science that the safety assessment of a recombinant DNA modified organism should be based on the nature of the organism and the environment into which it will be introduced, not on the method by which it was modified.[26] As a social scientist, I am not competent to pass judgement on matters of biosafety. But I do have confidence in substantial majority opinion of natural scientists and therefore refrain from any further comment.

From an ethical point of view there is, however, one demand to be made. In as much as risk assessments of the technology-inherent kind can be controversial, it must be insisted that research and experimentation involving potential technology-inherent risks be carried out under the best biosafety conditions possible and the most stringent regulatory framework available. Although there has been significant progress with regard to the state of the art of biosafety in a number of countries, poor developing countries should not become the testing ground for potential technology-inherent risks.[27] The export of risks from technologically highly developed countries into poor countries is illegitimate, even were local law to permit it.

4. *Technology-transcending Risks*

The technology-transcending risks that need to be discussed in the context of genetic engineering, biotechnology and intellectual property rights in food crops of developing countries are as noted above:

- Aggravation of the prosperity gap between North and South;
- Growing disparities in the distribution of income and wealth within poor societies; and
- Loss of biodiversity.

(a) *Aggravation of the Prosperity Gap between North and South*

What is usually discussed under this heading is an international trade issue of a very general nature, i.e. economic risks for (some![28]) developing

[25] S.M. Gendel, "Biotechnology and Bioethics" in St. M. Gendel, A.D. Kline, D.M. Warren and F. Yates (eds.) *Agricultural Bioethics. Implications of Agricultural Biotechnology* (Iowa State University Press, Ames, 1990), 341.

[26] See G.J. *Persley, Beyond Mendel's Garden: Biotechnology in the Service of World Agriculture* (The World Bank, Washington, DC.,1990), chap. 7, 67ff.

[27] See F. Wambugu, E. Zandvoort and K.V. Raman (eds.), *Biotechnology and Risk Assessment in an African Perspective* (Special Issue of the *African Crop Science Journal* on Biotechnology/Biosafety), Vol. 3, 1995 (Sept.).

[28] Here again it is not admissible to pronounce on the "developing countries" lumped

countries due to a loss of export opportunities. With genetic engineering and biotechnology it will become possible to produce in the laboratory or in temperate zones goods that have hitherto been grown exclusively in the tropics. This prospect gives rise to concerns that the resultant competitive edge could drive a number of tropical products off the market. The example commonly used to shed light on this issue is the production of vanilla aroma in the laboratory using biotechnological techniques, with existence-threatening effects on several tens of thousands of vanilla-producing small farmers in poor African countries.

Similar but even more far-reaching consequences could materialise in connection with cocoa. Genetically improved cocoa varieties could not only result in higher yields and a concomitant drop in prices. They could also lead to the dislodging of small hold production in the poor West African countries by plantation-scale farming in the newly industrialised economies of Asia. A comparable outcome might happen with vegetable oils.

Furthermore, countries like Cuba or Mauritius, which depend on sugar cane for a decisive share of their export earnings, could find themselves extremely hard pressed should industrial manufacture of the low-calorie protein sweetener thaumatin or similar substances come broadly to supplant sugar cane.[29] The story of thaumatin is one that fits very much into the context discussed here. Some 10 years ago Nigerian researchers at the University of Ife identified the sweetener thaumatin in the berries of *Thaumatococcus danielli*, which is common in the forests of that part of Nigeria. At that time, no industry was interested in using the fruit as a sweetener. With the advent of biotechnological possibilities, the gene for thaumatin—is a protein weight-for-weight some 1,600 times sweeter than sugar—has been cloned and is now being used for the industrial production of sweetener in the confectionery industry. Patents on the process have been registered, but the people from whose lands the gene was obtained never received any compensation.

Where genetic engineering and biotechnology in food crops of developing countries are concerned this category of risks is not of importance, as the farmers who grow food crops are not in danger of being threatened by

together, as this impact differs very much between countries which are net agricultural exporters, e.g., and those which must import much of their food. See P. Commandeur, G. von Roozendaal, *The Impact of Biodiversity on Developing Countries. Opportunities for Technology-Assessment Research and Development Cooperation*, a study commissioned by the Büro für Technikfolgen-Abschätzung (TAB) in the German parliament, Bonn, 1993, chap.3.

[29] Cf. A. Sasson, *Biotechnologies and Development* (UNESCO, Paris, 1988), 269–76; see also S. Jacobson, A.Jamison, H. Rothman (eds.), *The Biotechnical Challenge* (Cambridge, 1986), 96 ff; H. Hobbelink, *Bioindustrie gegen die Hungernden* (Rororo, Reinbeck, 1989), 46 ff. According to Robert Walgate in R. Walgate, *Miracle or Menace. Biotechnology and the Third World* (PANOS DOSSIER) (The Panis Institute, London, 1990), 161.

genetically engineered substitutes for their crops.[30] Nevertheless the risk of aggravation of the prosperity gap between North and South must be addressed because of its tremendous importance: From a *holistic political perspective* it cannot make sense to uncouple the North from the agricultural raw materials of the South, for this would plunge a large part of humanity into dire misery. It is incompatible with sustainable development, and hence a peaceful future for all the inhabitants of our planet, if life goes on getting better for a relatively small segment of the world's already affluent population, while for billions of others their already skimpy living standard stagnates or even shrivels.

In the perspective of *economic rationality*, however, it has to be expected that superior goods will conquer the market. Copper can serve as an example. Its price is determined by the metal's electrical conductivity. Once electric current can be conducted cheaper and better by glass or carbon fibre, for instance, copper will in due course no longer be used for this purpose—with corresponding consequences for demand and thus price. The substitution will take place even though crumbling prices may lead in countries like Zambia or Chile to mass unemployment, with all the human distress it brings.

The same market "logic" tells us to expect that if "lab vanilla" or "lab sugar" should prove cheaper or exhibit some other edge—healthier than the real thing, for example—over products previously imported from the South, then substitution will follow. Ultimately this process cannot be forestalled, not even by sizeable government intervention, which is not desirable anyway.

The solution to the product substitution problem must therefore lie in a concerted international endeavour to diversify the production structure in vulnerable countries and not in counter-market intervention. Here, better governance[31] and more appropriate long-term structural planning from the governments of the countries in danger, as well as a bigger allocation of funds from the international development establishment to the support of diversification efforts are urgently required. A comprehensive risk/benefit analysis of the substitution of agricultural export commodities from the tropics would also have to examine the alternative use of the land left fallow by substitution for increasing local food production, and perhaps ecologically opportune changes in how it is used as well—for afforestation in the framework of the "joint implementation" of the Climate Convention, for example.

In the context of the aggravation of the prosperity gap between North and

[30] There are, however, other technology-transcending risks coming from the "North" such as inappropriate food aid and subsidised export of surplus grain to developing countries, both having a deflating effect on food prices and creating a taste for foreign foods. Both effects work to the economic disadvantage of food crop producers in the South.

[31] World Bank, *Governance and Development* (Washington, DC,1992).

South there is one further important issue that has to be examined: who shall compensate whom for the use of genetic material from developing countries and how much shall the compensation amount to?

There is widespread fear that private enterprises and research institutes could gain control of the genes of plants native to the developing world free of charge, as it were, and use them for developing and producing superior varieties that would then be sold back to developing countries at high prices. Suppose a private seeds company discovered a property in an Ethiopian barley strain making it resistant to certain plant diseases, and genetically transferred this property to a wheat variety that would afterwards be commercialised in Ethiopia. Obviously, the farmers of Ethiopia, male and female, have contributed something by selecting and preserving this variety over a long period of time. It is also obvious that without the research and development work of the seeds company the "something" would not have been turned to use outside Ethiopia or in food grains other than the native barley. So, both parties, the farmers of Ethiopia and the seeds company, have contributed to the new wheat variety, and therefore both have some kind of an intellectual property right and thus a right to compensation.

The basic question of whether remuneration is due has been clearly and positively answered by Article 19 of the Rio Convention on Biological Diversity (UNCED 1992) and the virtually unanimous consensus of the agencies engaged in development. While the general political decision in favour of compensation has been taken, the technical details of how it should be handled in specific nations are still unclear. What especially needs unequivocal regulation is who should compensate whom for what, and how much this compensation should be. As a rough first approach I would recommend the following:

Who?	Those who benefit!
For what?	For varieties and species that have been cultivated and preserved by active agriculture; the unimproved genetic wealth of the world's Vavilov centers are the common heritage of humankind.[32]
How much?	Let us look at this in terms of a licence agreement and leave the price to the mechanism of supply and demand.

A step in the direction of satisfying both sides' claims to fair compensation would be to work out binding national and international regulations. Urgently needed, they should be designed to keep open access to the genetic riches of the developing countries and at the same time enable the people who have helped to build and conserve this wealth through decades of

[32] This does, however, not exclude that commercial enterprises which have an interest in the biological inventory of a specific biotope must pay a negotiated amount of money for the right of prospecting. See in this context the contract between Costa Rica's Conservation Programmme and National Biodiversity.

indigenous selection and traditional agriculture to profit equitably from the commercial returns on gene exports. From a development policy point of view it is desirable that funds that result from compensation of such genetic material support those who over centuries through their hard agricultural work helped to preserve the varieties in question. Money resulting from a fair compensation arrangement should not land in the private pockets of a corrupt upper-class which, because its members are politically powerful, has ready access to the pot.

It should not be difficult to find a simple and effective way to establish fair compensation. The INBio-Merck contract is a pilot; other mechanisms could deal with the matter by looking at the issue in the way of a licensing agreement, whereby those who use the genetic material from a traditional agricultural society pay a licence fee into a fund for the support of the national agricultural research of the gene-exporting country. As the Consultative Group for International Agricultural Research (CGIAR) already exists and does excellent work for the poor farmers of the world, one would not have to create a new institution instead of CGIAR or its subsidiary, the International Service for National Agricultural Research (ISNAR) could be requested to draft a proposal outlining how to deal with such compensation fees in a fair and constructive way.

From a business ethics point of view I would recommend that as long as there are no binding national regulations, seed corporations should not take a free ride but look at the issue in the way of a tacit licensing agreement and set aside the usual percentage of sales for the support of agricultural research in developing countries. It is a demonstrated fact that research supported by the development assistance efforts of a private enterprise can be successful.[33]

(b) *Risks Rooted in Growing Disparities in the Distribution of Income and Wealth in Poor Societies*

The use of genetically modified seeds adapted to the specific conditions of difficult biotopes can no doubt provide most desirable impulses to national agricultural development and tremendously benefit the farmers who use them. In a socially and politically deficient setting it can hardly bring about improvements in the condition of those who are not able to use the new varieties. Wherever unjust social and political power structures determine the distribution of wealth, income and access to the means of production, the lower social strata face great obstacles to economic and social progress. Perpetuated poverty is the result.

Where land ownership and tenancy systems, access to extension services, credit and marketing channels, as well as to new technologies, are governed

[33] See K.M. Leisinger, K.M. Schmitt and ISNAR (eds.), *Survival in the Sahel. An Ecological and Developmental Challenge* (ISNAR, The Hague/Basel, 1995).

by a socio-political power structure that favours only a small minority, technological progress cannot possibly be neutral in impact. The answer to the question who benefits and how much from the advent of new technologies and to what extent economic and social progress can be achieved depends decisively on the social and political configuration in place. Disease-resistant cassava, millet richer in protein or rice tolerant to stress can contribute to prosperity and thus enhanced food security only if the new varieties and other social advances come within the reach of the broad mass of the population, male and female. Whether this is possible and within what time depends on the political will to create the necessary national development framework. As poor farmers tend to be risk-minimising and not output-maximising even under the best social circumstances early adopters stand to gain more.

Today's perspective on the "green revolution" shows that, in countries where small farmers were supported by agricultural extension services, where they had access to land, inputs and credit—in other words, where the agricultural development framework assisted the endeavours of the small farmers—they were able to benefit much and early. Even where the "green revolution" made the "rich" richer, because they could use the new technologies earlier, on better land, with better inputs and less expensive credits—the poor also benefited over time, becoming less poor as agricultural modernisation proceeded. This may not be the best of all social results one can imagine, but in a world where more than 1.3 billion people live in absolute poverty such achievements should not go unappreciated.

Like the "green revolution", genetically engineered varieties for food crops are a land-saving technology, and as such can be of particular importance for those who have little or only marginal land. Whether or not the potential benefits become economic and social reality for the small farmers is not a question of the technology but of the social quality of the development policy. If land and tenure reforms are implemented, if there is support for the small farmers and other elements of a development-friendly environment, the benefits of a new technology can be scale-neutral. Where 90 per cent of the land belongs to 3 per cent of the population and where the agricultural extension and credit services are only available to the big landholders, the introduction of a new technology will lead to the deterioration of income distribution. The economic and social impact of genetic engineering and biotechnology can only be as good as the socio-political soil in which the resulting new varieties are planted.

Any technical advance, progress in genetics included, can only benefit those who have access to and understand the technology well enough to apply it properly. Every restriction on access, be it lack of schooling or feudal power-structures, has the effect of aggravating income discrepancies—pronouncedly so, when the technology is very potent.

These facts and causal connections are very important in any train of moral reasoning about intellectual property rights, genetic engineering and biotechnology. While the technology-transcending social risks of new technologies do exist, they are not caused by the technology as such and therefore cannot be prevented by that technology. The ethical "blame" and the need for reforms rest with the socio-economic framework within which these risks become reality. Today's state of the art in development policy points clearly to the reforms and institutional changes that have to be initiated in order to get at the roots of socio-economic problems.[34] The fact that the appropriate political will is the exception to an often deplorable rule ought to be scrutinised in the context of development ethics.

(c) *Loss of Biological Diversity*

A last technology-transcending risk that calls for discussion is the highly complex ethical and ecological problem of loss of biological diversity.[35] The total number of species on earth is not known. Various estimates range as high as 111 million, cautious estimates put the number close to 14 million, of which only about 1.7 million have been scientifically described.[36] Biodiversity provides the raw materials—combinations of genes—are the essential building blocks of plant varieties upon which sustainable agriculture depends.

Today, the speed of the loss of biodiversity is perceived to be faster than ever in human history. Various projections suggest that during each decade from 1975 to 2015 between 1 and 11 per cent of the world's species will have been committed to extinction.[37] While most laymen perceive the extinction problem in the context of animals like the African elephant, the rhino, the Asian tiger or the spotted owl, the real problem is not with species you can stir up emotions about: 95 per cent of lost species are very small insects, plants, microbes, fungi, algae, viruses or bacteria.

The extent of biological impoverishment all over the globe has been a source of great concern for many years.[38] More recently, the issue has been taken up again in the context of genetic engineering and biotechnology. To address so critical an issue in every conceivable context may be legitimate

[34] I. Serageldin, *Nurturing Development. Aid and Cooperation in Today's Changing World* (The World Bank, 1995).

[35] For an introduction to this complicated problem area, see P.R. Ehrlich, "The Loss of Biodiversity. Causes and Consequences" in E.O. Wilson (ed.), *Biodiversity* (National Academy Press, Washington, DC, 1988), 21 ff. see also N. Myers, *The Sinking Ark: A New Look at the Problem of Disappearing Species* (Pergamin, New York, 1979), as well as the special edition of *Ambio* (Journal of the Human Environment): Economics of Biodiversity Loss vol. XXI, No. 3, May 1992.

[36] See The World Resources Institute/UNEP/UNDP/World Bank, *World Resources. A Guide to the Global Environment* (1996–97, (Oxford University Press, New York, 1996), 247.

[37] *Ibid.*

[38] See J.H. Vogel, *Genes for Sale. Privatization as a Conservation Policy* (Oxford University Press, New York 1994), chap. 2; see also P.H. Raven, "Disappearing Species: A Global Tragedy" in *The Futurist*, Vol. 19, No. 5, 1985, 8–14.

from a political point of view, with the aim of generating more public—and hence political—awareness. To put the blame for the loss of biodiversity on genetic engineering and biotechnology may be a sexy tactic for advocacy groups, because "big business" is involved. Factually, however, it is wrong and therefore detrimental to conservation policies.

To avoid any misunderstanding, undoubtedly greater public and political awareness is necessary, because the loss of biological diversity is immensely regrettable for æsthetic, ethical, philosophical, ecological and economic reasons: with each species lost, the natural economy of individual nations and the world as a whole is diminished forever.[39] Because biological diversity and ecological stability are interconnected, biological systems become more vulnerable (less robust) as they become less diverse.[40] As cultural diversity is closely intertwined with biological diversity, further losses occur through depletion of the world's cultural heritage.

The loss of biodiversity is uniquely deplorable, since extinction of a species involves the irrecoverable loss of genetic resources whose value for Man and nature has never even been determined. Genetic engineering and biotechnology can make use of biodiversity in ways that were not possible before by identifying, isolating and using genes for purposes that are basically outside the original species. One can only speculate whether tropical rain forests, wetlands or reefs contain basic materials for decisive breakthroughs in the treatment of diseases which today are still regarded as incurable. One simply does not know whether an endangered plant contains a gene that might be of vital importance for a major food crop. As, to date, less than a tenth of 1 per cent of naturally occurring species have been used, we do not know what is at stake with the ongoing loss of genetic resources.[41]

For every complex problem there is one *simple solution*, and it is wrong. The main responsibility for the loss of biological diversity lies definitely *not* with genetic engineering and biotechnology. The paramount reasons for the reduction of biological diversity are human activities and, as a result of population growth, the spread of human beings into hitherto untouched ecosystems. In particular the destruction of tropical forests is one of the tragic results of this development.[42] According to various estimates, as much as 50 to 75 per cent, perhaps even 90 per cent, of all species are native

[39] Cf. P.R. Ehrlich, A. Ehrlich, "The Value of Biodiversity", in *Ambio*, Vol. 21, No. 3, 1992, 219–26.

[40] See R. Edwards, "Tomorrow's Bitter Harvest", in *New Scientist* 17.Aug. 1996, 17ff.

[41] C. Perrings , C. Folke, K.G. Müller, "The Ecology and Economics of Biodiversity Loss: The Research Agenda", in *Ambio*, vol. 21, No. 3, 1992, 205.

[42] For details see: Enquete Commission "Vorsorge zum Schutz der Erdatmosphäre" of the German Bundestag (eds.), op. cit. p. 495 ff. The dying-out of species has always been a concomitant of evolution, but the speed and extent of this process have increased dramatically as a result of the destruction of forests, growing pollution, and other changes in the habitats of threatened species.

to the tropical rain forests. Since these forests are currently being destroyed more rapidly than all other habitats on earth, the extinction of species is today more massive than ever before in the history of mankind—presumably one species every hour since the mid-1980s.[43] What stepped up global warming will do to biodiversity can only be guessed.

The potential impact of genetic engineering and biotechnology on the number of species available to mankind is minimal. Farmers who gain access to varieties that are resistant to or tolerant of plant diseases and animal pests as well as to stress factors, such as poor soil quality, will not continue to cultivate inferior varieties. If traditional varieties are not preferable in taste or attractive for cultural reasons, it will simply not be in the farmers' interest to use them if they are vulnerable to fungi or fall easy prey to insect pests. Precisely because farmers find new varieties advantageous, the number of food crop varieties has diminished throughout the world over the last 100 years; farmers discontinue cultivating of traditional varieties because modern varieties are more remunerative.

To fight against genetic engineering and biotechnology because they make available superior varieties to the small farmer in developing countries is the wrong way to join battle against the continuing loss of biodiversity. If one shares the conviction that a loss of biodiversity is regrettable for many reasons—and I do share this conviction—then the main battlefield must be national conservation strategies for tropical forests, mangroves and other wetlands, rivers, lakes and coral reefs.

For the safeguarding of traditional food crop varieties which are under substitution pressure from improved varieties two synergistically applied strategies will bring success: *in vivo* and *in vitro* conservation. Both strategies need a strong national commitment and reliable international support.

If one wants preservation of biodiversity *in vivo*, one has to give financial or other incentives to small farmers of both sexes in developing countries to continue to cultivate varieties which they otherwise would not cultivate. It would be politically unrealistic and economically unfair to the small farmer community to expect it to forego an available benefit here and for the sake of the long-term global availability of a genetic resource. The need for capacity building, engaging local residents and other stakeholders as well as for promoting co-operation between organisations and institutions has been established.[44] As the protection of genetic crop resources in their natural agro-ecosystems seems to be advantageous, *in vivo / in situ strategies* need specific strong support. At present the small farmers in developing countries have no incentive to conserve-another "tragedy of the commons".

[43] Enquete Commission, "Vorsorge zum Schutz der Erdatmospäre" of the German Bundestag (eds.), *Schutz der Tropenwälder. Eine internationale Schwerpunktaufgabe* (Bonn, 1990),495.

[44] K.R. Miller, *Balancing The Scales: Guidelines for Increasing Biodiversity's Chances Through Bioregional Management* (World Resources Institute, Washington, DC, 1996).

If one wants conservation *in vitro*, one must make sure that international agricultural research institutes all over the world have adequate resources for their gene banks. Here fair compensation for genetic material comes in again: if the preservation of certain varieties becomes economically interesting because they contain genes which are valuable for other purposes, new motivations for the continued cultivation of traditional crops develop.

The benefits of genetic conservation are long term and rarely predictable, whereas commercial profit expectations are rather short term and depend to a large degree on predictability.[45] Hence the motivation behind patenting and other forms of intellectual property rights will in most cases not be conservation as such. Nevertheless, granting intellectual property rights to scarce genetic information could become part of a successful conservation strategy, as it would assign value to resources that are otherwise considered to be "free".[46]

Traditional plants and their genetic information have long been important to agriculture and medicine; genetic engineering and biotechnology are opening up new frontiers. As matters now stand those small and big, private and state, male and female farmers who conserve traditional varieties, and with them genetic information, have today no financial incentive for conservation and would become only residual claimants to the royalties paid by those who use that preserved information.[47] Ultimately someone will have to pay for conservation: it should be those who benefit!

5 The Ethical Analysis: Ambivalence of Technological Progress

Coming to a conclusion about the ethical aspects of intellectual property rights in the context of genetic engineering and biotechnology in food crops of developing countries is like discussing technical progress in general: we must live with ambivalence:

On the one hand, there are clear benefits from genetic engineering and biotechnology. They have the potential to increase production and productivity, enhance the environment, and improve food safety and quality.[48] As intellectual property rights—regardless of who owns them—demonstrably

[45] The Crucible Group, *People, Plants and Patents. The Impact of Intellectual Property on Biodiversity, Conservation, Trade and Rural Society*, (IDRC, Ottawa, 1994), 5.

[46] Not for wild species, see M.A. Gollin, "An Intellectual Propery Right Framework for Biodiversity Prospecting", in W.V. Reid *et al. Biodiversity Prospecting: Using Genetic Resources for Sustainable Development* (World Resources Institute, Washington, DC, 1993), 159–98. See also The Crucible Group, n. 45 above; for a critical point of view see M.B. Marques, *Patenting Life. Foundations of the Brazil–United States Controversy* (Fundaçao Oswaldo Cruz, Rio de Janeiro, 1993).

[47] See J.H. Vogel, *Genes for Sale. Privatization as a Conservation Policy* (Oxford University Press, New York, 1994).

[48] See A. Krattiger, in: F. Wambugu, E. Zandvoort, K.V. Raman, (eds.), *Biotechnology and Risk Assessment in an African Perspective* (Special issue of the *African Crop Science Journal* on Biotechnology/Biosafety) Vol. 3 1995 (Sept.), p.i.

trigger further research and innovation, they also constitute a positive element in the context of innovation in the field of genetic engineering and biotechnology.

These desirable contributions to the common good have to be set against a number of economic, social and ecological risks, most of which are of a technology-transcending nature, i.e. neither caused nor preventable by the technology as such. In this respect, progress with genetic engineering and biotechnology is no different from any other form of technological and societal progress, which, as the German theologian Helmut Gollwitzer said, is "nothing other than the unremitting struggle to secure its positive aspects, learning to live with the dangers that come with it and surmounting the impairments it causes".[49] Exactly what constitute the "positive aspects", "dangers" and "impairments" in a given case is the stuff of dispute. The valence of a certain effect of technological progress is very much a function of individual value judgements. Solutions in the sense of a definitive decision on the ethical dilemma thus conjured up are not possible. Depending on how someone judges the worth of a good gained or lost through the march of technology, either the gain or the loss will bulk larger.

Technological innovation is no panacea—it is just one stone in a large and complex socio-economic mosaic. Whether the economic blessing becomes a social curse depends on the political and the broad social ramifications. A technology can only be as good as the warp and woof of a society permits.

Social and ecological risks materialise because a gap opens between human scientific technical prowess and human willingness to shoulder moral and political responsibility. The risks lie in the political, economic and social milieu in which technology is applied. If and when poor small farmers have access to land, to agricultural extension services, to marketing opportunities, to working equipment and to fair terms of credit, then higher-yielding seeds adapted to the biotope and resistant to pests can be developed with the use of genetic engineering and biotechnology, and bring noteworthy advantages and more food to the mass of small farmers.

As far as the biosafety issue is concerned, risks that are not allowed to be taken in industrial countries with their stringent regulatory framework should not be exported to developing countries. If genetically engineered organisms and biotechnological procedures are used in developing countries, state of the art quality management must be applied, taking into consideration the specific conditions of the countries concerned.[50] But even then leftover risks will remain. Risks—calculable risks—must be taken, otherwise technological progress becomes impossible. Such risks should not be

[49] H. Gollwitzer, *Krummes Holz—Aufrechter Gang: Zur Frage nach dem Sinn des Lebens. 10. Auflage* (Christian Kaier Verlag, München, 1985), 142.

[50] See e.g. R. Fredrikson, S. Shantaram, K.V. Raman, (eds.), *Environmental Impact and Biosafety: Issues of Genetically Engeneered Sorghum*, Special Issue of *African Crop Science Journal*, Vol. 3, No. 2, 1995.

insouciantly accepted—but the worst possible problem-solver in this case would be technophobia.

As Carl Friedrich von Weizsäcker has put it, you do not make a bicycle safer to ride by wedging the handlebars fast. In 1957 he pointed out that if humankind today wished to do without technology and the planning that goes with it, then it would have to be prepared and able to decimate the number of people in the world.[51] He was referring to the world population at the time, two and a half billion people, who owed their very lives to industry, transportation and intensive agriculture—in short, to technology. Despite its perils, wherever technological progress has taken place—in the past mainly in the industrial West—it has created the material foundations of prosperity and security for broad classes of society. The developing world will not be able to develop economically and socially without it either.

There is no way of getting around the ambivalence that is intrinsic to every technical advance. In the context of the application of genetic engineering and biotechnology in food crops of developing countries, the dilemma posed by technical change can be between the political objective of national food security and the interests of poorer farmers: Without a change in technology there may be an imbalance between supply of and demand for basic food commodities while a changing technology could make it more difficult for smaller farmers, forcing them to spend more time and resources to adjust to the new production conditions.[52]

But the knowledge that ambivalence and ethical dilemmas exist should also not paralyse us. On the contrary, it must serve to clarify the course of action and expand our horizon of responsibility. Only action that is informed by an awareness of the ambivalence makes the socially meaningful deployment of top-class technology possible. Participative technology assessments and co-operation between different stakeholders will enhance the positive impact of technological change.[53]

The developing countries are faced with the formidable task of doubling their food output over the next 25 years, and this—in contrast to how it has so often been done in the industrial countries—in ways sparing of the environment and resources. Population pressure has already begun to affect the environment in large parts of the developing world. Because of intensive land use and widespread biomass shortage, cultivated soils are being depleted of essential nutrients and organic matter. Fisheries, livestock and forestry resources are also under increasing strain. Unless countries with

[51] C.F. Von Weizsäcker, *Die Verantwortung der Wissenschaft im Atomzeitalter. 7. Auflage* (Kleine Vandenhoeck-Reihe, Göttingen, 1986), 67.

[52] See G.J. Persley, *Beyond Mendel's Garden: Biotechnology in the Service of World Agriculture* (The World Bank, Washington, DC, 1990), chap. 4, 40ff.

[53] See W. Van den Daele, A. Pühler, H. Sukopp, *Grüne Gentechnik im Widerstreit. Modell einer partizipativen Technikfolgenabschätzung zum Einsatz transgener herbizidresistenter Pflanzen* (VCH-Verlag, Weinheim/Basel, 1996).

high population growth achieve a social transformation that results in a substantially lower birth rate and unless they start regenerating their resource base, they will continue to move towards a major social and ecological disaster.[54]

In order to secure positive economic and social development possibilities in the South and the North, what is needed are political and social national as well as international reforms.[55] At the same time, along with its utilitarian alignment it would be desirable that technological progress take on a socio-ethical orientation.[56] If genetic engineering and biotechnology were oriented to a greater extent on the needs of the poor people in the developing countries, particularly on those of smallhold farmers, they could become indispensable to the whole development effort.

More publicly financed research North and South is summoned to make a bigger contribution to finding expedient solutions. The emphasis is on *public* research, because the fruits of public research can be passed on to small farmers at cost or, via government channels, even free of charge. This cannot be done with the results of research sponsored by private enterprise. When the research priorities are determined by the financial return on investment, the needs of those who have the purchasing power are likely to have high priority, whereas the needs of the poor small farmers (if and where they are different) are likely to receive a low priority. For this reason public research must be strengthened. The Consultative Group on International Agricultural Research (CGIAR), with its focus on the needs of the developing countries, could play a conspicuous role in such an effort. In a number of countries, agricultural biotechnology seminars are already under way to assess research priorities and turn them into feasible programmes.[57]

More ought to be done in this respect. And there must be more and more intensive co-operation between the private and the public sectors. Were the private sector to become more receptive to the needs of the international development effort and the international research community, funds already in short supply and valuable time could be saved. The special knowledge and know-how and the different experience—and patented intellectual

[54] For a comprehensive analysis of the global population problem and solutions see: Klaus M. Leisinger, K. Schmitt, *All Our People. Population Policy with a Human Face* (Island Press, Washington, DC, 1994).

[55] For details see I. Serageldin, *Nurturing Development. Aid and Cooperation in Today's Changing World* (The World Bank, Washington, DC, 1994).

[56] For an introduction see M. Qizilbash, "Ethical Development" in *World Development*. Vol. 24. No. 7, 1209–21 and the references.

[57] See J. Komen, J.I. Cohen, Z. Ofir, (eds.), *Turning Priorities into Feasible Programs* (ISNAR, The Hague, 1996). See also J. Komen, J. Cohen, Lee, Sing-Kong, (eds.), *Turning Priorities into Feasible Programs* (ISNAR, The Hague, 1995). For lessons from the country studies see C. Brenner, *Integrating Biotechnology in Agriculture. Incentives, Constraints and Country Experiences* (OECD Development Centre, Paris) 1996.

property as well—that are at the disposal of the private sector but are used only selectively for lucrative markets in the industrial countries could be passed on via donated transfers or very favorable licensing terms to public research institutes in developing countries. This can be done, as a concrete example shows: Ciba has made available a gene of *Bacillus thuringiensis* to IRRI, the International Rice Research Institute. Co-operation with the private sector and other "coalitions against famine" could be an important unconventional way to make progress faster and less expensive.

In many respects the conclusions set forth by the Club of Rome in one of its reports apply to our discussion: "[l]iving as we do at the onset of the first global revolution, on a small planet which we seem hell-bent to destroy, beset with conflicts, in an ideological and political vacuum, faced with problems of global dimensions which the fading nation states are impotent to solve, with immense scientific and technological possibilities for the improvement of the human condition, rich in knowledge but poor in wisdom, we search for the keys to survival and sustainability".[58]

Sustainable development—and sustainable food security—will not be achievable without better governance and a new dimension of solidarity between the "rich" and the "poor" of this world—but also not without new technologies such as genetic engineering and biotechnology.

[58] A. King, B. Schneider, *The First Global Revolution. A Report by the Council of the Club of Rome* (Simon & Schuster, London, 1991), 193.

14

RIGHTS, COMPENSATION, INDIGENOUS KNOWLEDGE SYSTEMS AND THE STRATEGY OF GLOBAL INTELLECTUAL PROPERTY MANAGEMENT: THE CHALLENGE

Joseph D. Ben-Dak *

I Introduction

This is a very exciting time to talk about applications of bio-resource-derived technology, and especially biotechnology applications that have direct relevance to the emerging world such as agricultural biotechnology and especially the commercialisation of bio-engineered plants. A number of products have been introduced into the market-place now which provide a basis for talking about real products and real issues.

The number of the people in the world should probably double in 40 or 50 years. We must realise that in the lifetime of many of our children, they will be sharing with this planet with 10 billion other people.

Today we use about 6 million square miles to cultivate the food for the world. According to Robert Farley of Monsanto Company, if we had not made increases in agricultural technology from 1950 to the present day, we would have had to use about 15 million square miles, the size of both of North and South America combined, to meet today's needs for food, feed and fiber. The pressures on land to feed 8 to 10 billion people will be enormous. Without new technology, demands will be chaotic. The advances in recent years that we have witnessed include plant breeding, the use of agro-chemicals and mechanisation and irrigation. Biotechnology presents a new tool and can have a significant impact on the future. The plant biotechnology promises to deliver a stream of new products and new industries related to areas such as bio-fuels, chemicals and polymers, health and nutrition, food processing and improved agronomically significant plants. We can see the first wave of products entering the marketplace which have better tolerance to herbicide, insect or disease resistance. We are seeing the

* Principal Advisor, Technology and Science, UNDP and Chief, Global Technology and Business Group. The author would like to record his indebtedness to Mark Austin, H. Walter Haeussler, Leonard Mackey, Dr Heinz Goddar and the Rural Advancement Foundation International (RAFI) for useful contributions and exchanges.

potential of fruits and vegetables with better storage properties and flavour. Even newer products can generate plant materials that reduce health problems by reducing carcinogens or certain fatty acids. We even see plants that can produce biodegradable plastics or pharmaceuticals or vaccines.

The use of animals for the production of vaccines and various therapeutic materials has been going on for many years. Now, however, there is the opportunity to create genetically modified animals that are living "bio-reactors" which generate high value added products. This is a very different use from the way Man has traditionally used animals and may in any given country raise ethical implications, as well as issues related to the subsequent use of the flesh of these animals in the food chain.

The use of biotechnology to create transgenic animals, or animals which have been administered recombinant DNA products to enhance performance, such as bovine somatatropin to increase milk, provide the possibility for enhanced production of protein, but also raised biosafety concerns.

In any event, it is clear that animal husbandry, when combined with biotechnology, has a potential for being a powerful tool to enhance the economic well-being of the farm population and can even be the basis of new industries.

Perhaps the most sophisticated and highest value-added bio-resource-based industry component is that related to the biomedical industry, where products are produced which have a prophylactic or therapeutic effect on humans or animals, with respect to specific disease states or general physiological wellbeing. The scope of products that are generated by such industries varies from simple chemical compounds to complex bio-reactive molecules such as, protein molecules, hormones, enzymes, monoclonal antibodies, genes, gene fragments, and genetic receptors, and the like. In addition to treatment modalities, such biomedical companies can also produce diagnostic materials and kits to allow for the testing of physiological states and conditions and the determination of the presence or absence of disease or suceptability to disease.

These commercial areas, because of their high value-added element and, because of the sophistication that exists in the developed world with respect to the medical and biomedical industry, present a real challenge to developing countries to compete. But where the industry initially can develop to meet unique local or regional needs, or where it has a proprietary position either through its own intellectual property rights or intellectual property rights licensed from others, such a company can make a substantial impact on a developing country's economy, not only directly but indirectly.

As high technology infrastructure in a developing country grows, one of the goals of the development policy should be the training of personnel, and the return of native personnel from outside the country who have been educated in the technology, so that together with accumulated skills, knowledge and experience, in-country staff can develop and operate independent medical biomedical businesses.

Developing countries do not form a homogeneous block. They do not have equal scientific capabilities, social structures or economic goals. There is no such thing as a typical country, so that one-size-fits-all when it comes to bio-resource technology, how it will be used, and how it will benefit and affect an industry, in particular, or the country in general. For example, developing countries have unequal capability to develop biotechnology and to deal with its overall impacts. Developing countries can be divided into a number of categories: (1) countries with no biotechnology capability; (2) countries with a growing research programme and an acceptable policy, but with little actual development; (3) countries with biotechnology capability with linkage to more advanced countries for training of scientists and for technology transfer in both directions; and finally, (4) countries with a modern up-to-date biotechnology programme, a national policy and strong connections within the country between the public and the private sectors and between both those sectors and their equivalent sectors in more advanced countries.

In any country, the social and the political processes must be considered as well as the positive and the negative impacts of biotechnology or other bio-resource-based technology on the national structure. High technology is a necessary, but not a sufficient, condition to advance social good in the food, fibre, medicine, vaccines and other areas. Any country has to deal with the uneven playing field throughout the world with a multiplicity of skills and systems: there must be a constant review of worldwide developments in the areas such as biotechnology and a study of the likely impacts on the region in question, so that the policies can be established and take advantage of opportunities and avoid or reduce potential negative impacts. There must be a continuing effort to increase north/south, south/north and south/south interactions and understanding of bio-safety, bio-conservation, and national capacity development of both science and markets. There must be the availability of negotiating skills to enhance the bargaining power of the developing countries with various sources of technology and funding. There must be in-country participation of all social, economic and political groups in the policy-making process regarding the direction and nature of biotechnology development. There must be development programmes aimed at creating and maintaining necessary skills sets, and motivating those trained people to more developed areas, and to prevent paying too high a price for external developments. There must be rational co-operation between national public and private sectors to increase industrial capacity in the country. There must be policies to increase public sector biotechnology research and development trusts where the technology is not necessarily economically attractive to the private sector in the short run. And finally, there must be policies which promote business investment, business development and education, which are sufficient and necessary for the particular country, not only in its present time but for its next logical development stage. Overarching all of this there must be a logical policy and regulatory oversight system to foster responsible development while protecting the public, if rapid growth and international investment is expected.

II Issues and Contexts

There is potential for a fundamental tension between the philosophy and terms of TRIPS and those of the Convention. TRIPS is directed *inter alia* to (1) recognising that IPR are private rights which can be licensed, transferred or sold only if and to the extent the holder of the rights so desires, with a few limited exceptions; and (2) upgrading standards of protection and enforcement of IPR in each country of the WTO.

The Convention is directed *inter alia* to assuring that technology necessary to meet the objectives of the Convention is developed and transferred where it is needed. Moreover, the interests of contracting parties that provide genetic resources, especially developing countries, are specially treated. In general, under the Convention, the owner of technology is required to transfer and license it. This is contrary to the general philosophy of TRIPS.

Many nations executed the Convention without reservation. But note, for example, the reservation of the United States in signing the Convention: "[a]s a matter of substance, we find particularly unsatisfactory the texts treatment of intellectual property rights, technology transfer and biotechnology". Resolution of this potential tension, if and when it arises, as well as reservations such as those expressed by the United States, will require enlightened negotiation of the specific facts involved to reach a satisfactory result.

The Biodiversity Convention (the 1992 Convention on Biological Diversity) has brought into focus the need to conserve biological diversity, yet sustainably use components of that biodiversity, while dealing with the issue of the "fair and equitable sharing of the benefits arising out of the utilization of genetic resources".

On the other hand, in the scientific research establishments, as well as the industrial organisations in the industrialised world, biodiversity derived biotechnology research as yielded benefits which are recognised as having great potential. Intellectual property rights are frequently obtained in the property obtained or derived from biological-genetic resources. At about the same time the Biodiversity Convention was progressing through its stages of creation, ratification and implementation, the World Trade Organisation (WTO) through the GATT/TRIPs agreements was causing developing nations to re-examine their attitudes and approaches towards intellectual property rights. In a very practical sense, this has moved the debate from the position of whether a developing country should have intellectual property laws, to the place where the question is now, how soon within a finite time frame will a country adopt minimal intellectual property law standards conforming to the TRIPs requirements.

Preamble: "conservation and sustainable use of biological diversity is of critical importance . . . for which purpose access to and sharing of both genetic resources and technologies are essential". This preamble is important, as in a fundamental way it represents the essential agreement between first and third world.

Perhaps the most significant change in direction created by the Biodiversity Convention was the expression of sovereign control over genetic resources rather than the older "common heritage" principle. The concept of sovereign control over genetic resources provides a foundation for the control of access to these resources, with the access being on mutually agreed terms with informed consent. This becomes the basis for gaining equitable compensation for the use of the genetic diversity.

Another new direction of the Biodiversity Convention was the recognition of the rights of indigenous peoples and their practices, as well as community knowledge in the sustainable use of genetic resources. This of course raises significant questions concerning protecting the indigenous peoples' knowledge and practices, since group rights traditionally have not been amenable to protection in intellectual property rights systems. The Biodiversity Convention points out the need to address the issues but does not give answers.

Article 1 *Objectives:* "the fair and equitable sharing of the benefits arising out of the utilization of genetic resources appropriate transfer of relevant technologies taking into account all rights over resources and to technologies". The purpose of the Objectives cited above can be taken as the indicator of the scope of both the possible and necessary dialogue.

Article 15(1) of the Biodiversity Convention makes it clear that sovereign rights over genetic diversity can be made the subject of national legislation. This clearly reverses the earlier concept of free access based on the common heritage of man. Article 15(5) requires that there must be mutually agreed upon terms for access, with informed consent.

Article 15(5): "*Access to Genetic Resources* shall be subject to prior informed consent of the contracting party providing such resources, unless otherwise determined by that party". Here the Convention opens the Pandora's box of questions as to the status of previous, uninformed consent and the consequent issue what mechanisms should be used to register and track consent.

With respect to intellectual property rights, Article 16(2) states that "in the case of technology subject to patent and other intellectual property rights, . . . access and transfer [should be] provided on terms which recognize and are consistent with the adequate and effective protection of intellectual property rights". This language directly reflects the language of the TRIPs agreement (The Agreement on Trade Related Aspects of Intellectual

Property Rights) which is a portion of the GATT-TRIPs agreement developed by the World Trade Organisation.

Article 16 *Access to and Transfer of Technology:* this article calls for the transfer of technology and transfer (or licensing) of IPR as essential for the attainment of the objective of this Convention (paragraph 1). This is so under fair and most favourable terms, including on concessional and preferential terms where mutually agreed, and, where necessary, in accordance with the financial mechanism established by Articles 20 and 21 (paragraph 2). Moreover, developing countries which provide genetic resources are to be provided access to and transfer of technology and rights under intellectual property which makes use of those resources (paragraph 3). Further, parties to this Convention are to co-operate to ensure that patents and other intellectual property rights are supportive of and do not run counter to the objectives of the Convention (paragraph 5).

Adding great controversy, however, is Article 16(5) of the Biodiversity Convention which reads, "[t]he Contracting Parties, recognizing that patents and other intellectual property rights may have an influence on the implementation of this Convention, shall cooperate in this with regard subject to national legislation and international law in order to ensure that such rights are supportive of and do not run counter to its objectives". Many have argued that this section allows developing countries to demand that intellectual property rights do not interfere with the transfer of technology and the economic benefit that may flow to the developing country.

It has been pointed out frequently that the opening words of paragraph 5 do not make it clear whether intellectual property rights are considered supportive or non-supportive of the objectives of the Convention. This was deliberate and represents the tension between north and south, which was the same tension which was apparent in the GATT/TRIPs negotiations. Clearly TRIPs requires that patent protection be available for all technologies without discrimination (raising *inter alia* the issue of patenting life forms).

Ironically, the mere review of the realities of such transfers breeds the rare case of all these conditions being met.

Article 19, *Handling of Biotechnology and distribution of the benefits:* Contracting parties that provide genetic resources, especially developing countries, are to participate in biotechnological research activities and have priority access to the results and benefits arising from bio-technologies based upon such resources.

Here we find only lip service being paid to the reality of these provisions.

The following references are to Articles and paragraphs of TRIPS.

Preamble—"Recognizing that intellectual property rights are private rights".

Article 28, *Rights Conferred*—a patent shall confer on its owner the exclusive right to prevent others from making, using, offering for sale, selling or importing the invention covered by a patent. Note here that the "owners" definition in the farmer's rights dialogue is disputed.

Article 30, *Exceptions to Rights conferred:* members may provide limited exceptions to the exclusive rights provided by Article 28, provided such exceptions do not unreasonably prejudice the legitimate interests of the patent owner, taking account of the legitimate interests of third parties. Here individual country degrees of freedom in definitions are stipulated as possible.

Article 31, *Other use without authorization of the right holder*: This Article *limits* the circumstances and terms under which a patent holder may be compelled to license its patent; i.e., "compulsory licensing".

Article 39, *Protection of Undisclosed Information*—this Article provides for protection of information which is secret, has commercial value and has been subject to reasonable steps by a person lawfully in control of the information to keep it secret.

It appears that the creative tension between the Biodiversity Convention and the GATT/TRIPs intellectual property provisions will have a useful effect in causing the north and south to come to terms with an intellectual property rights-based system. That is a system which promotes the equitable sharing of benefits between north and south and which on one hand recognises the need to change intellectual property laws to deal with issues such as indigenous peoples' rights and traditional knowledge, while recognising that to create commerce and encourage infrastructure investment by the developed world and the developing world, a basic, uniform intellectual property system which recognises farmers' rights, indigenous peoples' rights and national sovereignty over biodiversity and which allows for more confident equitable technology transfer, not only from south to north but from north to south and also to south to south.

III The Recognition of Rights

A significant subset of issues that must be resolved is the relationship of indigenous knowledge to intellectual property rights. There is a clear need to integrate existing intellectual property laws with the need to recognise the intellectual property and indigenous knowledge. It may be that a separate scheme of intellectual property protection has to be developed which is distinct from, but interactive with, the present patent laws.

Clearly any process that seeks to define or regulate or administer indigenous peoples' rights should have real involvement of indigenous people in the organisation and in the process.

Having said the above, it is not always clear who speaks with authority for the indigenous people, and it may be that the person or NGO who asserts he speaks for a particular indigenous body may not have clear authorisation from that body to represent it.

Article 8 of the Biodiversity Convention establishes a duty to respect, preserve and maintain knowledge of practices and innovations related to the biodiversity-related knowledge of indigenous people and local and traditional communities. The Article also suggests the promotion of this knowledge and practice and encourages equitable sharing of benefits for use. Ultimately, however, this becomes a national issue, which in large part has be resolved through national legislation and agreement between a particular country and its indigenous peoples. Indigenous knowledge is again referred to in Article 17 and Article 18 of the Biodiversity Convention. None of the provisions in the Biodiversity Convention actually provids a definition of rights or protection.

The Secretariat to the Biodiversity Convention has prepared a review of the issues (UNEP/CBD/IC/2/14,20 May, 1994) and lists a number of approaches which include state recognition of communal rights, state recognition of appropriately defined forms of indigenous property rights including control of access to their land, better access to legal support, access to financial and technical resources for their own capacity building and the encouragement of marketing and production of their own products rather than developed country derivatives of those products.

In any event, requiring the intellectual property protection regime to track the origin of biodiversity-derived inventions i.e. the so-called Certificate of Origin Concept, is a highly useful concept. Some argue that the Certificate of Origin would be useless because unscrupulous people will simply ignore the requirement. But it is pointed out, for example, under US patent law that there is a duty of disclosure of all relevant prior art and information which may invalidate the patent application if the examiner is aware of it. If that disclosure is not made, any resultant patent can be invalidated. On that same footing, the international intellectual property regime could adopt the principle that disclosure must be made and, if good faith disclosure is not made, then the patent is unenforceable. This then takes the burden off the Patent Examiner or the International Patent Offices and puts it upon the individual or organisation seeking a patent. If the technology becomes viable, the individual will not want their patent found invalid and therefore they will comply. One can then more readily track the origin of materials, and indigenous people can feel that they have a very focused mechanism by which to bring parties to the bargaining table early in the process.

The simplest method for supporting indigenous rights and providing benefits to indigenous people is to allow the indigenous group to control access to its territory's biodiversity and for the group to give certificates of origin or have the power to enter material transfer agreements rather than the national government or in conjunction with the national government. This then, coupled with the inclusion of references to certificate of origin in intellectual property rights, makes a clear situation where the person wishing to use the indigenous information must reach an agreement with the indigenous community.

There are many initiatives worthy to be considered by multilateral organisations, governments, non-governmental organisations and other stakeholders which address the issue of recognition of rights.

In addition to certificates of origin as a rights-tracking device, a study of materials transfer agreements and specific contracts with a view to establishing a series of model agreements that may be considered by governments, corporations and indigenous communities.

Develop further the Model Law on Folklore by both UNESCO and WIPO with a view to encouraging national legislation and an international convention in support of recognition of inherent rights in indigenous knowledge.

Another approach is to conceive of rights, not as something owned, but literally as something earned. With indigenous peoples, this earning of rights would be defined around certain characteristics of their lifestyle, so that earning the rights is inherent in their daily activities. This is best exemplified by the idea of the role of indigenous communities in *in situ* conservation with FAO, the Consultative Group on International Agricultural Research and in the context of the Biodiversity Convention.

Knowledge is an important component of rights, in the proactive sense of being able to claim what is "rightfully" one's own. In this sense, dissemination of knowledge to indigenous populations about their rights is a key element in having them recognised. The preparation of a popular information kit to provide key information to indigenous people would go a long way in this direction. It should be prepared in close collaboration with key organisations and it should form the basis for seminars and discussions within indigenous peoples' organisations and communities.

An extension of the above concept is the idea of taking responsibility for husbanding one's rights. The convening of a meeting with indigenous organisations and informatics experts to discuss needs and means for safeguarding the development of indigenous knowledge and its exchange with others would be a significant step in this path.

The major area for combined efforts in producing the best strategy by securing rights in productive capacity seems to be in developing IPR in fields of *unique products*: i.e. technologies based on best, sustainable win-win utilisation of less developing countries' special fauna, flora, materials and human resources. This is taken up further in a later section.

IV Mediation Mechanisms

The Biodiversity Convention has done a great service to the world community in focusing attention on the rights of indigenous peoples in the context of "fair and equitable sharing" of compensation for intangible property. Unfortunately, no compensation scheme has been set forth in the Biodiversity Convention and, to an extent, the uncertainty surrounding the compensation issues with respect to indigenous peoples has actually retarded interaction between the north and the south with respect to bio-exploration and the sustainable use of biodiversity in tribal or ancestral land, and therefore use of and compensation for indigenous knowledge.

The United Nations Human Rights Commission Working Group on Indigenous Peoples is preparing a draft declaration on the rights of indigenous peoples, which attempts in part to address intellectual or community property rights.

Presently there is needed an ombudsman service/honest broker-deal assistance organisation/escrow service that might help facilitate bringing certainty to an uncertain area and perhaps catalyse the creation of model legislation.

It is the experience of a number of existing relationships between developing countries or organisations in developing countries and countries in the developed world that they deliberately avoid sample collection in indigenous areas to avoid dealing with the uncertainty surrounding indigenous peoples' deal-making and compensation. Thus, instead of indigenous people benefiting, they are frequently passively excluded from benefits because of uncertainty.

The proposed organisation would have potential roles in educating the indigenous community as to its rights, and the reality of the negotiating process. It could provide negotiation assistance in an open and forthright manner, such that both sides would be comfortable with the organisation's involvement. The organisation conceivably could provide implementation assistance in seeing that the deal negotiated was implemented and that the proceeds were properly administered. Alternatively, where there is dispute or controversy surrounding the indigenous people, for example controversy with their own government over what land they can control and what rights they have, or any other issues which make direct dealing impractical, as a last resort, the organisation could serve as an escrow organisation allowing the developed world to utilise information that they have apparently appropriately acquired but are uncertain how much or to whom to give compensation. This organisation could be a *sui generis* organisation or could be under the auspices of the UNDP, UNIDO, the World Court or even the clearing house mechanism for technology exchange envisioned by the Biodiversity Convention but not yet implemented.

V Compensation Strategies

Compensation issues can be divided into two broad categories: (1) what strategies or mechanisms can be utilised to ensure that compensation is both collected, tracked and allocated in a proper due course; and (2) what is the appropriate medium of compensation itself?

In line with issue (1), further study is needed of inventors' certificates and materials transfer agreements as a means of compensating indigenous communities and of safeguarding the intellectual integrity of these communities are worthy of study. Also, the possibility of establishing a special trust fund for the remuneration of indigenous knowledge on a programme and project basis as part of FAO's Farmers' Rights initiative has merit. Once the idea of rights is established clearly in the first place, creative strategies can be developed to ensure compensation is properly delivered.

Yet the issue of the compensation strategy begs the question (2) what is useful and appropriate compensation, not in quantitative terms as to how much (who negotiates the better deal) but in qualitative terms.

One of many issues which complicate the question of compensation for the use of traditional genetic resources is that, in addition to all the other problems, developed countries tend to think of compensation in terms of monetary compensation. For the most primitive indigenous people, insertion of money into their economy may be neither appropriate or productive. From the viewpoint of the developing country or the indigenous people within a developing country, depending on the state and condition of their own development, other things may be more important, for example, investments in capacity building including training, equipment, general technology, creation or expansion of local research and sampling capabilities, to free supply of products or services and, lastly, the more traditional up-front payment and royalty payments on a standard licence agreement for any products developed. The Biodiversity Convention in Article 15 seems to encourage technology passage back to the developing country, but it must be recognised that such agreements may be good to a particular developing country in general, but may not be adequate or appropriate compensation if indigenous people are to have fair and equitable sharing.

We are in danger now of "losing sight of the forest for looking at the trees". While there is a need for further evolution of the IPR system, both within individual countries and within the international community, the seeds of the real solution to compensation lay already in the language of both TRIPS and the Biodiversity Convention, for both of them remind us that the goal of these processes is sustainable development.

The Convention, Article 20(4), *Financial Resources*, states:

"Developing country implementation of these commitments under the Convention will depend on the effective implementation by developed countries of their commitments relating to financial resources and transfer of technology."

TRIPS, Article 66(2), *Least Developed Country Members*, states:

"Developed country members shall provide incentives to enterprises and institutions in their territories for the purposes of promoting and encouraging technology transfer to least developed country members in order to enable them to create a sound and viable technology base."

Both of these agreements speak of the inherent process of technology transfer to the developing countries, for the implicit purpose of capacity building and sustainable development. This is combined with the reality that it will not always be possible to compensate a single individual appropriately for a specific piece of genetic material. In fact, in the context of biodiversity and indigenous knowledge, such a compensation scheme may turn out to be the exception rather than the rule.

The overall focus must therefore be on the large-scale transfer of technology and capacity building on the regional and sub-regional basis, and the fostering of sustainable livelihoods for individuals and groups.

In order to fulfil this mandate, the developed countries need a conceptual framework from within which issues of compensation can be subsumed. Catalysis and the unique product framework provide such a context.

VI Catalysis and Unique Product Development

Catalysis is the process of accelerating positive transactions and developments within the private sector of developing countries, in large measure by identifying individuals, institutions and processes to foster that change. Positive is here understood to mean in line with the goals of sustainable human development. This is especially important in the developing country context, as many developing countries lack what might be called an "entrepreneurial infrastructure" that fosters business development and evolution.

So how do catalysis and unique products tie in to the IPR dilemmas posed earlier? Specifically, they provide both a framework and a context by which developing countries, developed countries, NGOs and private sector enterprises, especially multinationals, can create activities whose net effect is to redress the imbalances implicit in the Biodiversity Convention. The effects of such activities, which include the role of IPR, can focus on indigenous populations, countries or regions and will have a more significant effect than stand-alone IPR compensation schemes alone, while avoiding the impossibilities of exact assignment in communal knowledge or biologically-based rights agendas. This framework also helps address the previously discussed issue that in many cases with indigenous populations, monetary compensation *per se* can be a culturally inappropriate reward.

Catalysis activities deal with human infrastructure issues related to sustainable development. Within the developing country these may include:

- Establishment of national science and technology policy, including the formation of a national oversight and co-ordinating body dealing with issues ranging from government regulations, national technology goals and agendas, science education, trustful use of biotechnology, intellectual property rights, etc.;

- Identification and creation of enterprise support networks, both formal and informal;
- Training in local scale business management, entrepreneurial development, and more sophisticated management systems;
- Creation of databases for access to resources, market information, distribution, etc.;
- Access to financing;
- Establishment of centres of excellence;
- Networking of government, academic, NGO and private-sector research centres;
- Identification of catalytic individuals and enterprise mentors such as government officials, military personnel, leaders of women's groups, retired executives, etc;
- Definition of appropriate regional technology requirements and plans for transfer and adaptation of the same;
- Conversion of military enterprises to sustainable activities;
- Creation of distribution co-operatives and clearing-houses, especially for international marketing and export.

On a country scale a catalytic compensation system might include the following elements. In exchange for access to certain quantified germplasm, a multinational corporation might fund an up-front programme that provided, for example:

- Personnel resources to develop a national science policy;
- On-going entrepreneurial training workshops;
- Community Internet access sites (hardware, software, instruction and promotion to the community about its utility);
- A downstream royalty based upon multinational corporation's success that funded certain additional activities into the future.

If the multinational corporation felt ill-equipped to provide such services, or preferred to maintain a more arm's length relationship, provision of these "IPR compensation services" could be subcontracted to consulting firms, international agencies, NGOs or a UN body such as UNDP. Such a programme comes far closer to filling the mandate of the international conventions as well as the needs of essentially community-based IPR, than did Merck's $1.3 million for 10,000 biological specimens from Costa Rica.

An example of an arrangement on a smaller scale, perhaps by a company working with a small indigenous group within a country, might be the creation of a local bank with seed funds strictly earmarked for low-interest loans to fund local producer co-operatives coupled with basic management training skills. Future royalty payments would further fund this local development bank with a strict mission of funding local enterprises and engendering local productive capacity.

The concept of unique products can be thought of first of all by contrast to commodity products, as being a high value-added product. The advantage of adding value to products locally is simply that more of the value paid by the end-user or consumer of the product is retained by the local producer. However, the concept of unique products goes one step further by looking not only at adding more value to the product locally but discerning market advantages in the regional environment which can give it a unique position, thereby helping further to secure the economic advantage of the original value-added.

Within the unique product conception, there are potentially four intellectual property right components. They are:

- The local natural resource base for the product, flora, fauna, mineral, etc.;
- The local knowledge base regarding the use and practice of the natural resource;
- The techniques for handling and/or processing the resource into its traditional form;
- New or additional techniques to transfer the traditional use into contemporary product form.

Thus, by way of medical example, the genetic material of the local plant constitutes the first-level IPR; the knowledge of the plant and the means of cultivating it constitute the second; the techniques for extracting or processing or fermenting constitute the third category; while the fourth represents its translation into final product form, for example, laboratory purified and compounded with certain chemicals or stabilisers, etc.

As with the example of catalysis above, the unique products framework allows significant opportunity for the IPR licensing partner to have significant inputs as part of the community compensation process, however, rather than at the level of human infrastructure, it is directly at the enterprise level.

In the perspective of a rights and compensation scheme, the licensor, presumably a corporation from a developed country, could work with the indigenous group either (1) in the context of the specific subject of interest or (2) in parallel with it.

Following the example of the medicinal product mentioned above, the in-context scenario (1) would focus on bringing added technology and productive capacity to the developing country group and jointly producing the unique product. In this case the licensor is adding to the intellectual property rights already contributed by the indigenous group, namely the genetic material, the knowledge of its use, and the techniques for its preparation. The licensor participates with the local partner licensee in the production and retains or shares certain distribution rights with the licensee.

In scenario (2) where the relationship is structured in parallel, the licensor obtains certain rights to genetic material from within the domain of the indigenous group, but, as part of the initial compensation, provides unique product development assistance to the group in the form of technology, productive capacity, development expertise or market/distribution access for the unique product other than that of the material originally sought by the licensee. Thus if the licensee was interested in cell lines from individuals in the group, or microbes from soil samples, etc., it might assist in the formation of producer co-operatives for clothing articles based on traditional craft techniques and, more importantly, link them to markets and customers in developed countries.

The following case study illustrates all of these concepts:

- Traditional intellectual property rights;
- Catalysis;
- Unique product development.

Most important, however, is the fact that the total system, structurally in terms of rights, compensation and intent, respects the framework of TRIPS and especially of the Biodiversity Convention.

VII The Ghana Story as an Exemplary Case

This story begins several years ago with an under-funded developing country organisation with then unformed intellectual property rights in the field of medicine based on local flora. The organisation was in danger of dissolving.

Through resources in the international IPR field, the Global Technology Group (GTG) of UNDP came in contact with the Centre for Scientific Research into Plant Medicine (CSRPM) located in Mampong-Akwapim, Ghana.

At approximately the same time, a US-based company, HealthSearch Inc. (HSI) contacted the CSRPM with an interest in collaboration. HSI was a small company and could not afford the kind of investments large pharmaceuticals can. GTG saw this as an opportunity to create a South–North win-win situation, that could be nurtured through the catalysis and unique product framework.

After an initial assessment, a small grant was provided to the Centre to conduct clinical trials in conjunction with the University of Ghana Medical School at the Teaching Hospital of Korle Bu, located in Accra. Likewise, the Centre entered into a joint venture agreement with HSI for the purpose of developing, manufacturing, marketing and distributing products based on or derived from plant medicines in CSRPM's master formulae list.

These trials focused on quantifying derivatives of *Capparis erythrocarpos* root bark which has a history of use in the treatment of pain, fever, rheumatism and arthritis in traditional Ghanian medicine. Initial phytochemical screening by the CSR staff indicated it contained triterpenoid/steroidal glycosides, reducing compounds, alkalolds, coumarins, triterpenes and seponins. Preliminary animal studies carried out at the Centre indicated a dose dependent analgesic and antipyretic effect.

The Global Technology Group introduced the Centre to Peter Hyland of London, whose background in pharmaceutical management includes experience in developing countries. Also, GTG initiated contacts in the Ghanian government at the ministerial level including the Ministers of Science, Environment and Health as well as at the World Bank. Though the World Bank did not become a source of project funding, they strongly supported it and lent their credibility to the project, which, along with the support of the Ghanian ministers, helped to increase the visibility of the project.

In this case, the GTG is functioning as the catalytic agent, by linking CSRPM to resources and opportunities it would not otherwise be able to activate. By creating a grant for clinical testing, it was moving traditional indigenous knowledge to the level of unique product and, with GTG support, it was further extended into a licensing agreement and patent process.

HSI applied for patents on the capparis derivative in the United States. and initial work on FDA trials was begun at the University of Pittsburgh, and then merged with and became a wholly-owned subsidiary of PhytoMedica Health Products (PhytoMedica), thus increasing the product base and know-how available to the Centre. PhytoMedica later merged with Ryker to become Phyto-Riker Pharmaceuticals (PRP).

As a result of the initial interest created at the government level, an opportunity arose to acquire the Ghana Industrial Holding Corporation's GIHOC Pharmaceutical Company Limited, and thereby privatise the manufacturer. GIHOC manufactures a large line of health supplements such as vitamins as well as medicinal products ranging from Aspirin to Penicillin. At this point, and in order to complete the privatisation, the company made a successful initial public offering (IPO) in the New York market. The original CSRPM members were now stakeholders in a well-financed corporation.

At present, the company is making a major commitment to the entire African continent and has just formed the Africa Pharmaceutical and Health Care Alliance (APHCA). The APHCA stresses the utilisation of new medicines, niche generic products and special treatment programmes to develop certain sections of the business community. The purpose of these programmes are:

- Foster business ownership by local individuals;
- Promote the competitive vitality of such firms;
- Expand programmes for local procurement of materials and supplies.

APHCA will expand through six markets in Africa with a current planned total of 62 products, including those originally under development by the

Centre for Scientific Research into Plant Medicines, as well as those manufactured by GIHOC and additional products licensed into the system from elsewhere.

The market expansion in Africa will follow a regional approach as shown:

- Region 1: Ghana;
- Region 2: West Africa English-speaking;
- Region 3: West Africa French-speaking;
- Region 4: East Africa;
- Region 5: Southern Africa;
- Region 6: Northern Africa.

Future plans call for addressing international markets through distributors. Already collaborations have begun with China and Cuba.

This example involved a small developing country organisation with local genetic material and indigenous knowledge, a small North company, and the UNDP/GTG in a catalytic role. The process resulted in a unique product, that is the transformation of local flora and indigenous knowledge into a product that is now locally produced, high-value added, unique in the sense of its chemical nature and utility, and protected by intellectual property rights. This is a model that could be replicated by other small, medium or large corporations.

However, the truly important concept is that the *net compensation* for the rights to the native genetic material and indigenous knowledge *is not only* the involvement and financial benefit of the individual stakeholders (including the government of Ghana) to the enterprise.

The Net Compensation for the IPR is:

- The capacity building that has taken place in Ghana;
- The transfer of technology to Africa;
- The (soon) new availability of medicines continent-wide;
- The fostering of local entrepreneurship.

This is the real compensation.

This is the result of catalysis and unique products perspective.

This is the spirit and intent of the TRIPS and the Biodiversity Convention.

PART TWO
Abstracts and Outlines

Panel I

Strategies of Industrial Property Protection in the USA, Japan, Europe and Developing Countries

CHAIR: KLAUS P. HOELLER[1]

---

1 Global Approach to Building Strong Trade Marks[2]

W. Dexter Brooks[3]

The speaker presented a case study on Coca-Cola and highlighted the following essential elements of successfully managing the famous trade mark:

1. **Scope of Operations**
   - Sale of soft drink syrups and concentrates
   - Licensing trade marks to bottling partners and fountain customers
   - Expanding and reinforcing image of Coca-Cola trade mark
   - Offering top-quality products and service to customers
   - Providing consumers worldwide with consistent, inexpensive source of top-quality refreshment
   - Retail sale—$ 18 billion
   - 1,000 independent owned bottlers
   - Countries
   - Per cent of total soft drink sales
   - Coca-Cola system—$ 90 billion
   - Replacement value—over $ 100 billion
   - In-house counsel—200 outside counsel

2. **Portfolio of Intellectual Property Rights**
   - Secret of soft drink formula
   - Coca-Cola trade mark
   - Coke trade mark
   - Distinctive contour bottle
   - Proprietary fountain dispensers
   - Proprietary vendors
   - Coca-Cola megabrand—asset worth $ 42.8 billion
   - 15,000 trade mark registrations
   - 2,000 trade marks pending
   - New markets – China, Vietnam, Budapest, Prague and Eastern European Markets

[1] Vice President and Director of Patents, Trade Marks and Licenses, BASF Aktiengesellschaft, Ludwigshafen, Germany.

[2] For the full paper see page 3.

[3] Senior Staff Counsel, Legal Division, The Coca-Cola Company, Atlanta, USA.

3. **Licensing and Policing Policies**
   - Agreements with bottlers, wholesalers, advertising agencies
   - Agreements with suppliers for merchandise for non-beverage use
   - Agreements with suppliers concerning development of improved technology
   - Litigation activity
   - Infringement and counterfeiting actions
   - Substitution or passing-off actions
   - Trade disparagement actions
   - Licensing activity
   - Bottlers, wholesalers, advertising agencies
   - Merchandise licensing
   - Patent and technology

4. **Global Trends**
   - Communication media
   - Decline of mass markets
   - Global markets
   - Trading blocks

5. **US Trade Mark Recent Decisions**
   - *Playboy Enterprises, Inc.* v. *Frena*
   - *Two Pesos Inc.* v. *Taco Cabana, Inc.*
   - *Qualitex Co.* v. *Jacobson Products Co.*
   - *White* v. *Samsung Electronics America, Inc.*

6. **Future Legal Issues**
   - Communication media
   - Decline of mass market
   - Global markets
   - Trading blocks

2 Industrial Property Protection—Lifeline for the Pharmaceutical Industry[4]

Thomas B. Cueni[5]

The speaker emphasised the paramount importance of effective patent protection for the pharmaceutical industries:

Patents and the pharmaceutical industry form a symbiosis which is inseparable. Industrial property protection, in particular, patents form the lifeline for the research-based pharmaceutical industry. Investment of, at present,

[4] For the full paper see page 13.
[5] Secretary General, Interpharma, Basle, Switzerland.

more than $ 500 million for the research and development of one new medicine reaching the market can only be justified because industrial property protection grants a limited exclusivity for the commercial exploitation of such an invention.

The address covers four aspects:

- some of the myths leading to a lot of controversy with regard to pharmaceutical product protection in developing countries;
- the recent improvements in upgrading protection of industrial property world-wide;
- current IP issues seen from the perspective of the European R&D-based pharmaceutical industry;
- the communication problems of patent experts as exemplified in the debate about biotechnology patents in Europe, and, in particular, Switzerland.

Following on an exploration of recent achievements such as the minimum standards of the Uruguay Round TRIPS and the Supplementary Protection Certificate granting a maximum effective patent protection of 15 years from launch of a new medicine, the paper addresses current issues. It outlines the need for an improvement and clarification of the TRIPS agreement, expresses concern about preferential treatment of generics, and highlights the trade-distorting aspects of parallel trade in medicines within the European Community. Unfortunately, the European Court of Justice has in the past consistently put free trade rules above the protection of industrial property. It is hoped that the Court of Justice will at least partially restore the balance and accept that differences in patent protection within the EU create unacceptable trade distortions.

Explaining the importance of the "BiotechDirective" for the future of biotechnological research in Europe, the author addresses the communication challenge which the industry is faced with, and highlights key issues relating to the patenting of life-forms.

3. Strategies of Intellectual Property Protection in Japan

Kensuke Norichika[6]

The speaker emphasised the importance of intellectual property protection in Japanese industrial culture:

- Industrial property protection has contributed much to the development of the Japanese economy.

[6] Executive Director, Softic, Software Information Center (former General Manager, Intellectual Property Division, Toshiba Corporation), Tokyo, Japan.

- Intellectual property protection is the key to open the future of Japan.
- The strategic approach is essential in the field of intellectual property protection.
- Strategic patenting is generally the most important.
- The strategic enforcement of intellectual property rights is now the keen concern of top management.
- An intellectual property strategy should be established in each company.
- The intellectual property strategy should be harmonised with other business strategies such as the research and development (engineering) strategy, the marketing strategy, the legal strategy and the international business management strategy.
- The assessment of intellectual property activities should be done by top management.
- Top management should take responsibility for the outcome of intellectual property activities.
- The risk management of intellectual property problems is inevitable today.

4. The LEGO Group and Intellectual Property Rights

Henning Skovmose[7]

The speaker presented a case study on LEGO and highlighted the following essential elements of successfully managing the trade mark of LEGO toys:

1. **Short description of LEGO Group**
   Classical family enterprise:
   - Manufacture
   - Sales
   - Product Development
2. **Godtfred Kirk Christiansen**
   - Owner of the firm
   - Inventor of the brick
   - His interest in IP work
   - The great patent
3. **Fighting copying in early years by patents**
4. **Other rights—new products: The process of developing new rights for new products**

[7] General Counsel, The LEGO Foundation, Billund, Denmark.

5. **A new generation**
   - Kjeld Kirk Kristiansen: marketing man with a trade mark concept and an interest
6. **Present days' importance of laws on unfair competition, passing off, trade dress protection, marketing practices etc.**
7. **Famous trade marks and 3-dimensional ones**
8. **The two guidelines**
   - Trade marks
   - Fair play
9. **What is legally possible may not be the right thing to do**
10. **Taking the initiative and keeping it: the importance of timing**
11. **A couple of policy statements**
    - We will protect widely
    - We will defend effectively rights acquired
    - We will retain the best possible advisors
    - We will invest own efforts in support of any case
12. **The value, if any, of having a reputation for being aggressive**

Panel II
Selected Financial Aspects of Industrial Property

CHAIR: HEINZ GODDAR[8]

---

1. Industrial Property Rights and Private Sector Development: Lessons for Developing Countries[9]

Carlos A. Primo Braga[10]

The speaker emphasised the following elements in defining the relationship of developing countries and IPR's:

The conventional economic rationale for the protection of intellectual property rights (IPRs) is often framed in terms of the incomplete appropriability of knowledge. IPRs can be understood as second-best solutions to the problems created by the "public good" nature of knowledge. To the extent that they enhance "appropriability", IPRs are expected to foster investment in research and development (R & D) and knowledge creation. They create, however, a static distortion as they constrain the current consumption of knowledge, by increasing the market power of title holders. In short, IPRs involve a "bargain" between the producers of knowledge and society, which is mediated by the government.

The long-term trend with respect to IPRs protection in developed economies has clearly been in the direction of the strengthening of these rights. More recently, many developing countries have also begun to reform their IPRs regimes, reflecting new international commitments, domestic economic reforms and external pressures. This paper reviews what are the potential implications of stronger IPRs (particularly industrial property rights) in the developing world for economic development.

The paper analyses the main implications of stronger IPRs for technology transfer, R & D investment, foreign direct investment and trade flows. It also discusses the cost of IPRs strengthening in terms of anti-competitive practices, balance-of-payments impact and the displacement of "pirates". It argues that, as developing countries pursue market-based reforms and outward-orientation, the dynamic benefits of protecting IPRs tend to dominate short-term costs. Still, the challenges of implementing such reforms should not be minimised. The strengthening of IPRs requires a strong commitment from governments to the administration and enforcement of the IPRs regime in order for the private sector to benefit from these changes.

[8] Attorney-at-Law, Patent Attorney, Partner of Boehmert & Boehmert, Munich, Germany.

[9] For the full paper see page 23.

[10] Manager of the Information for Development Program and of the TechNet (Technology Network) initiative at the World Bank.

2 Intellectual Property Rights in the Balance Sheet and Specific Tax Problems in Cross-Border Licensing [11]

Dirk Krüger[12]

The speaker emphasised that IPRs often amount to a considerable corporate value. Questions of accounting and taxation of IPRs have increased, far from being adequately settled.

1. **Introduction**
2. **Intellectual Property Rights in the Balance Sheet**
   - Fixed assets
   - Current assets
3. **Cross-border Licensing**
   - Transfer pricing
   - Treaty protection
   - Anti-treaty shopping provisions
   - Controlled foreign companies provisions
4. **Closing Comments**

3 Security Interests in Intellectual Property[13]

Harry C. Sigman[14]

The speaker drew attention to the importance of an effective and harmonised world-wide system for security interests in intellectual property. He presented the applicable state and federal law in the United States:

As more of the world's wealth comes to be embodied in intangible assets, particularly in intellectual property ("IP"), and as owners seek to maximise the leverage available from their assets, the ability to grant effective security interests in IP becomes increasingly important. By effective I mean a system that allows the rights to be created easily, quickly and inexpensively, that provides clear rights *inter partes* and predictable and certain priorities *vis-à-vis* third parties, and that provides efficient, reliable and fair enforcement mechanisms. This entails, ideally, a sophisticated financial market-place and a well-designed legal regime. Even, and perhaps especially, developing

[11] For the full paper see page 37.
[12] Professor, Arthur Andersen, Wirtschaftsprüfungsgesellschaft Steuerberatungsgesellschaft mbH, Frankfurt am Main, Germany.
[13] For the full paper see page 46.
[14] Attorney-at-Law, Los Angeles, U.S.A.

countries, however, will find it advantageous to create the legal environment necessary to facilitate such transactions. The ultimate goal is a modern, efficient and harmonised world-wide system for security interests in IP. I will describe the applicable state and federal law in the United States. Given the time allotted to the initial oral presentation, it will of course not be possible to discuss the applicable law in detail; my goal will be to stimulate and provoke.

As you are all knowledgeable in the field of IP, I will say nothing about US substantive IP law except to observe that because the USA is a federal nation, rather than a unitary one, it is always necessary to take into account the respective roles of federal and state law. Generally speaking, most of the substantive patent and copyright law is federal, trade mark law is far more of a mix and trade secret law is mostly state law. Personal property security law, on the other hand, is primarily state law. Fortunately, it is far less variegated than other state law subjects, because it is largely embodied in Article 9 of the Uniform Commercial Code ("UCC"). Nevertheless, there may well be an overlay of federal involvement even here, particularly with respect to the public filing of notices of possible security interests. Generally speaking, state, not federal, law governs substantive issues relating to security interests in IP. Over 40 years ago a federal appellate court ruled that state law governs the enforcement of a security interest in a copyright. None of the federal IP statutes provides a comprehensive body of security law to displace the UCC.

In 55 Code sections, Article 9 sets forth a single coherent comprehensive legal framework for security interests in personal property, both tangible and intangible. Subject to a very limited number of exclusions, Article 9 governs all such security interests, no matter the nature of the debtor, no matter the nature of the secured party, no matter the nature of the collateral, including property not yet owned by the debtor and even as yet non-existent property, and no matter the nature of the obligation secured. It covers both possessory and non-possessory security interests, with respect to the latter, usually providing for public notice by means of filing.

Article 9 governs consensual security interests in personal property regardless of form. In the creation of security interests, Article 9 provides for a minimum of formality and allows *inter partes* rather broad party autonomy, with very few mandatory provisions.

Article 9 provides a detailed regime of priorities, spelling out who prevails in contests between a secured party, on the one hand, and various competing interests, ranging from another secured party to a lien creditor, a buyer of the collateral, a donee of the collateral, etc. The level of refinement leaves little to the courts, and thus provides maximum predictability. A lender or seller who knows that his position is vulnerable to no or only a few specified competitors can measure his risk on an informed basis and extend a greater amount of credit at a lower price, i.e., the value of the asset as collateral is maximised.

Article 9 deals with rights and obligations after default, i.e. enforcement remedies. I will say very little about this, observing simply that in addition to the familiar judicial remedies, Article 9 provides a seemingly revolutionary enforcement mechanism.

The priorities regime depends on the availability of public notice. Article 9 provides basic rules for the filing system, but does not provide a detailed implementation design. Article 9 was written around 1950, well before the computer age. Each state designed its own filing system. There is a great variation in the financial resources of the different states, and the states moved into the computer age in different ways and at different speeds. Thus, today, we have a variety of systems ranging from one state that still has an essentially primitive uncomputerised paper system, to several states that already accept paperless electronic filings. Indeed, there exists a national standard format for electronic filing that offers the potential to facilitate worldwide filing and searching, using shared databases.

IP falls within the UCC category of "general intangibles". Filing is required to perfect a security interest in such collateral. The proper place to file against general intangibles is the debtor's "location". Although intangibles have no *situs*, a debtor is located in only one place and that place is usually easy to determine. Article 9 provides that a debtor is located for this purpose "at his place of business if he has one, at his chief executive office if he has more than one place of business, otherwise at his residence". There is a four-month grace period in which to re-file if the debtor's location changes.

Some US filing issues should not present a problem elsewhere, as most nations are unitary, not federal. It would be highly inefficient to place IP security interest filings in the specific offices that otherwise govern the issue or ownership of the various forms of IP. Typical financing is not limited to a single patent or a single copyright; rather, all the debtor's IP, together with all its non-IP assets, are likely to be pledged to a lender providing blanket financing. A filing system built on a debtor-based index, such as the UCC system, rather than an asset-based system such as is common in copyright and patent registries, is far better suited to facilitating sophisticated financing of multiple types of collateral of a changing composition and including future assets. Thus, it is, generally speaking, more efficient to put all security interest filings in a single office without regard to the nature of specific items of collateral.

The challenge is to design, legislate for and implement a modern legal regime that facilitates effective security interests in IP, with an efficiently operated electronic worldwide database, and with substantive IP law being harmonised across borders.

4. The Valuation of Intellectual Property Rights

Thierry Sueur[15]

The speaker emphasised the importance nowadays of the valuation of intangible assets, namely intellectual property rights and presented different approaches:

Study of different approaches

- the cost approach: the cost involved in reproducing the intellectual property rights that you want to evaluate.
- the market approach: what are, if any, the financial conditions of comparable or similar transactions.
- the income approach: calculation of the discounted cash flows due to intellectual property rights.

[15] Air Liquide S.A., Intellectual Property Department, Paris, France.

Panel III
Industrial Property Rights in the Context of Antitrust Legislation

CHAIR: ROLAND VON BÜREN[16]

---

1. Technological Information and the Essential Facilities Doctrine of U.S. Antitrust Law[17]

David J. Gerber[18]

The speaker focused on the potential impact of US antitrust laws on the capacity of dominant firms to protect their technological information. In this context he presented the doctrine of "essential facilities" which may under some circumstances require a firm in a dominant position to provide information or products to other firms.

When might a dominant firm be required to divulge proprietary information or license its technology? The problem is obviously critical to many international firms, not only because of the increasingly important role played by technology in international business operations, but also because of the expansion of international intellectual property rights protection.

In the United States there are few legal constraints on decisions by business firms to transact or refuse to transact business with particular parties. Normally, a firm may unilaterally refuse to sell or deliver services to any other firm if it so wishes. Under some circumstances, however, United States antitrust laws impose obligations to deal on monopolists and firms acting in concert. This means that owners of intellectual property rights operating in the United States may sometimes be subject to legal obligations to provide access to technology or information related to technology. The main area of concern involves situations in which such firms may be accused of "monopolising" a market by limiting access to products or information that are necessary for maintaining competition on that market. This presentation discusses some of the circumstances under which such obligations may be imposed and factors to consider in assessing the impact of the United States antitrust laws in this area.

I will first discuss some of the characteristics of the US antitrust law

[16] Professor of Commercial, Competition and Intellectual Property Law at the University of Berne, Switzerland; Chairman of the Federal Competition Commission.

[17] For the full paper see page 58.

[18] Professor of Law, Chicago-Kent College of Law, Illinois Institute of Technology, Chicago, U.S.A.

system that are relevant to assessing the impact of substantive law norms. This will include discussion of issues such as the role of private litigation in the enforcement of US law, the role of treble damage awards, and the impact of US discovery procedures and concepts of international jurisdiction.

This discussion will serve as the context for consideration of the legal bases for imposing a duty on a dominant firm to license technology or provide other firms with information regarding its technology. In US law such obligations derive from section 2 of the famous Sherman Act, which prohibits monopolisation and "attempts to monopolise". Under that provision a doctrine of "essential facilities" has developed which may under some circumstances require a firm in a dominant position to provide information or products to other firms. The presentation will explore those circumstances and discuss the ramifications of these aspects of US antitrust law.

2. Patents and Antitrust [19]

Valentine Korah[20]

The speaker focused on the interfaces of competition law and intellectual property. She emphasised the importance of intellectual property rights in encouraging investment and innovation and the dangers of a wide interpretation of the Magill case and compulsory licensing.

- Importance of intellectual property rights in encouraging investment in innovation.
- *Ex post*, some intellectual property rights may remove the incentive to invest in follow through innovations.
- How much protection is required to provide the incentive to the right amount of innovation? Not knowable.
- Sometimes when there is new technology, the initial patents granted prove to be very wide—should competition law require compulsory licensing in extreme cases? Assessment of a reasonable royalty would be confiscatory and arbitrary and possibility of compulsory licensing would marginally reduce the incentives to invest in the original innovation, but might increase the incentives to follow through research and reduce the cost to consumers to have additional suppliers.
- *Internal combustion engine, computers*, but initially turned to copyright and ideas no longer novel when inventors applied to patents, *biotechnology*, although the most basic invention was not patented, some subsequent patents were very broad.

[19] For the full paper see page 68.

[20] Professor Emeritus of Competition Law at University College London, London, GB.

- Would be better for this to be taken into account under intellectual property law when the patent granted, because inventor would have more certainty, but no one realises how wide the rights are at the beginning. Should EC competition law intervene as a backstop when patents later found to be much to broad?
- EC competition law is not as firmly focused as American antitrust on the interests of consumers, but is concerned also with foreclosing third parties. From the early 1970s, intellectual property rights were perceived as entry barriers and treated with hostility—exhaustion (Articles 30 and 36 EC Treaty), exclusive licenses (Article 85 EC Treaty)—collective acquisition of two technologies for achieving a result led to compulsory licence at controlled price (*IGR Stereo).*
- Article 86 EC Treaty forbids the abusive exploitation of a dominant position and refusals to supply have been condemned, sometimes invoking an essential facility doctrine and often without. Our requirements for compulsory licensing might well go further than in the USA, because the interest of competitors is respected whether or not this is in the interests of consumers or the economy as a whole.
- *Magill* case—disreputable form of copyright in information, contrary to civil law conceptions of copyright. Wording of judgment would require compulsory licensing of basic patent to the holder of an improvement patent.
- Danger if this be widely construed. Press release from Court and Legal Service of the Commission believe that this should be limited to the exceptional circumstance of the case, where there was copyright in information.
- FTC in Washington DC held hearings in November and December 1995 into the desirability of compulsory licensing.
- The question is should competition law ever intervene to reduce intellectual property rights by requiring compulsory licensing of very important patents or other intellectual property rights.

3. Industrial Property Management in a Multinational Corporation[21]

Marshall C. Phelps, Jr.[22]

The speaker presented two strategies of managing intellectual property in the context of antitrust legislation, rules and regulations: either the company takes the course of a "close" strategy and retains IP for internal use only, or the company decides for an "open licensing" approach. The speaker emphasised the benefits of an "open licensing" strategy.

I intend to approach this subject largely from a business perspective—especially that of large, high-tech, multinational firms with substantial IP assets. This discussion will begin by noting the fundamental choice facing such companies:

- Retain IP for internal use only,
- License openly.

IBM has taken the latter course and I will give a brief historical view of IBM's practices, including:

- Antitrust suits and investigations
- IBM's 1956 US Consent Decree
- IBM's EC Undertaking
- The genesis of IBM's licensing practices

I will argue that an "open licensing" approach (non-discriminatory patent licences, selective technology licences and joint ventures in development, manufacturing, sales and service) in our case has led to significant benefits, including:

- new products
- open systems
- interoperability
- new markets
- creation of IP
- substantial licensing revenues

Conversely, a "closed" strategy is less efficacious in today's high-tech world: first, because it is probably impossible to dominate even a small environment for long, due to the need to interface to the offerings of others: Secondly, because there are real limitations on the refusal to license or sell:

[21] For the full paper see page 88.

[22] IBM Corporation, Vice President, Intellectual Property and Licensing Services, New York, U.S.A.

- "essential facilities" doctrines
- compulsory licensing initiatives (government mandated or judicially imposed)
- standards/consortia driven initiatives (ETSI)
- need for IP of others

Thirdly, the pace and scope of technology advances make such restrictive practices self-defeating.

Finally, I will argue for enhanced IP protection throughout the world. And, while sound industrial property schemes are essential to encourage innovation and create competition, there have been cases of over-reaching, and government action may be appropriate.

In such events, any government faces real difficulties, however, in fashioning timely and effective remedies. I will argue against inappropriate remedies which broadly penalise, but instead for remedies addressing individual situations on a timely basis.

Panel IV

Strategies of Dispute Settlement in Industrial Property

CHAIR: ROLAND GROSSENBACHER[23]

---

1. The Employment of Experts in Mediating and Arbitrating Intellectual Property Disputes[24]

Robert Goldscheider[25]

The speaker elaborated on the role, contribution and advantages of qualified experts and arbitrators in IP disputes and presented some case studies:

1. Roles of Experts in Litigation and ADR Involving Intellectual Property

- Analysing technology, particularly relating to patent infringement, and the availability of non-infringing alternatives;
- Projecting the financial dimensions of patent, trade mark and copyright infringements, as well as the misappropriation of trade secrets and know-how, usually in the form of lost profits;
- Providing opinions as to damages, frequently expressed as "reasonable royalties", that should be paid to the proprietors of such intellectual property rights as a result of such infringements and misappropriations; these exercises often involve simulating negotiations between the proprietor and accused infringers; and
- Commenting about standard industry attitudes and practices which could provide better understanding of the disputes that inspired the legal proceedings.

2. Commentaries about the special considerations in long term licensing relationships that can differ from interpretations of standard commercial contracts

- No "loophole mentality";
- Are there fiduciary duties?
- Experts must provide a dimension of input different from counsel and the judicial authorities.

3. Expert approaches to the valuation of patented and unpatented technology

4. Providing a "real world" dimension to the resolution of legal disputes

[23] Chairman of the Swiss Federal Institute of Intellectual Property, Berne, Switzerland.
[24] For the full paper see page 93.
[25] Chairman, The International Licensing Network, Ltd., New York, U.S.A.

2. Patent Dispute Resolution in the Research Based Pharmaceutical Company

Nicholas P. Malatestinic[26]

The speaker explored the purpose and strategy of protecting and enforcing the research-based pharmaceutical company's intellectual property rights and the presentation concluded that alternative dispute resolution is not a practical substitute for infringement litigation.

3. Implications of the TRIPS Agreement for Dispute Settlement in Industrial Property[27]

Adrian Otten[28]

The purpose of this presentation was to explore the implications of the WTO Agreement on Trade-Related Aspects of Intellectual Property Rights (TRIPS Agreement) for the resolution of disputes in industrial property, in particular the interface between domestic legal proceedings about private rights and international dispute settlement proceedings between states about treaty rights.

After a brief introduction to the TRIPS Agreement, the presentation will discuss the relevance to dispute resolution of the provisions of the TRIPS Agreement concerning minimum substantive standards, procedures for the acquisition and maintenance of rights, domestic procedures and remedies for the enforcement of intellectual property rights, and dispute settlement between states. The question of direct applicability of TRIPS provisions in national legal proceedings is also addressed. The GATT dispute settlement proceedings about Section 337 of the United States Tariff Act and their relation to the dispute between Akzo and Du Pont concerning certain aramid fibres is used as a case study.

The paper concludes that the implications of the TRIPS Agreement for this resolution of disputes in and between WTO Members on industrial property, including those between private parties, can be summarised as follows:

[26] Formerly Bristol-Myers Squibb Co., International Patent Counsel, New York, U.S.A.

[27] For the full paper see page 102.

[28] Director, Intellectual Property and Investment Division, World Trade Organization, Secretariat, Geneva, Switzerland.

- the substantive intellectual property law that is at stake in national proceedings will have to conform with the minimum requirements of the TRIPS Agreement, often involving a considerable increase in the level of protection;
- domestic enforcement proceedings and also proceedings before industrial property offices will have to provide for the procedures and remedies set out in the TRIPS provisions in Parts III and IV of the Agreement;
- in some countries, TRIPS provisions, whether on substantive standards or on enforcement, will be directly applicable by national courts. In some others, national courts may wish to take them into account in interpreting national law;
- dispute settlement proceedings between WTO Members on intellectual property will often be prompted by specific difficulties brought to the attention of governments by private parties. In some cases these difficulties may result from domestic legal proceedings, which are considered to have been procedurally defective in relation to TRIPS obligations or which have interpreted national law in a way considered to be TRIPS inconsistent.

4. The Role of Litigation in Corporate Intellectual Property Strategy[29]

Melvin Sharp[30]

The speaker—former Chief Patent Counsel of Texas Instruments—reviewed his experiences with the role of litigation as a corportate IP strategy before the changing background of the IP environment in the USA.

- Litigation has become a practical reality in the electronics field when intellectual property rights are used to pursue business objectives seeking a competitive advantage such as substantial royalty income or increased market share.
- The background, evolution and results of Texas Instruments licensing policies seeking substantial royalty income will be reviewed. These licensing policies integrate business objectives, patent enforcement and litigation strategy.
- Moreover, investment in start-up companies in the electronics field must account for litigation by entrenched patent holders who will

[29] For the full paper see page 111.

[30] Attorney-at-Law and Counselor in Intellectual Property Law and Related Matters (former Chief Patent Counsel of Texas Instruments), Dallas, Texas, U.S.A.

reluctantly give up market share. For example, litigation and intellectual property strategy of new entrant Cyrix Corporation into the microprocessor field dominated by Intel will be reviewed.

- Litigation will continue as the major form of dispute resolution for intellectual property rights where substantial imbalances of patent portfolios exist because the value of intellectual property rights (and the R & D it represents) are too high to treat otherwise.

Panel V
Ethical and Ecological Aspects of Industrial Property Rights

CHAIR: THOMAS COTTIER[31]

---

1. Rewarding Creativity for Conserving Diversity in the Third World: Can IPR Regime Serve the Needs of Contemporary and Traditional Knowledge Experts and Communities in Third World?[32]

Anil K. Gupta[33]

The speaker pleaded for a new framework for safeguarding the IPRs of knowledge-rich economically poor individuals and communities in third world countries and presented a new global system of registration for grassroots innovations (Honey Bee)

Regions of high biodiversity are often inhabited by the poorest people. The irony is that many local healers and other herbal experts do not even charge for their services to the community. They conserve biological diversity despite remaining poor themselves. Their superior ethics can not be a reason for our inferior ethics. The fact that the younger people are no more inclined to acquire and improve this knowledge further increases the risk of knowledge erosion. The contemporary innovations suffer even worse fate compared to traditional knowledge. In the absence of any institutions to recognise, respect and reward the grassroots creativity, the intellectual properties are exploited by national and multi-national corporations inviting a charge of biopiracy. The projected losses to third world on this account could be many times more than the suspected loss to developed countries due to copyright and IPR piracy in the third world.

I summarise the arguments of those activists, NGOs and policy makers who oppose the provisions of TRIPs and justify the need for local knowledge to remain in common domain. I critique then the proposals of Community intellectual property rights in so far as these subsume all local knowledge under the rubric of traditional knowledge and all individual knowledge under Community knowledge. The framework for safeguarding

[31] Professor of European and International Economic Law at the University of Berne, Switzerland.

[32] For the full paper see page 119.

[33] Coordinator, SRISTI, Professor, Indian Institute of Management, Ahmebad, India.

the IPRs of knowledge-rich economically poor individuals and communities is presented next. A case is made for the following changes: (1) a global registration system of traditional knowledge as well as contemporary innovations, (2) the newness and non-obviousness of traditional knowledge should be seen in the light of available repertoire on the subject and the transaction costs involved in easily accessing the same, (3) the norms regarding exhaustion of the rights due to publication of local knowledge should be reconsidered and modified so that incentives to share the knowledge by local communities with outsiders are not affected adversely, (4) every patent office in a western country should insist that the patent applicant declares that the knowledge and resources used in a patent have been obtained lawfully and rightfully, (5) the challenge to marry two rather conflicting goals of easy and quick opportunity for lateral learning (through local language publication) among people and sharing of benefits through value addition in the same knowledge as attempted by Honey Bee network should be addressed.

Since it will be very difficult for any and every community to seek the protection of its knowledge and inventive recipes for various purposes such as herbal pesticides, human or veterinary medicines, vegetative dyes, etc., a registration system should be developed as explained below.

SRISTI and the Honey Bee network have been pleading for a global system of registration for grassroots innovations. The Honey Bee database (one of the world's largest databases of its kind) has more than 2,300 innovations, with the names and addresses of the innovative/creative community and/or individuals along with the name of the communicators through whom we learned about these innovations. A registry will prevent any firm or individual to seek a patent on community knowledge as well as on knowledge and innovations produced by individuals without some kind of cross licensing. It will be possible to achieve the following results from such a registry: (1) acknowledgment of individual and collective creativity, (2) the grant of entitlements to grassroots innovators to receive a share of any returns that may arise from commercial applications of their knowledge, innovations or practices with or without value addition, (3) linking the golden triangle of entrepreneurship by linking investments, enterprise and innovations—small-scale investors in North and South cannot afford to go to various countries, scan the diversity of knowledge and resources, negotiate contracts and invest up front huge investments for value addition—(4) an autonomous authority of which local community representatives will be the majority members could be entrusted with the responsibilities of having access to all the contracts, (5) each entry in the register will be coded according to an universal system like ISBN. The postal pin code of the habitat of the community or individuals registering innovations will be incorporated in the indexation system so that geo-referencing of innovations can be done, (6) the entry in the register will at the first stage be mere acknowledgment of creativity and innovation at grassroots level. But later some of the innovations will be considered appropriate for the award of inventors' certificates or a kind of petty patent which is a limited purpose and limited duration protection. The essential purpose of this innovation is also to enable the potential investors (a co-operative of consumers, producers, an entrepreneur or a large firm in private or public sector) to access the innovations and explore opportunities of joint ventures or licensing of innovations for research and commercialisation—the transaction costs of both the investors and innovators will be reduced through the registry—(7) the award of a certificate will also increase the entitlement of innovator/s to access to concessional credit and risk cover so that the transition from collector or producer of herbs to developer and marketeer of value-added products can take place in cases where innovators deem that fit, (8) the registration system will also be part of knowledge network linking problem solving people across the world at grassroots level (see discussion on the knowledge network in thc later section).

We realise that most governments in developing countries do not have resources even to pay the salaries of public administrators, to expect them to provide benefits to conservators of diversity and developers of innovations is not a realistic goal. If the private or public or co-operative sector has to share the benefits, it should obviously make profits. IPRs do play a significant role in generating these profits. However, very broad patents like the one in the case of transgenic cotton (which was later rescinded) are in the interest of neither science nor business efficiency in the long term.

So far as sustainable technologies are concerned such as herbal pesticides, growth regulators, vegetative dyes etc, the South can provide technologies to North. But if such innovations are used without appropriate reciprocities, then the knowledge systems which produced these innovations will not last very long. It is true that many poor people in the third world are creative and innovative but they cannot afford costly attorneys. A systems has to be evolved to provide this help through public interest institutions or initiatives. Inventor assistance programmes like the ones tried by the Franklin Law Pierce Centre should be tried out at global scale and in many countries immediately. The patentees in the case of innovations like the ones based on neem trees should agree to share part of their profits with an international innovations support and biodiversity conservation fund. The paper makes a case for adapting patent systems to not only accommodate the creative urges of local communities but also ensure that this vibrant and dynamic laboratory for developing sustainable technologies and products does not die down just because a community of IPR experts could not fathom its long-term potential.

2. Ethical and Ecological Aspects of Industrial Property Rights in the Context of Genetic Engineering and Biotechnology[34]

Klaus M. Leisinger[35]

The speaker gave a thorough presentation on the risks and benefits of biotechnology and genetic engineering in developing countries and further elaborated on ethical and ecological issues in this context.

To describe the role of biotechnology and genetic engineering for developing countries in general is almost impossible: on the one hand, there are no simple cause and effect relationships in complex social systems with intricate interdependencies; on the other hand, the collective term "developing countries" is too sweeping: it takes in countries so different in economic and social terms, as well as with regard to their capacity to absorb the fruits of research and technology, that generaliSations are defied. This is also true for a more focused consideration—the roles of biotechnology and genetic engineering with respect to food security or improved health.

One thing is certain: there is a role and it can be a very positive one, as biotechnology and genetic engineering add new tools to the armoury in the fight against hunger and disease. However, as there are no technical solutions to political and social problems, biotechnology and genetic engineering can be no "silver bullets" for structural development problems.

The challenges to an appropriate food production system in coping with a rapidly growing world population and increasingly shrinking, or at least more and more scanty, natural resources are immense. There are great hopes that biotechnology and genetic engineering will help develop new seed varieties that will make consistently high yields possible in an environmentally compatible way.

There are a number of ethical and ecological issues to be discussed in the context of the use of biotechnology and genetic engineering in developing countries—among the most important being equity and biological diversity. Appropriate ways to deal with these issues include fairness in international relations, innovative forms of co-operation and the readiness to go beyond the minimum if it comes to defining obligations of different partners in development.

Sustainable development—and hence a world approaching the goals "Health for All" and "Food for All"—will be achievable neither without

[34] For the full paper see page 130.

[35] Executive Director and Delegate of the Board of Trustee of Novartis for Sustainable Development, formerly Ciba-Geigy Foundation for Cooperation with Developing Countries, and Professor of development sociology on the philosophical-historical faculty of the University of Basel, Switzerland.

better governance and a new dimension of solidarity between the "rich" and the "poor" of this world, nor without new technologies such as biotechnology and genetic engineering.

3. Rights, Compensation, Indigenous Knowledge Systems and the Strategy of Global Industrial Property Management: The Challenge[36]

Joseph D. Ben-Dak[37]

The speaker highlighted the rights and obligations under the Biodiversity Convention ('Convention') and its relationships to the WTO–TRIPS agreement ('TRIPS') with particular emphasis on technology transfer and licensing of intellectual property rights (IPR).

This paper first presents some general comments on the provisions of the Convention and of TRIPS and the relationship of the respective provisions to each other. Significant provisions relating to technology transfer and licensing of IPR are then summarised.

There is potential for a fundamental tension between the philosophy and terms of TRIPS and those of the Convention. TRIPS is directed *inter alia* to (1) recognising that IPR are private rights which can be licensed, transferred or sold only if and to the extent that the holder of the rights so desires, with limited exceptions; and (2) upgrading standards of protection and enforcement of IPR in each country of the WTO. The Convention is directed *inter alia* to assuring that the technology necessary to meet the objectives of the Convention is developed and transferred where it is needed. Moreover, the interest of contracting parties that provide genetic resources, especially developing countries, are specially treated. In general, under the Convention, the owner of technology is required to transfer and license it. This is contrary to the general philosophy of TRIPS.

Many nations executed the Convention without reservation. But note, for example, the reservation of the United States in signing the Convention: "As a matter of substance, we find particularly unsatisfactory texts treatment of intellectual property rights, technology transfer and biotechnology". Resolution of this potential tension, if and when it arises, as well as reservations such as those expressed by the United States, will require enlightened negotiation of the specific facts involved to reach a satisfactory result.

Summarising, the following actions should be considered by multilateral

[36] For the full paper see page 153.

[37] Principal Advisor, Science and Technology and Chief, Global Technology Group, UNDP.

organisations, governments, non-governmental organisations and other stakeholders:

- Further study of inventors' certificates and materials transfer agreements as a means of compensating indigenous communities and of safeguarding the intellectual integrity of these communities.
- Further development of the Model Law on Folklore by both UNESCO and WIPO with a view to encouraging national legislation and an international convention in support of indigenous knowledge.
- The possibility of establishing a special trust fund for the remuneration of indigenous knowledge on a programme and project basis as part of FAO's Farmers' Rights Initiative.
- A study of materials transfer agreements and specific contracts with a view to establishing a series of model agreements that may be considered by governments, corporations, and indigenous communities.
- A discussion of the role of indigenous communities in *in situ* conservation with FAO, the Consultative Group on International Agricultural Research and in the context of the Biodiversity Convention.
- The preparation of a popular information kit to provide key information to indigenous people. It should be prepared in close collaboration with key organisations and it should form the basis of seminars and discussions within indigenous peoples' organisations and communities.
- The convening of a meeting with indigenous organisations and informatics experts to discuss needs and means for safeguarding the development of indigenous knowledge and its exchange with others.

The major area for combined efforts in producing the best strategy seems to be in developing IPR in fields of *unique products*: i.e. "technologies based on best, sustainable win-win utilization of less developing countries special fauna, flora, materials and human resources".

The Global Technology Facility has grown in response to the post-Rio heightened need. Many countries in the South feel that their fuller potential of environmental and human *productivity* needs urgent and concrete assessment. Thus, GTF complements the work of the private sector and sustainable livelihood groups in BPPS by focusing on new country macro-level or sectoral employment strategies by proposing new product lines, new modes of using technology mixes of local, home grown technologies and products *with* "imported" state-of-the-art, particularly enriching and useful transfers. GTF complements the work of management development and governance by addressing technology management issues, such as the environmentally sound technology appropriate for truly *consequent-conscious policy-making* at country, regional or megapolis levels.

To the country office efforts, GTF offers flexibility in support modalities that is based on a particularly large volunteer expertise base in some 1,600 technology classifications, often in same or neighboring countries, in addition to consultancies and missions of the more usual UNDP and inter-agency style. GTF is particularly strong in a rather pragmatic mix of South–South and North–South mixes of responsive expertise and business "gatekeepers" to local initiatives and indigenous entrepreneurship, building on a *participatory* development of local poor communities micro-insights (or fuller concepts) about products, employment, organisation toward precisely defined mature evolvement with the international market-place.

The GTF is either the proponent or an active collaborator in some 400 global professional engineering or technology transfer organisations wherein GTF is the main or only United Nations representative. Among these networks, country offices could access such groups as

- Licensing Executive Society International (LESI) incorporating thousands of legal and other practitioners and scholars in about 40 countries including Malaysia, India, South Africa. These are available to perform advisory or mediating tasks relevant to Unique Products, Catalysis, UNFT or ECO-INWARDS, often on a total voluntary basis.
- World Business Network (WBN), an electronic community and a community of enterprises participating in world trade involving for example, 20,000 (presently) Chinese subscribers. This network allows for easy access to UNFT information and global introduction or any business of our country office supported programmes.
- University of Sao Paulo's The School of the Future base network of teachers, scholars, research centres, schools (at all educational levels) etc. In some 60 countries including South America—committed to education programming for unique product development.
- Financial networks including innovative public offering in countries that begin to develop financial markets for environmental technology and systematic privatisation in UNFT related business e.g. Ghana, Vietnam, Zimbabwe.

Members of the Organizing Committee

VINCENZO M. PEDRAZZINI
Isler & Pedrazzini AG
Gotthardstrasse 53
Postfach 8053
CH–8002 Zürich
Switzerland

DR. PETER A. PESTALOZZI
Pestalozzi, Gmuer & Patry
Löwenstrasse 1
CH–8001 Zürich
Switzerland

PETER WIDMER
Fuhrer Marbach & Partner
Konsumstrasse 16 A
CH–3007 Bern
Switzerland

List of Participants

Argentina

Berti, Laura M.
Laura Berti y Cia S.A.
Cordoba 1525
1055 Buenos Aires

De las Carreras, Daniel
Allende & Brea
De las Carreras &
Chaloupka
Maipu 757 5th floor
1006 Buenos Aires

Magnanini, Carlos
Clarke Modet & Cia.
Lavalle 190
1047 Buenos Aires

Muir, Roberto
Marval, O'Farrel & Mairal
Carlos Pellegrini 885
1338 Buenos Aires

Noetinger, Fernando
Noetinger & Armando
Carlos Pellegrini 1125, EP
1009 Buenos Aires

Palacio, Hector
Palacio & Asociados
Tucuman 141 8 Piso
1049 Buenos Aires

Australia

Bentley, Cyril M.
Griffith Hack & Co.
PO Box 1285K
Melbourne, VIC 3001

Brownscombe, David E.
RTZ–CRA
55, Collins Street
Melbourne, VIC 3000

Corbett, Terence
Davies Collison Cave
1 Little Collins Street
Melbourne 3000

Dowling, Michael
Arthur Robinson &
Hedderwicks
530 Collins Street
Melbourne, VIC 3000

Haliday, Ronald A.
Cullen & Co.
240 Queen Street
Brisbane, QLD 4001

Padbury, Mary
Blake Dawson Waldron
Level 39
101 Collins Street
Melbourne, VIC 3001

Royal, Malcolm J.
Phillips Ormonde &
Fitzpatrick
367 Collins Street
Melbourne, VIC 3000

Smith, Stuart M.
Shelston Waters
60 Margret St.
Sidney, NSW 2000

Smoorenburg, Richard
Watermark
290 Burwood Road
Hawthorne, VIC 3122
Stearne Peter A.
Davies Collison Cave
Patent Attorneys
10 Barrack Street
Sidney, NSW 2000

Austria

Alge, Daniel
Sonn, Pawloy, Weizinger
& Wolfram
Riemergasse 14
1010 Wien

Markart, Friedrich
Vereinigung Österreichis-
cher Industrieller
Postfach 61
1031 Wien

Sonn, Helmut
Sonn, Pawloy, Weinzinger
& Wolfram
Riemergasse 14
1010 Wien

Bangladesh

Salahuddin, Abdullah
Mohammad
Remfry & Son
56, New Esketon Road
GPO Box 885
Dhaka 1000

Belgium

Duvivier, Marie-Hélène
Interbrew S.A.
Vaartstraat 94/4
3000 Leuven

Meyers, Liliane
Solvay S.A.
Rue de Ransbeek 310
1120 Bruxelles

Turner, Amedée
Oppenheimer Wolff &
Dennelly
250 Avenue Louise
1050 Brussels

Brazil

Arnaud, Antonio M.P.
Pinheiro, Nunes, Arnaud &
Scatamburlo P.C.
Rua Jose Bonifacio 93
Sao Paulo 01003–901

Dale, Denise
Momsen, Leonardos & Cia
Teofilo Ottoni 63–10
Andar
Rio de Janeiro 20090–080

Dannemann, Gert Egon
Dannemann Siemsen
Bigler & Ipanema
Moreira
Rua Marques de Olinda, 70
Rio de Janeiro 22251–040

Do Nascimento, Waldemar
Rua Tabapua, 627
4533 012 Sao Paulo

Fabbri, Helio
Advocacia Pietro Ariboni
S/C
Av. Paulista/352/5th Fl./CJ
51
PO Box 9967
01310 Sao Paulo

Faria Correa, Jose Antonio
Dannemann, Siemsen,
Bigler & Ipanema
Moreira
Rua Marques de Olinda, 70
Rio de Janeiro 22251–040

Leonardos, Fernanda
Momsen, Leonardos & Cia
Teofilo Ottoni 63–10
Rio de Janeiro 20090–080

Leonardos, Gabriel F.
Momsen, Leonardos & Cia
Teofilo Ottoni, 63–10
Rio de Janeiro, 20090–080

Leonardos, Gustavo
Momsen, Leonardos & Cia
Teofilo Ottoni 63–10
Rio de Janeiro 20090–080

Leonardos, Luis
Momsen, Leonardos & Cia
Teofilo Ottoni 63–10
Rio de Janeiro 20090–080

Marrylees, David
Dannemann, Siemsen,
Bigler & Ipanema
Moreira
Rua Marques de Olinda, 70
Rio de Janeiro 22251

Siemsen, Peter Dirk
Dannemann, Siemsen,
Bigler & Ipanema
Moreira
Rua Marques de Olinda, 70
Rio de Janeiro 22251–040

Bulgaria

Bojinova, Fanny
Bojinov & Bojinov Ltd.
17, Karnigradska St.
PO Box 728
1000 Sofia

Daraktschiew, Todor D.
Agenz Ofeibea
Busludsha 64
1463 Sofia

Slabova, Roumiana
Irin Patent Ltd.
3, Leonardo da Vinci St.
PO Box 15
1202 Sofia

Sokolova, Feodora
Irin Patent
PO Box 15
1202 Sofia

Canada

Abu-Ghazaleh, Luay T.
TMP Agents International
1 Westmount Square, #840
Montréal, QBC. H3Z 2P9

Botting, Brian
Industry Canada
235 Queen Street
5th Floor West
Ottawa, Ont. K1A 0H5

Boudreaul, Jean
Gouvernement du Quebec
MICST
776 Sherbrooke Ouest
Montréal H3A 1D4

Clark, Joan
Ogilvy Renault
1981 Mc Gill College
Avenue
Montréal H3A 3C1

Eades, Norris M.
Kirby, Eades, Gale Baker
PO Box 3432, STN.D.
Ottawa, ONT. K1P 6N9

Hill, Donald A.
PO Box 2999
Ottawa K1P 5Y6

Leger, Jacques A.
Leger Robic Richard
55 St. Jacques
Montréal H2Y 3X2

McCourt, Conor D.M.
McCarty Tetrault
#4700 Bank Tower
Toronto Dominion Centre
Toronto M5K 1E6

Mitchell, Robert
Swabey Ogilvy Renault
1981 McGill College,
#1600
Montréal, QBC H3A 2Y3

Perry, Rose-Mary
Gowlin, Strathy &
Henderson
2600–160 Elgin Street
Ottawa K1P 1C3

Salame, Nabil M.
TMP Agents International
1 Westmount Square, #840
Montréal QBC. H3Z 2P9

Chile

Alessandri, Arturo
PO Box 1317
Santiago

Beuchat, G.E.
Beuchat, Barros &
Pfenninger
Serrano 14 6th Floor
PO Box 456–V
Santiago

Claro, Felipe
Clari y Cia.
Gertrude Echenique 30
Piso 13
Santiago

Langlois, Felipe
Johansson & Langlois
Marchant Pereira #954
1834 Santiago

China

Lin, Bonan
CCPIT Patent and Trademark
CCPIT Building
1 Fuxingmenwai Street
100860 Beijing

Mu Dejun
SINDA Intell. Property Ltd.
41 Xueyuan Road, Haidan
Beijing 100088

Wang Shen
CCPIT Patent and Trademark CCPIT Building
1 Fuxingmenwai Street
100860 Beijing

Xie Lina
SINDA Intell. Property Ltd.
41, Xueyuan Road, Haidan
Beijing 100088

CIS

Arievich, Eugene
Baker & MacKenzie
B. Strochenovski 22/25
113054 Moscow

Beliaeva, Elena N.
Patent Bureau
Karl Marx, 40–34
220030 Minsk

Dunaev, Yuri
Dunaev & Vlasova
Tarasivska 18
252033 Kiev

Gordodissky, Mikhail L.
SOJUZPATENT
Iliinka, 5/2
103735 Moscow

Guerman, Valeri
INTELS
Pokrovka, 27
103062 Moscow

Kim, Sergey Romanovich
INNOTEC
B-Semenovskaya Street, Bld. 49
Office 402
105023 Moscow

Kolodjazhnij, Jurij
Ministerium Wissenschaft und Technische Politik
Twerskaja Uliza 11
103905 Moskwa

Krjukow, Vladimir
Ministerium Wissenschaft und Technische Politik
Twerenskaja Uliza 11
103905 Moskwa

Mikashina, Ludmila
Grischenko & Partners
37 Reytarska
252034 Kiev, Ukraine

Okhinchenko, Tamara
Nordpatent
Nevsky Pr. 58
191011 St. Petersburg

Osharova, Irina
Intels Agency
14A, Borschagovskaya
Suite 41
252150 Kiev

Sergueev, Vladimir
Ars-Patent
Shvedsky Per. 2–332
191186 Saint-Petersburg

Shamrina, Elena
Pakharenko & Partners
9, Pushkinskaya Str. Apt. 11
252034 Kiev

Shevelya, Mykola
Shevelya Pisarenko & Partner
Acad. Pavlova 313, Apt. 8
310168 Kharkiv

Skobkariova, Ludmila
PAG
Kommunisticheskaya 36–5
220029 Minsk

Soloviova, Svetlana
OMI Ltd.
Ap. 107
Timoshenko Str. 11
252212 Kiev

Svirchevskiy, Victor
Ukranian Fund of Inventors
Reiterska 19
252034 Kiev

Vakhnina, Tatyana Alexeynva
INNOTEC
B-Semenovskaya Bld. 49
Office 402
105023 Moscow

Vasileva, Nina M.
INTELS
Mezhinsky 8, Apt.17
220012 Minsk

Vinogradov, Sergey G.
PAG
Kommunisticheskaya 36–5
220029 Minsk

Columbia

Castro, Ramiro
Brigard & Castro
P.O.B. 3692
Bogota

Cavelier, German
Cavelier Abogados
Carrera 4A No. 72–35
Bogota 8

Rubio, Humberto
Rubio & Cia.
Carrera 7 No. 74–64
Suite 506
Bogota

Croatia

Boskovic, Davor
Producta Ltd.
Srebrnjak 81 A
10000 Zagreb

Kopcic, Nikola
State Patent Office
Avenija Vukovar 78
10000 Zagreb

Korper, Zemva Dina
Korper & Haramija
Prilaz Gj. Dezelica 16
10000 Zagreb

Sikiric, Dragutin
Sikiric Law Office
5, Jurisiceva
10000 Zagreb

Tomasovic, Sanja
Pliva D.D.
Ulica Grada Vukovara 49
10000 Zagreb

Vasiljevic, Vesna
Pliva D.D.
Ulica Grada Vukovara 49
10000 Zagreb

Cyprus

Demetriou, Athos S.
Markides, Markides & co.
1–1A Heroes Street
PO Box 4325
1703 Nikosia

Theodoulou, Christos A.
Law Officers
PO Box 965
Larnaca

Dcnmark

Meidahl, John
H. Lundbeck A/S
Ottiliavej 9
2500 Kopenhavn

Raffnsoe, Knud
International Patent Bureau
Hoje Taastrup Boulevard
23
2630 Taastrup

Skovmose, Henning
The Lego Foundation
Aastvej 3
7190 Billund

Sogaard, Henry
Plougmann, Vingtoft &
Partners A/S
Sanct Annae Plaos 11
1021 Kobenhavn

Stellinger, Jens-Holger
Giersing & Stellinger A/S
Teglporten 3
3460 Birkeroed

Ecuador

Andrade, Luis A.
Amazonas 2374
Quito

Fabara, Maria Rosa
Larreategui & Fabara
De Almagro 1730 y
Republica
Quito

Egypt

Bakir, Mohamed M.
Bakir International Office
26 Sherif Pacha SI
Cairo

Reda, Yahya
Arab Lawyers Y. Reda Co.
Build. 59
A. Gouza
Cairo

Estonia

Koitel, Heinu
Patendi- Kaubamärgi- &
Ögusbüroo
PO Box 1759
0009 Tallinn

Urgas, Enn
Patent Bureau Turvaja Ltd.
Kaupmehe 8
EE0001 Tallinn

Finland

Aarnio, Hannu
Outokumpu Oy
Riihitontntie 7D
02201 Espoo

Dahlstroem, Krister
Oy Kolster Ab
Stora Robertsgatan 23
00121 Helsinki

Ihamoutila, Riikka
Kone Corporation
Munkkiniemen Puistotie
25
00331 Helsinki

Kilpinen, Aarre L.J.
Nokia Telecommunications
Oy
PO Box 44
02601 Espoo

Koeykkae, Aira
Outokumpu Oy
Kuparitie 5
28101 Pori

Kolster, Bjoern
Oy Kolster Ab
00121 Helsinki

Korpi, Kristiina
Neste Oy
Patent Services
PO Box 310
06101 Porvoo

Lipsanen, Jari
Seppo Laine Oy
Loennrotinkatu 19a
00120 Helsinki

Rantanen, Pekka
Kone Corporation
Myllykatu 3
PO Box 667
05801 Hyvinkaeae

France

Aghayan, Shahin
9, Rue d'Anjou
75008 Paris

Bloch, Gerard E.
Bloch & Associés
2, Sq. de l'Avenue du Bois
75116 Paris

De Beaumont, Michel
1 bis, Rue Champollion
38000 Grenoble

Gaultier, Geoffroy
10, Square Henry Pate
75016 Paris

Hangard, Daniel
INPI
26 bis, Rue Saint-Petersbourg
75800 Paris Cedex 08

Mollet-Vieville, Thierry
Duclos-Thorne-Mollet-Vieville
130 Fbg St. Honoré
75008 Paris

Montagnie, Luc
Institut Pasteur
75000 Paris

Ores, Bernard
Cabinet Ores
6 Avenue de Messine
75008 Paris

Ores, Irène
Cabinet Ores
6 Avenue de Messine
75008 Paris

Phelip, Bruno
Cabinet Harle & Phelip
21, Rue de la Rochefoucauld
75009 Paris

Sueur, Thierry
L'Air Liquide SA
75, Quai d'Orsay
75007 Paris

Sueur, Yvette
Sueur & Helgoualch
78, Rue Carnot
95240 Cormeilles-en-Parisis

Germany

Adrian, Johann
Humboldt-Universität
Marienstrasse 19/20
10117 Berlin

Axster, Oliver
Pünder, Volhard, Weber & Axster
Cecilienallee 6
40416 Düsseldorf

Bardehle Heinz
Patent- und Rechtsanwälte
Bardehle & Partner
Galileiplatz 1
81679 München

Bopp, Thomas
Gleiss Lutz Hootz Hirsch & Partners
Maybachstrasse 6
70469 Stuttgard

Einsele, Rolf W.
Daimler-Benz AG
Patente und Lizenzen HPS 0533
Epplestrasse 225
70546 Stuttgard

Flaccus, Rolf-Dieter
Bussardweg 12
50389 Wesseling

Fritsche, Rainer
Eisenführ Speiser & Partner
Herterichstrasse 18
81479 München

Goddard, Heinz
Böhmert & Böhmert
Franz-Joseph-Strasse 38
80801 München

Goeken, Klaus
Eisenführ, Speiser & Partner
Martini Strasse 24
28195 Bremen

Hoeller, Klaus P.
BASF AG
Patent Abteilung, ZDX
67056 Ludwigshafen

Kinne, Reinhard
Tiedtke-Bühling-Kinne et Al
Bavariaring 4
80336 München

Kouker, Ludwig
Böhmert & Böhmert
Hollerallee 32
28109 Bremen

Krüger, Dirk
Arthur Anderson & Co. GmbH
Mergenthalerallee 10–12
Postfach 53 23
65728 Eschborn

Lange, Reinhart
Gaedertz Vieregge Quack Kreile
Kaiser-Friedrich-Ring 66
65185 Wiesbaden

Leistner, Georg
Friedrich Krupp AG Hoesch-Krupp
Altendorfer Strasse 103
45143 Essen

Lindner, Manfred K.
Walter Eggers Lindner
Gottfried-Boehm-Ring 25
81369 München

Mager, Kurt
Schering AG
Müllerstrasse 178
13342 Berlin

Meyer-Dulheuer, K.-H.
Keil & Schaafhausen
Eysseneckstr. 31
60322 Frankfurt a. M.

Moritz, Hans-Werner
Beiten Burckhardt Mittl & Wegener
Leopoldstrasse 236
80807 München

Müller, Frithjof E.
Ter Meer Müller Steinmeier & Partner
Mauerkircher Strasse 45
81679 München

Münich, Wilhelm
Kanzlei Münich, Rösler und Steinmann
Wilhelm-Mayr-Strasse 11
80689 München

Popp, Eugen H.K.
Meissner, Bolte & Partners
Widenmayerstrasse 48
80538 München

Reimann, Thomas
Puender, Volhard, Weber & Axster
Cecilienallee 6
40474 Düsseldorf

Reinhard, Markus
Reinhard & Söllner
Hausen 5b
85542 Kirchheim

Siegfried, Jürgen
Beetz & Partner
Steinsdorfstrasse 10
80538 München

Söllner, Udo
Patentanwälte Söllner & Reinhardt
Hausen 5b
85551 Kirchheim

Solf, Alexander
Solf & Zapf
Candidplatz 15
81543 München

Turi, Michael
Samson & Partner
Widenmayerstrasse 5
80538 München

Von Fuener, Alexander
Von Fuener Ebbinghaus Finck
Mariahilfplatz 2 & 3
81541 München

Von Meibom, Wolfgang
Wessing
Berenberg-Gossler
Zimmermann Lange
Königsallee 92 a
40212 Düsseldorf

Wacker, Paul-Alex
Kuhnen, Wacker & Partner
Alois-Steinecker-Strasse 22
85354 Freising

Wicke, Reinhard
BASF AG
ZDX Patente und Lizenzen
67056 Ludwigshafen

Wickler, Andreas
Böhmert & Böhmert
Hollerallee 32
28209 Bremen

Greece

Argyriadis, Korinna
Argyriadis-Metallinos-Schinas
Sina Str. 14
10672 Athens

Lyberis, Nikolaos
Law Offices Vayanos Kostopoulos
Tournara 37
10682 Athens

Oekonomidis, Dimitri
Sina Street 9
10680 Athens

Papaconstantopoulou, Penelope
32, Efterpis Street
Holargos
15561 Athens

Paraharalabus, Catherine C.
Evretechnika-C.Papaharalabus Law Offices
23 Analipseus Street
15235 Vrilisia Athens

Papaharalabus, Costas P.
Evretechnika
23 Analipseos Street
15235 Vrilisia Athens

Zomba Coletti Economou Sophia
Cabinet Zombia
78, Ave. Konst. Palaiologou
146 71 Athens (Politia)

Hongkong

Dajian Wu
China Patent Agent (H.K.) Ltd.
23 Harbour Road
Wanchai

Scholefield, Paul
Deacons Graham & James
3–6/F Alexandra House
Chater Road
Hongkong

Shi Xiaomei
China Patent Agent (H.K.)
23 Harbour Road
Hongkong

Hungary

Beliczay, Laszlo
S.B.G. & K. Patent and Law Offices
Andrassy Ut 113
1369 Budapest

Gödölle, Istvan
Gögölle, Kekes, Meszaros & Szabo
Keleti Karoly U. 13/b
1024 Budapest

Kereny, Judith
Danubia
Patent & Trademark Attorneys
16, Bajcsy-Zsilinszky
1368 Budapest

Kovari, Gyoergy
Advopatent
Foe U 19 PO Box 11
1251 Budapest

Kovats, Zerna
S.B.G. & K. Patent and Law Office
Andrassy Ul 113
1062 Budapest

Mak, Andras
S.B.G. & K. Patent and Law Office
Andrassy Ut 113
1062 Budapest

Somfai, Eva
Somfai & Partners
Industrial Rights Co. Ltd.
Pozsonyi U 38
1137 Budapest

Szentpeteri, Adam
S.B.G. & K. Patent and Law Office
Andrassy Ut 113
1062 Budapest

Iceland

Ragnarsson, Olafur
Patice
Skeifan 19
Reykjavik

India

Ahuja, Sudhir
D.P. Ahuja & Co.
52 Syed Amir Ali Avenue
Calcutta 700019

Gupta, Anil
Indian Institute of Mangement
Vastrapur
380015 Ahmedabad

Indonesia

Tanuatmadja, Hendra
Hata Int. Legal Counsellors
Jl. Jend Sudirman Kav. 36
Wisma Ben. Hil. Floor 6, RA 9–10
10210 Jakarta Pusat

Iran

Laghaee, Ali
Dr. Ali Laghaee & Associates
Vali-e-Asr
19656 Teheran

Israel

Friedman, Mark
Dr. Mark Friedman & Co.
Haomanim 7
Tel Aviv 67897

Goldenberg, Amnon
S. Horowitz & Co.
31, Ahad Ha'am
65202 Tel Aviv

Hess, Yitzhak
Dr. Yitzhak Hess & Partners
PO Box 6451
61063 Tel Aviv

Noam, Meir
23 Hillel Street
91320 Jerusalem

Rapaport, Erich I.
Cohen Zedek & Rapaport
29, Bezalel Street
Tel Aviv 04683

Shtadler, Svetlana
Orbotech Ltd.
PO Box 215
70651 Yavne

Italy

Bottero, Claudio
Porta, Checcacci & Botti Srl
Viale Sabotino 19/2
20135 Milano

Domenighetti, Diana
Dr. Ing. Racheli
V.S.M. del Corso, 4
20144 Milano

Giannesi, Pier Giovanni
Pirelli Spa
Viale Sacra 222
20126 Milano

Karaghiosoff, Giorgio A.
Via Pecorile 27/d
17015 Celle Ligure

Macchetta, Francesco
Gruppo Lepetit S.A.
Via R. Lepetit, 34
21040 Gerenzano (VA)

Pallini, Diego
Notar Bartolo & Gervasi
Viale Bianca Maria, 33
20122 Milano

Pellegrino, Giovanni
Via Bocaccio 27
20123 Milano

Prato, Roberto
Studio Torta
Via Viotti 9
10121 Torino

Riccardi, Sergio
Riccardi & Co.
Via M. Melloni 32
20129 Milano

Righetti-Pelosi, Renata
Bugnion Spa
Via Farini 81
20159 Milano

Saglietti, Luigi
Studio legale Saglietti & Associati
C.so Vittorio Emanuele II
10121 Torino

Sama, Daniele
Sama Patents
Via G.B. Morgagni 2
20129 Milano

Schwarzer, Ivo
Bugnion Spa
Via Pelliccerie 2
33100 Udine

Sorenti, Paolo
Bianchi e Associati
Visconti die Modrone 18
20122 Milano

Trevisan, Luca
Trevisan & Cuonzo
Via Brera 6
20121 Milano

Zorzoli, Franco
Riccardi & Co.
Via M. Melloni 32
20129 Milano

Japan

VIII. Handa Massao
H. Handa & Associates
Sanei Bldg. 4f
2–3–8 Wada Suginami-Ku
166 Tokyo

Hara Kenzo
Patent Law Firm
Daiwa Minamimorimachi Bldg.
2–6–2 Chome Kita Tenjinbashi
Osaka 530

Hattori Masaki
Hattori & Associates
Arex Bl. 1–4–12
Marunouchi, Naka-Ku
Nagoya 460

Ikeda Kazuma
K. Ikeda & Associates
Fair Bldg. N. 201
5–27, Izumi 1-Chome, Higashi
Nagoya 461

Ikeuchi Hiroyuki
Ikeuchi & Sato Patent Office
Umeda Plaza Bldg. Suite 401
3–25, Nishitenma 4-Chome Kita
530 Osaka

Ishida Jun
Yoshida Kanayama Ishida & Ass
1–34–12 Kichijoji-Honcho
Musashino-Shi
180 Tokyo

Ishii Sadaji
AIPPI Japan
7 F Toranomon Building
8–1 Toranomon 2-Chome Minato
Tokyo 105

Itoh Susumu
Itoh-Shin Patent Office
Musahi Bldg. 4–4, Nishishin-Juku, 7-Chome, Shinjuku-Ku
Tokyo 160

Itoh Tadahiko
Itoh Internat. Patent Office
32nd Floor YGP Tower,
20–3 Ebisu, E-Chome, Shibuya-Ku
PO Box 5008
Tokyo 150

Kataoka Hiroshi
Kataoka International
33 Yoshida Kami-Oji-Cho
Sakyo-Ku
Kyoto 606

Kawasaki Takao
Kawasaki Patent Office
9–2 Toramomon 1-Chome
Minato-Ku
Tokyo 105

Kawawa Takaho
Kawawa & Partners
5–14–16 Minato-Ku, Shiba
Tokyo 108

Kobayashi Sumiko
Abe, Ikubo & Katayama
Fukuoka Bldg. 8th Floor
Yaesu, Chuo-Ku
104 Tokyo

Kohno Akira
Kohno & Co.
Nagata-Cho Hoso Bldg, #306
2–21 Akasaka Minato-Ku
Tokyo 107

Marushima Giichi
Canon Inc.
3–30–2 Shimomaruko, Ohta-Ku
Tokyo 146

Matsui Shoji
4–8 Sonehigashi Machi
2-Chome, Toyonaka
Osaka 561

Nakajima Kazuo
Shiga Intern. Patent Office
3–23–3 Takadano Baba
Shinjuku-Ku
Tokyo 169

Nakamura Minoru
Nakamura & Partners
3-3-1 Marunouchi
Chiyoda-Ku
Tokyo 100

Nogawa Shintaro
Patent Office
5–1–3– Nishitenma, Kita-Ku
Osaka 530

Nomura Yasuhisa
Nomura Patent Office
Nibanchou Building
8–20 Nibanchou
Chiyodaku
Tokyo 102

Norichika Kensuke
Software Information Center
Toto Building
5–1–4 Tornamomon
Minato-Ku
Tokyo 105

Ochi Hirofumi
Takino & Associates
Hiroo SK Bldg. 4th Floor
2–36–13 Ebisu Shibuya-Ku
Tokyo 150

Ono Hisazumi
Ono & Associates
Nihonshuzokaikan 4 F.
1–21 Nishishinbashi 1-Chome
Tokyo 105

Ooya Ken-Ichi
Hiraki & Associates
2–7–7 Toranomon
105 Tokyo

Osuga Yoshiyuki
Osuga & Associates
6–1–18 Kojimachi
Chiyoda-Ku
Tokyo

Ota Keiichi
Ota & Associates
Toranomon Bldg. 505
1–1–12 Toranomon,
Minato-Ku
Tokyo 105
Saikyo Keiichiro
Saikyo Patent Office
Shikishima Bldg. 6th Floor
2–6 Bingomachi 3-Chome
Chuo-Ku
Osaka 541

Satoh Masami
M. Satoh & Associates
Shino Bldg. 8f
8–12–1 Nishi-Shinjuku
160 Tokyo

Shimizu Tetsuo
Shimizu & Daigo
1–3–8 Nihonbashi-Honcho
Chuo-Ku
Tokyo 103

Takatsuki Takeshi
T. Takatsuki & Associates
Dai 2 Toranomon Denki
Bldg.
No. 1–10, Toranomon 3-
Chome
105 Tokyo

Tanaka Shigemitsu
Mitsubishi Heavy
Industries
Patent & Licence Dept.
3–1 Minatomitai 3-Chrome
220–84 Nishi-Ku,
Yokohama

Tessensohn John A.
Yamamoto Patent Law
Offices
Crystal Tower, 15th Floor
1–2–27 Shiromi, Chuo-Ku
Osaka 540

Tsukuni Hajime
Tsukuni & Associates
SVAX TS Bldg.
22–12 Toranomon 1-
Chome, Minato-Ku
Tokyo 105

Yamamoto Shusaku
Patent Law Offices
Crystal Tower, 15th Floor
1–2–27 Shiromi Chuo-Ku
Osaka 540

Yamazaki Toshiomi
Dr. Sonderhoff Law Office
No. 20 Mori Building
7–4 Nishishinbashi, 2-
Chome
Tokyo 105

Latvia

Anokhine Vladimir
Agency Tria Robit
23–207 Aizkraukles
1006 Riga

Dolgitser Nina
Patent Agency KDK
PO Box 180
1084 Riga

Fogel Abraham
Alfa-Patents
4 Marstalu Street
1050 Riga

Fortuna Alexandra
Patent Office 'Foral' Sia
Raina Blvd. 19
1159 Riga

Makeeva Svetlana
Latiss Agency
Office 1
63, Gertrudes Street
1011 Riga

Petersons Armins
Petersona Patents
Ausekla Str. 2
Suite 2, PO Box 61
1098 Riga

Sergeyeva Valentina
Intels Agency
56/58 Ventspils Street
1046 Riga

Lebanon

Saba, Suhail
Saba & Co.
PO Box 11–9420
Beirut

Zahr Hisham
Saba & Co.
Arabia House
131 Phoenicia Street
Beirut

Lithuania

Gerasimovic, Liudmila
Agency Liudmila
Gerasimovic
Patent Attorney
Basanaviciaus 16/5–41
PO Box 2816
2000 Vilnius

Laurinaviciute, Rita
Metida
Pilies 8/1–2
2600 Vilnius

Lenkutiene, Marija
Kazimiera
Patentiniu Paslaugu
Centras
UAB
J. Basanaviciaus 11/1
2600 Vilnius

Zaboliene, Reda
Metida Patents &
Trademark Agency
Pilies 8/1–2
2600 Vilnius

Luxembourg

Freylinger, Ernest T.
European Patent Attorney
Route d'Arlon
PO Box 48
8001 Strassen

Mexico

Becerril, Ricardo
Becerril, Coca & Becerril
PO Box 265
Mexico, D.F. 11590

Perez de la Sierra, Carlos
Calderon y de la Sierra
Campos Elisos 400, Piso 6
Col. Lomas de
Chapultepec
11000 Mexico City

Mongolia

Bayart, G.
Balco Ltd.
Patent and Trademark Agency
Suite 319, Bagatoiruu 49
Ulaanbaatar 13

New Zealand

Hardie, John D.
J.D. Hardie & Co.
44–48 Emily Place
Auckland

Howie, Bill
A J Park & Sons
6th Fl, Huddart & Parker Bdg.
Post Office Square
Wellington

Nigeria

Allan, Marlies
Allan & Ogunkeye
8/10 Broad St. (13th Floor)
51769 Ikoyi
Lagos

Durosinmi-Etti, Lookman
Etti, Edu & Co.
6th Floor Aib Plaza
Off Akin Adeshola Street
Lagos

Kayode, Omolara
O. Kayode & Co.
47/57 Martins Street
Lagos

Ohikhuare, John E.W.
Mexi Commercial
3, Fayemi Street, Ilasamaja
POB 2579 Marina
Lagos

Norway

Balle, Morten
Bryns Patentkontor A/S
Karl Johansgt. 25
0106 Oslo

Byklum, Knut
Byrns Patentkontor A/S
Karl Johansgt. 25
0106 Oslo

Coward, Bjarne Gorgus
Byrns Patentkontor A/S
Karl Johansgt.25
0106 Oslo

Dawes, Dag
Bryn & Aarflota A/S
Kongens.Gata 15
Postboks 449 Sentrum
0104 Oslo

Foss, Toril
Patentstyret
Norwegian Patent Office
Postboks 8160 Dep.
0033 Oslo

Grette, Gunnar
Smith Grette Wille
Drammensveien 6
Postboks 1397 Vika
0114 Oslo

Gulbrandsen, Sigurd
Norsk Hydro A.S.
Bygdoy Alle 2
0240 Oslo

Gustad, Trond
Oslo Patentkontor AS
Holtegata 20
0306 Oslo

Hamsoe, Gunnar
Hamsoe Patentbyra
Vagsgt. 43
4300 Sandnes

Helgerud, Jan e.
Bryns Patentkontor A/S
Karl Johansgt. 25

Ranger, Per Olaf
Patentstyret
Norwegian Patent Office
Postboks 8160 Dep.
0033 Oslo

Smith, Joergen
Patentstyret
Norwegian Patent Office
Postboks 8160
0033 Oslo

Tofting Arild
Bryns Patentkontor A/S
Karl Johansgt. 25
0106 Oslo

Wahl, Elfrid
Tandbergs Patentkontor AS
Uranienborg Terrasse 19
Postboks 7085
0306 Oslo

Woxholth, Geir
University Faculty of Law
Karl Johansgate 47
0162 Oslo

Pakistan

Yawar, Irfan Khan Mohammaed
United Trademark & Patent Services
Top Floor, West End Bldg
Lahore 54000

Paraguay

Berkemeyer, Hugo
Berkemeyer & Salomoni
Benjamin Constat 835
Asuncion

Fernandez, Wilfrido
Zacarias & Fernandez
Buongermini 11/4
Asuncion

Peru

Alvarez, Hector
Rodrigo, Elias & Medrano
Av. San Felipe 758
11 Lima

Barreda, Fernando
Berreda Moller
Las Begonias 441
Lima 27

Philippines

Bunye, Patricia
Villaraza & Cruz Law Offices
118 Perea Street
PO Box 3539 Makati Central
1229 Legaspi Village

Calma, Renato G.
Bito, Lozada, Ortega & Castillo
140 Alfaro Street, Salcedo
Manila

Ferrer, Inocencio Jr.
Villaraza & Cruz
PO Box 3559 Makati Central
Legaspi Village
1229 Makati

Francisco, Emma
Magellan Capital Holdings
Ortigas Bldg.
Ortigas Avenue
Pasig

Narciso, Edilberto S.
Bengzon Narciso Cudala Pecson Bengson & Jimenez
PO Box 1690
1229 Makati City

Poblador, Manuel A.
Poblador Azada & Bucoy
186 Salcedo Street
Legaspi Vil.
Makati City

Quirino Aleli, Angela G.
Anagara Abello Concepcion Regala & Cruz
Accra Bldg. 122 Gamboa Str.
770 Makati City

Portugal

Arnaut, Jose Luis
Raul Cesar Ferreira, Lda.
Rua do Patrocinio, 94
1350 Lisboa

Bessa Monteiro, Cesar
Veiga, Gomes, Bessa, Monteiro
Marques Bom
Marques Fronteira 8, 3 Dto.
1070 Lisboa

Cruz, Jorge
J. Pereira da Cruz, Ltd.
R. Vitor Cordon 14
1200 Lisboa

Cunha Ferreira, Goncalo
Cabral, Cunha, Ferreira & Ass.
Rua D. Joao V, 9–2 Dto.
1250 Lisboa

De Sampaio, Jose
J.E. Dias Costa, Lda
Rua do Salitre 195 R/C
1250 Lisboa

Gomes Montiz Pereira, Manuel
Gastao da Cunha Ferreira Lda
Arco de Conceicao, 3–10
1100 Lisboa

Romania

Ghita, Constantin
B-Dul Take Ionescu 24–28
1900 Timisoara

Larion Elisabeta-Sonia
Rominvent S.A.
N. Balescu Blvd. 22
PO Box 37–71
Bucharest

Nicolae, Ioan
Indipendent Propini Agent
Fabrica de Chibrituri 42
75222 Bucharest

Oproiu, Margareta
119, N. Titulescu
78157 Bucharest

Rata, Grigore
Cabinet Enpora
Sos. Iancului 7
Bl.109b, Et.1 Ap.46
73371 Bucharest

Voicu, Alexandra
A.G.V., Srl.
9, Magheru Blvd.
70161 Bucharest

Slovakia

Kertesz, Josef
Slovakofarma
Zeleznicna 12
920 27 Hlohovec

Kovalcik, Vladimir
Slovakofarma
Zeleznicna 12
920 27 Hlohovec

Slovenia

Borstar, Dusan
Ljubljanska 91
61230 Domzale

South Africa

Burrell, Tim
Spoor and Fisher
Rochester Place
173, Rivonia Road
PO Box 41312
Craighall 2024

Du Plessis, Esme D.
Adams & Adams
1140 Prospect Street
Pretoria 0001

Hahn, Hans
Weber Wentzel Bowens Hahn & Hahn
222 Richard Street
Pretoria 0083

Parker, Llewellyn D.
John & Kernick
Kernick House Howick Close
Waterpall Park
PO Box 3511
Midrand 1685

Van Biljon, Carel P.
D.M. Kisch Inc.
PO Box 668
Johannesburg 2000

Van Niekerk, Nico M.
Webber Wetzel Bowens
Patag Building
222 Richard Street
Hatfield
Pretoria 0083

Vermaak, Nicolaas J.
D.M. Kisch Inc.
PO Box 668
Johannesburg 2000

South Korea

Cho Chul Hyun
Patent & Law Office
CPO Box 348
Seoul

Cho Tae-Yeon
Lee International
Kwang Hwa Moon
PO Box 1504
Seoul 110–615

Chung Kwang-Sun
Patent & Law Firm
823–22 Sun Kok Building
Yoksam-Dong
Kangnam
Seoul 135–080

Kim Myung –Shin
Myung-Shin & Partners
12th Floor Jindo Building
37 Dowha-Dong, Mapo-Ku
Seoul 121–040

Kim Tae Won
T.W. Kim International
Patent & Law Office
Jeongnam Bldg. 202,
814–3 Yoksa
135081 Kang Nam, Seoul

Kim Won-Ho
You Me Patents & Law Firm
825–33 Yoksam-Dong
Kangnam-Ku
Seoul

Kim Woo Kyung
First Law Offices of Korea
Dongwon Bldg, 3rd Floor
275 Yangjae-Dong
Seocho-Ku
Seoul

Kim Yeon-Soo
45 Doshaning Building
648–23 Yeoksun-Dong
Kangnam
Seoul 135–080

Kim Yong Ho
Y.H. Kim Patent & Law Office
1305–2 Seocho-Dong
Seocho-Ku
Kangnam PO Box 1307
Seoul 137–070

Kim Yong-In
Intern. Patent & Law Office
648–23 Yeoksam-Dong
Kangnam-Ku
Seoul 135–080

Kwon Young Mo
First Law Offices of Korea
Seocho
PO Box 437
Seoul 137–130

Lee Heong Sook
Central Internat. Law Firm
Susong-Dong 80
Seoul

Moon Kyoung-Jin
Central Internat. Law Firm
Susong-Dong 80
Seoul

Park Jang Won
Park, Kim & Partner
200, Nonhyum-Dong
Kangnam-Ku
Seoul 135–080

Park Yong H.
Y.H. Park & Associates
52 Ika Kwangbok-Dong
Chung-Ku
PO Box 426
Pusan 600–031

Shin Dong-Jeon
Park & Shin Patent Law Firm
824–25 Yeoksam Dong, Kangnam
Seoul 135–080

Sohn Kyung-Han
Aram Intern. Law Office
&F., Daejung Bldg.
51–7 Banpo-Dong,
Seocho-Ku
Seoul 137–040

Son Won
C.H. Chun, Son & Kim
KPO Box 103
Seoul 110–601

Yim suk-Jae
Wonjon Intellectual Property
823–1 Yeoksam-Dong
Kangnam-Ku
Seoul 100–665

Yoon Dong-Yol
Yoon & Lee Intern. Patent & Law Firm
648–23 Yoksam-Dong
Kangnam
Seoul 135–081

Spain

Bosch Rovira, Anna
Laboratorios Vita, S.A.
Avenida Barcelona 69
8970 Sant Joan Despi

Cabeza Marti, Alvaro
Clarke, Modet & Co.
Avda. Los Encuartes 21
28760 Tres Cantos

Cobas Barrios, Luis
Tecnieurop S.l.
Salustiano Olozaga 6
28001 Madrid

D Rivera Elzaburu, Alfonso
Elzaburu
Miguel Angel 21
28010 Madrid

De Larramendi, Luis H.
Elzaburu
Miguel Angel 21
28010 Madrid

Fernandez-Lasquetty, Javier
General Cabrera 11
28020 Madrid

Garnateo Ancillo, Jose
Clarke, Modet & Co.
Avda. Los Encuartes 21
28760 Tres Cantos

Isern, Jorge
Patentes y Marcas
Avda. Pau Casals 22
08021 Barcelona

Isern, Nuria
Patentes y Marcas
Avda. Pau Casals 22
08021 Barcelona

Testor, Carlos
Ungria Patentes y Marcas S.A.
Avda. Ramon y Cajal, 78
28043 Madrid

Ulloa, Gonzalo
Gomez Acebo & Pombo
Castellana, 164
28046 Madrid

Sweden

Bergentall, Annika
Goeteborg Patentbyra AB
Odinslundsg. 11
40221 Göteborg

Borgenhaell, Hakan
Rydin & Carlsten Advokatbyra
Norrmalmstorg 1
Box 1766
111 87 Stockholm

Forsberg, Lars
AB Tetra Pak
Ruben Rausings Gata
221 86 Lund

Granehult, Johan
Mannheimer Svartling Advokatbyra
Box 4291
203 14 Malmö

Karlsson, Berne
Telia Research AB
Marinensvag 30
136 40 Haninge

Kristansen, Alf
Albihn West AB
Box 142
401 22 Göteborg

Loevgren, Tage
Ericssons Radio Systems AB
Torshamnsgatan 21–23
164 80 Stockholm

Lundquist, Lars-Olof
L-O Lundquist Patentbyra AB
Herrardsgatan 6
651 03 Karlstad

Nihlmark, Per
Linnegatan 22
102 40 Stockholm

Nilsson, Katarina
Stora Corporate Reseach
Box 601
661 29 Affle

Sandstroem, Sven
Pharmacia AB
Diagnsotics
751 82 Uppsala

Stroem, Tore
Stroem & Gulliksson AB
Studentgatan 1
PO Box 4188
20313 Malmö

Svensson, Peder
Telia Research AB
Marinensvag 30
136 40 Haninge

Von Heidenstam, Peter
Heidenstam & Nicander
Strandvaegen 7 b
114 56 Stockholm

Willquist, Bo
Willquist & Partners AB
S T Larsgatan 23
582 24 Linköping

Switzerland

Addor, Felix
Eidgenössisches Institut für GeistigesEigentum
Einsteinstrasse 2
3003 Bern

Altenpohl, Martina
Wehrli Lutz Zimmermann und Partner
Forchstrasse 2
Postfach 1022
8032 Zürich

Barth, C.O.
IBM Research Laboratory
Intellectual Property Dept.
Säumerstr. 4
8803 Rüschlikon

Becker, Konrad
Novartis
Postfach
4002 Basel

Blum, François
Blum Manfrini Gaillard Avocats
8c Av. Champel
1211 Genève

Blum, Urs D.
E. Blum & Co.
Vorderberg 11
8044 Zürich

Bogsch, Arpad
World Intellectual Property Organisation (WIPO)
1200 Genève

Brinkmann, H.-Volker
Kraft Jacobs Suchard AG
Klausstrasse 4
Postfach 147
8034 Zürich

Brudere, Werner
Patentanwaltsbüro
Oberhittnauerstrasse 12
8330 Pfäffikon

Bühr, Daniel
Mador AG
Baarerstrasse 8
Postfach 348
6301 Zug

Bugnion, Ute A.S.
14, Rue du Rhône
1204 Genève

Burkhart, Hans
Alusuisse-Lonza Services AG
Bad. Bahnhofstrasse 16
8212 Neuhausen am Rheinfall

Celli, Alejandro
Froriep Renggli
Attorneys at Law
Bellerivestrass 201
8034 Zürich

Cottier, Thomas
Universtität
Juristische Fakultät
Hochschulstr. 4
3012 Bern

Cronin, Brian
Moinas Kiehl Savoye & Cronin
42, Rue Plantamour
1201 Genève

Cueni, Thomas B.
Interpharma
Petersgraben 35
4003 Basel

Curchod, François
Organisation Mondial de la Propriété Intellectuelle
34, Chemin des Colombettes
1211 Genève

Ducommun, Jean-Michel
Bovard AG Patentanwälte VSP
Optingerstrasse 16
3000 Bern 25

Eder, Carl E.
Patentanwaltsbüro Eder AG
Lindenhofstrasse 40
4052 Basel

Felderer, Christian
Zürich International
Mythenquai 2
8022 Zürich

Feldmann, Clarence
Patentanwaltsbüro
Kanalstrasse 17
8152 Glattbrugg

Fischer, Franz
Bovard AG, Patentanwälte VSP
3000 Bern 25

Frick, Hans Peter
Nestlé S.A.
Avenue Nestlé 55
1800 Vevey

Gernet, Samuel
Alusuisse-Lonza Services AG
Bad. Bahnhofstr. 16
8212 Neuhausen a. Rhf.

Grossenbacher, Roland
Eidgenössisches Institut für Geistiges Eigentum
Einsteinstr. 2
3003 Bern

Gurry Vei, Sylvie
Blum Manfrini Gaillard Avocats
8c Avenue du Champel
1211 Genève 12

Heinrich, Peter
Lenz & Stähelin
Bleicherweg 58
8027 Zürich

Heinrich, Werner
F. Hoffmann-La Roche AG
Grenzacherstrasse 124
4007 Basel

Hepp, Dieter
Hepp, Wenger & Ryffel AG
Marktgasse 18
9500 Will

Heritier, François
A. Braun Heritier Eschmann AG
Postfach 169
4027 Basel

Hilti Christian
Isler & Pedrazzini AG
Postfach 6940
8023 Zürich

Hool, Max
Fédération de l'Industrie Horologère Suisse
Rue de l'Argent 6
2501 Bienne

Hug, Pierre
Hug Interlizenz AG
Nordstrasse 31
8035 Zürich

Junet, Bernhard
Pestalozzi, Gmür & Patry
15, Bd. des Philosophes
1205 Genève

Kerr, Andrew
A.Kerr AG
Finkelerweg 44
Postfach 444
4144 Arlesheim

Kiehl, Hubert
Moinas Kiehl Savoye & Cronin
42, Rue Plantamour
1201 Genève

Kündig, Renata
Kündig Trademarks
Hallenstrasse 15
8008 Zürich

Küttel, Ellen
Isler & Pedrazzini AG
Postfach 6940
8023 Zürich

Kunze, Gerd
Walder, Wyss & Partner
Rue Crémières
1605 Chèxbres

Leisinger, Klaus M.
Novartis
Klybeckstrasse 141
4002 Basel

Lutz, Martin J.
Lenz & Stähelin
Bleicherweg 58
8027 Zürich

Meisser, Urs
Meisser & Meisser
Bahnhofstrasse 8
7250 Klosters

Merlotti, Yvan
Cabinet juridique
15, Boulevard Hélvétique
1207 Genève

Micheli, Bertrand
Micheli & Cie
Rue de Genève 122
1226 Genève-Thonex

Notegen, Eric-André
F. Hoffmann-La Roche AG
Grenzacherstrasse 124
4070 Basel

Oertli, Reinhard
ATAG Ernst & Young AG
Bleicherweg 21
8022 Zürich

Otten, Adrian
WTO Intellectual Property
& Investment Division
Rue de Lausanne 154
1211 Genève 21

Ottow, Jens M.
Hug Interlizenz AG
Nordstrasse 31
8035 Zürich

Pedrazzini, Vincenzo M.
Isler & Pedrazzi
Gotthardstrasse 53
8002 Zürich

Pestalozzi, Peter A.
Pestalozzi Gmür & Patry
Löwenstrasse 1
8001 Zürich

Pletscher, Thomas
Schweiz. Handels- und
Industrieverein
"VORORT"
Mainaustrasse 49
8034 Zürich

Rauber, Georg
Homburger Rechtsanwälte
Weinbergstr. 56/58
8035 Zürich

Roth, Bernhard M.
Novartis
Patentabteilung
Postfach
4002 Basel

Saladin, Martin
AIPPI
Bleicherweg 58
8027 Zürich

Schetters, Will
Mador AG
Baarerstrasse 8
Postfach 348
6301 Zug

Schwander, Kuno
Patentanwaltsbüro Eder
AG
Lindenhofstrasse 40
4052 Basel

Seifert, Hans Ulrich
Ritscher & Seifert
Kreuzstrasse 82
8032 Zürich

Simon, Jürg
Münstergrasse 38
3011 Bern

Stieger, Werner
Homburger Rechtsanwälte
Weinbergstr. 56/58
8035 Zürich

Strahlberg, Alfred M.
Strahlberg Trademarks
Funkstrasse 95/401
3084 Wabern

Sziele, Ivanka
Novartis
Postfach
4002 Basel

Treis, Michael
Baker & McKenzie
Zollikerstrasse 225
8034 Zürich

Von Büren, Roland
Institut für Wirschaftsrecht
Falkenplatz 18
3012 Bern

Von Meiss, Reinhard W.
SIG Schweizerische
Industrie-Gesellschaft
8212 Neuhausen am
Rheinfall

Wavre, Claude-Alain
Nestlé SA
55, Avenue Nestlé
1800 Vevey

Weber, Gertrud
Novartis Nutrition Ltd.
Monbijoustrasse 118
3007 Bern

Werner, Georges
Trösch Scheidegger
Werner AG
Siewerdtstrasse 95
8050 Zürich

Wibmer, Jeannette Karin
Altenburger & Partner
Atte Landstrasse 128
8702 Zollikon-Zürich

Widmer, Peter
Fuhrer Marbach & Partner
Konsumstrasse 16a
3007 Bern

Widmer, Ursula
Dr. Widmer & Partner
Schosshaldenstrasse 32
3000 Bern

Wild, Peter E.
A.W. Metz & Co. AG
Hottingerstrasse 14
8024 Zürich

Zimmerli, Adrian
Zimmerli, Wagner &
Partner
Löwenstrasse 19
8001 Zürich

Syria

Tarazi, Ibrahim
Saba & Co.
PO Box 460
Damascus

Taiwan

Ho Ted Chin-To
Wenping & Co.
8F, 77, Tun Hwa South Rd
PO Box 1869
106 Taipei

Tsai, Thomas Q.T.
Tsai & Kao
12F-3, 148 Sung-Chiang
Taipei

Thailand

Chirasavinuprapand
Supask
Int. Legal Counsellors Ltd.
18F Sathorn City Tower
South Sathorn Road
Bangkok 10120

Mongkolsit Chakrapat
Domnern Somgiat &
Boonma
719 Si-Phya Road
Bangkrag
10500 Bangkok

Nettaya Warnche
Domnern Somgiat &
Boonma
719 Si-Phya Road
Bancrak
10500 Bangkok

Uttasart Chavalit
Int. Legal Counsellors Ltd.
18/F Sathorn City Tower
South Sathorn Road
Bangkok 10120

The Netherlands

Berger, R.L.M.
Netherlands Industrial
Property Office
Patentlaan 2
2280 HV Rijswijk

Capel, Kees
Kneppelhout & Korthals
Advocaten
Boompjes 40
3000 AM Rotterdam

De Boer, W.R.
Gist-Brocades N.V.
Wateringseweg 1
Postbus 1
2600 MA Delft

Galama, Jan E.M.
Philips International
Prof. Holstlaan 6
5656 AA Eindhoven

Iemenschot, Jan
Van Exter Polak &
Charlouis
De Bruyn Kopsstraat 9
2280 GE Rijswijk

Kupecz, Arpad
Octrooibureau Los En
Stigter
Horstlaan 25
3971 LA Driebergen

Louet Feisser, Arnold
Trenite Van Doorne
De Lairessestraat 133
1075 Amsterdam

Mertens, Hans V.
Van Exter Polak &
Charlouis
De Bruijn Kopsstraat 9 F
2280 GE Rijswijk

Neervoort, Wim
Netherlands Industrial
Property Office
Patentlaan 2
2280 HV Rijswijk

Ottevangers, Sietse U.
Vereenigde
Octrooibureaux
Postbus 87930
2508 DH Den Haag

Schlkwijk, Piet C.
Akzo Nobel N.V.
Velperweg 76
6800 SB Arnheim

Schaper, Teartse
De Brauw, Blackstone
West-Broek
Paramaribostraat 7
2528 Den Haag

Van Assen, Jan W.B.
Octrooibureau Assenpatent
BV
Postbus 1029
2243 BA Wassenaar

Van Gennip, Han J.S.W.
Vereenigde
Octrooibureaux
Nieuwe Parklaan 97
2587 BN The Hague

Van Wezenbeek, Bart
Mogen International NV
Einsteinweg 97
2333 CB Leiden

Czech Republic

Horejs, Milan
Cermak, Horejs, Vrba
Narodni 32
110 00 Praha

Korejzova, Zdenka
Dr. Korejzova & Co.
Zirovnicka 5
106 17 Praha 10

Malusek, Jiri
Kania, Sedlak, Smola
Patent & Trademark
Agency
Mendlovo Nam. 1A
603 00 Brno

Pavlica, Ivo
Patentservis
Jivenska 1, PO Box 34
140 00 Praha 4

Reichel, Pavel
Kocian Solc Balastik
Jindrisska 34
110 00 Praha 1

Soukup, Pavel
Dr. Ivan Korecek Law and
Patent Office
Na Baste Sv. Jiri 9, Box
275
160 00 Praha 6

Traplova, Jarmila
Traplova, Hakr, Kubat
Law and Patent Offices
Pristavni 24
170 00 Praha 7

Vokalek Ales
Patentservis
Jivenska 1, PO Box 34
140 00 Praha 4

United Arab Emirates

Tarazi, Hani
Saba & Co.
Deira
Dubai

United Kindom

Abnett, Richard C.
Reddie & Grose
16 Theobalds Road
London WC1X 8PL

Adkins, Mike
Withers & Rogers
60 Holly Walk
Leamington Spa
CV32 4JE

Brereton, Graham
Glaxo Wellcome Plc
Glaxo Wellcome House
Berkeley Avenue
Greenford UB6 0NN

Brown, Jeremy
Linklaters & Paines
Barrington House
59/67 Gresham Street
London EC2V 7JA

Cockbain, Julian
Frank B. Dehn & Co.
179 Queen Victoria Street
London EC4V 4EL

Donovan, Colleen
Hammand Suchard
Moor House
119 London Wall
London EC2Y 5ET

Korah, Valentine
University College
Bentham House
Endsley Gardens
London WC1H 0EG

Muir ,Ian R.
Haseltine Lake & Co.
Temple Gate House
Temple Gate
Bristol B21 6PT

Nodder, Edward J.
Bristows Cooke &
Carpmael
10 Lincoln's Inn Fields
London WC2A 3BP

Prentice, Roy
R.R. Prentice & Co.
The Hop Exchange
24 Southwark Street
London SE1 1TY

Skinner, Vincent J.
British Gas Plc
59 Bryanston Street
London W1A 2AZ

Westmacott, Philip G.
Bristows Cooke &
Carpmael
10 Lincoln's Inn Fields
London WC2A 3BP

Williams, Janice
De Young & Co.
21, London Road
Southhampton SO15 2AD

USA

Adamo, Kenneth R.
Jones, Day, Reavis &
Pogue
901 Lakeside Avenue
Cleveland, OH 44114

Bale, Harvey, Jr.
Pharmaceutical Research
and Manufacturers of
America
1100 15th Street NW
Washington, DC

Ben-Dak, Joseph
UN Development
Programme
20 Villa Street
Mount Vernon, NY 10552

Braga, Carlos
The World Bank
IENTI
1818 H Street, NW
Washington, DC 20433

Brooks, W. Dexter
The Coca-Cola Company
Legal Division
One Coca-Cola Plaza
Atlanta, GA 30313

Converse, Robert E.
Finnegan, Henderson,
Farabow
Garret & Dunner
1300 I Street NW
Washington, DC 20005

Cotreau, William Joseph
National Cancer Institute
Technology
Development
23320 Forsythia Lane
Middleburg, VA 22117

Craig, Paul M.
Birch, Stewart, Kolasch &
Birch LLP
8110 Gatehouse Rd, #500E
Falls Church, VA 22040

De Grandi, Joseph A.
Beveridge De Grandi
Weilacher & Young
1850 M Street NW #800
Washington, DC 20036

Fawcett, Richard F.
Finnegan, Henderson
Farabow Garrett &
Dunner
1300 I Street NW
Washington, D.C.
20005–3315

Garrett, Arthur S.
Finnegan, Henderson,
Farabow, Garrett &
Dunner
1300 I Street, N.W.
Washington, DC
20005–3315

Gerber, David J.
Kent College of Law
Comparative Law
545 West Adams Street
Chicago, IL 60661

Gitten, Howard M.
Stroock & Stroock & Lavan
7 Hanover Square
New York, NY 10004

Goldscheider, Robert
The International Licensing Network Ltd.
1175 Park Avenue, # 3C
New York, NY 10128

Greason, Edward W.
Kenyon & Kenyon
One Broadway
New York, NY 10004

Hattori, Ken
Armstrong Westerman Hattori McLeland & Naughton
1725 K Street
Washington, DC 20006

Hill, David W.
Finnegan, Henderson, Farabow, Garrett & Dunner L.L.P.
1300 I Street NW
Washington, DC 20005–3315

Hoinkes, H. Dieter
US Patent & Trademark Office
6302 Broad Branch Road
Chevy Chase, MD 20815

Jorda, Karl F.
Franklin Pierce Law Center
2 White Street
Concord, NH 03301

Joyce, Joseph J.
Pepsico, Inc.
Law Department
700 Anderson Hill Road
Purchase, NY 10577

Kashiba, Yukio
Rogers & Wells
200 Park Avenue
New York, NY 10166

Kasper, Alan J.
Sughrue, Mion, Zinn, MacPeak & Seas
2100 Pennsylvania Avenue
Washington, DC 20037–3202

Kit, Gordon
Sughrue, Mion, Zinn, MacPeak & Seas
2100 Pennsylvania Avenue
Washington, DC 20037–3202

Krause, John A.
Fitzpatrick, Cella, Harper & Scinto
277 Park Avenue
New York, NY 10172–0194

Malatestinic, Nicolas P.
Bristol-Myers Squibb Co.
Rt. 206 & Provinceline Road
Princeton, NJ 08543–4000

Mayer, Richard L.
Kenyon & Kenyon
One Broadway
New York, NY 10004

McLeland, Le-Nhung
Armstrong, Westerman, Hattori, McLeland & Naughton
1725 K Street, N.W. Suite 1000
Washington, DC 20006

Myrick, Ronald E.
Fish & Richardson P.C.
225 Franklin Street
Boston, MA 02110

Nath, Gary M.
Nath & Associates
1835 K Street, N.W. #750
Washington, DC 20006-1203

Phelps, Marshall C. Jr.
IBM Corporation
500 Columbus Avenue
Thornwood, NY 10594

Roth, Norman W.
Roth & Goldman
523 W. 6th St. Ste.707
Los Angeles, CA 90014

Rothwell, Gideon F.
Rothwell, Figg, Ernst & Kurz
Columbia Sq. #701 East Tower
555 13th Street NW
Washington, DC 20004

Seas, Robert J., Jr.
Sughrue, Mion, Zinn, MacPeak & Seas
2100 Pennsylvania Avenue
Washington, DC 20037

Sharp, Melvin
Sharp, Comfort & Merrett
Suite 1710
13455 Noel Road
Dallas, TX 75240–6636

Sigman, Harry C.
Professional Corporation
PO Box 67EO8
Los Angeles, CA 90067–1408

Slattery, James M.
Birch, Stewart, Kolasch & Birch, LLP
8110 Gatehouse Rd, #500 E
Falls Church, VA 22040

Sloan, Robert V.
Sughrue, Mion, Zinn, MacPeak & Seas
2100 Pennsylvania Ave. N.W.
Washington, DC 20037

Virelli, Louis J.
Unilever Research U.S.
45 River Road
Edgewater, NJ 07020

Weber, Cindy
Sughrue, Mion, Zinn,
MacPeak & Seas
2100 Pennsylvania Avenue
Washington, DC 20037

Wetzel, James M.
9345 S.W. 46th Place
Gainesville, FL 32608

Wray, James C.
1493 Chain Bridge Road
McLean, VA 22101

Yugoslavia

Kisovec, Maria
Patent Agency Maria
Kisovec
Nsegoseva 74
11000 Belgrade

Pavlovic, Gordana
Cabinet Pavlovic
M. Jevrosime 53
11000 Belgrade

Popovic, Slobodan
Law Offices
Generala Zdanova 34
11000 Belgrade

www.ingramcontent.com/pod-product-compliance
Ingram Content Group UK Ltd.
Pitfield, Milton Keynes, MK11 3LW, UK
UKHW020203290926
15471UKWH00005B/1031

9 781841 130668